Nak

Judith

Anneke Wills

love

Anneke

www.hirstbooks.com

Anneke Wills: Naked

First Published April 2009
by Hirst Books

Hirst Books, Suite 285 Andover House, George Yard, Andover, Hants, SP10 1PB

ISBN 978-0-9557149-1-7

Design by Tim Hirst

Printed and bound by ASAP UK Ltd, Unit 8, Rushington Court, Chapel Lane, Totton, Southhampton, SO40 9NA
www.asapuk.net

Paper stock used is natural, recyclable and made from wood grown in sustainable forests. The manufacturing processes conform to environmental regulations.

All artwork in this book is by Anneke Wills. All photographs are from the author's personal collection, or © Yogi Gough. Rear cover photo by Bim.

www.hirstbooks.com
www.annekewills.com

So be true, absolutely true. Naked!

Bhagwan Shree Rajneesh
March 1977

Chapter 1

Norfolk

Where was I? Oh yes... In the spring of 1971, Polly and Jasper and I move into the grain-dryer building that runs along the side of the field of our new home. I love this land, filled with windmills, Saxon churches, vast salt marshes, huge skies and Dutch barns that remind me of Holland.

Last autumn our friend Jonathan had swept this barn out and painted fields and clouds on the walls, built a huge fireplace and chimney out of mud and stone, and a cardboard geodesic dome with a Victorian glass-fronted door in it! He and his girlfriend Linda will stay in our house in Fulham with Mickgough until it sells ... although Mickgough is in France completing the Van Gogh film. Rather than placing Polly and Jasper in the school in our village we think the larger school up on the coast will give them a wider friend-base. It's five miles away so I've become a chauffeur.

While our team of local builders are beginning the heavy renovation work on the farmhouse I'm making our temporary home comfortable. We have discovered a local auction house where they have a stock of 1950s three-piece suites and old carpets. So for under a fiver I've made us warm and cosy. Jonathan has built Polly and Jasper their own bedroom dome out of bamboo and a silk parachute. Jasper is roaring about on his tricycle. Polly is covering the walls with her paintings. We have water but no electrics so we cook on a camping stove, and on bath nights we fill a tin tub in front of the wood fire and they splash around with abandon.

We love the freedom that the space gives us. No TV, no radio, no newspapers. *So liberating!* At night we read stories by candlelight, and fall asleep at the same time. Apart from the builders banging away in the house the village is very quiet. On one side of the hedge lives an old retired Colonel. We can hear his wife constantly nagging him, so he abuses his little dog. We hear him shouting.

'Tobeh! Come heyah! Come heyah Sir, when I tell you… Tobeh!'

Across the road next to the pub is a row of cottages that until recently have been lived in by a local witch and his coven. Now they stand vacant and Jonathan and Linda are hoping to buy them. Charlie and Mrs Cox own the pub. They are a very kind Norfolk couple. She twinkles with sweetness and has an inspiring veg patch, and Charlie's gravely old voice is legendary. When we go in at lunchtime it's a place of deep peace. The antique clock on the wall ticks loudly as the old boys sip their pints companionably. A few remarks here and there, punctuated by Charlie's

'Ohh, aar, blast!'. He has the jowls of an old bulldog. The evenings are slightly more busy – all locals. On the corner is Mr and Mrs Roberts's Post Office and shop. We appreciate being accepted into this small community. We will all become very good friends. Mick comes up as often as he can get away from his work. He is enchanted by the charm of our new home in the barn. He sets about trimming the wicks of our oil lamps – he looks like an old alchemist. He and I are deeply bonded in our shared passion – the restoration of this beautiful Georgian farmhouse. We have a carpenter and joiner friend, Richard Newton, and he will hand-make the kitchen cupboards and replacement medieval windows for the older part of the house. His wife is Norwegian and she gets us our first duvets. Such freedom, no more bed-making! Many of the windows on the south side have got to be opened up – they were bricked in when they had a tax on windows in the 17th century – and we are going up into the roof and making a whole other floor with Dorma windows. One weekend there is a huge storm and the plastic covering the attic windows comes loose and Mickgough has bravely climbed up a very tall ladder and is straddled on the roof battening them down. I'm standing on the base of the ladder, frantic for him, and the children are cheering. We are all wearing sailor-smocks from the ships chandlers in Blakeney.

When we were filming *The Go-Between*, a local family sort of adopted us. He's a retired housemaster from the local public school – Greshams – and now has an antiques stall in the local town. His wife Nancy is a really outspoken character. Apparently there is a very grand long table in the old school hall – silver and candlesticks – and at the end of term teachers' dinner they are all pontificating away and Nancy who's a socialist is getting more and more frustrated at the snobby, narrow-minded nonsense and no-one is listening to her, so she takes hold of the white linen tablecloth and pulls it away. The silver, crockery, candlesticks and all are scattered in confusion… I like Nancy. They live in a beautifully restored farmhouse in Cley-next-the-Sea and we are generously plied with gin and local information. Their daughter has long blonde hair and like horses and also, Mickgough.

One of the chimneys of the farmhouse has collapsed and the building regulations say we must replace this massive space in the drawing room with a nine-inch flue. It drives me mad because I know this will cause problems. The fireplace is eight feet wide and three feet deep, with a massive beam across. Of course it smokes forever, until finally we give up and put a woodstove in. The huge kitchen will have a York Stone floor laid which will prove brilliant, as Mickgough loves his homes to be like railway stations, and so it will become.

I'm so busy with all of this I hardly have time to wonder if my idea to give up my 18-year long acting career and move into this country scene, to nourish our children, grow vegetables and mend our wobbly marriage, is sound or not. It seems in this moment to have brought us happiness.

♬ *Our house, is a very very very fine house, with two cats in the yard, life used to be so hard, now everything is easy …* ♬
- Crosby, Stills and Nash

At the end of the day after the builders have left, I walk around the large rooms of the house. I love it. I'm imagining how it will all look when it's finished, which we hope will be before it gets too cold in the barn, so that we can have our first Christmas in our new home.

But, sometimes late at night in the barn, I lay awake listening to the strange sounds ... the owls, the fierce Norfolk winds which make the windows rattle, and the children jump into bed with me, and I feel quite responsible. I'm hoping it will all work out well for us. I'm really missing my London friends and their support. I worry that Mickgough has to be away so much. He's in LA at the moment, making a film called *Trog* with Joan Crawford. There is a dusty telephone hooked up in the hall of the house so the guys shout down to me if he calls, however when I'm 'creating' I'm never happier. As my darling step-daughter Emma says,

'We love playing house, 'Neke.' Later, it will become my profession. For now, I am part of the building team. I've designed the kitchen and the bathroom with Richard the carpenter, I've stripped all the bedrooms of wallpaper, stained the wide-oak floors. We have found some rare goodies along the way – little tokens from past occupants. A First World War postcard, a comb, a malachite brooch, clay pipes, buttons... 'We've lived here, we've lived here...'

Polly wants a cat and Jasper wants a dog. So Blackberry – a sweet, tufty-faced mongrel adopts us, so does a black and white kitten called Gemini. She's our entertainment in the barn as she skedaddles up the Indian bedspreads that Polly and I have hung from the ceiling to make the sitting space cosier. Blackberry and Jasper are best buddies.

The local town has the most wonderful delicatessen called Larners. There I buy the 'goodies'. It's frequented by many retired army people – so the Indian spice department is very well stocked. It is here that we bump into Roddy Maude-Roxby – very surprised to see our old friend and to discover he has bought a farmhouse in the next village, which is really quite extraordinary as I've known him since Peter Cook days and Roger Lloyd Pack, who was in *The Go-Between*, has rented a small cottage not far away.

Nancy is quite deaf yet the surprising thing is, she always manages to hear you when you say,

'Who's for a gin and tonic?' She has introduced me to her dear friends David and Roger. They are in the process of buying The Townshend Arms in Stiffkey. We fall into instant friendship. They are a captivating couple. Roger from the West Country with his Rock Hudson good looks and Bristol burr, chuckling and supporting David, who has intense blue eyes, set in his Clint Eastwood face. They are designers, socialists and creators of huge magic and laughter. And they're gay – so Mickgough hopefully won't be jealous of them.

Chapter 2

The Good Life

We have half an acre of field and a huge 200 year-old Ash tree. We're having the field ploughed and before we can seed it we have to clear as many of the horseradish, docks and nettle roots as we can. Mickgough gets happily stuck in with a fork. Before he became an actor he went to agricultural college. His father had been a rubber farmer in Malaya and Mick had been brought up in Galway with an old uncle who was the Master of The Galway Blazers, so his happy memories were of running barefooted and free with his brother Pete in the Irish countryside. So this move to Norfolk is nourishing his spirit. He wants to plant a wild flower meadow.

'But won't it take a few years to get rid of the weeds?'

'No, no,' he replies. 'We'll just scatter the seeds around – they'll grow – you'll see …' But by the next spring we have a plan to keep it mowed. He also starts his woodshed – aah – how he loves his woodshed. He'll place his latest script on the side beam and be working on his lines as he chops and sorts it all into – number ones (twigs), number twos (split logs) and number threes (heavy logs). He's hung his Bafta award on a nail.

It's a wild and stormy night. We've invited Roddy and Jane for supper in the barn. The oil lamps are lit, the Bolognese bubbling. Polly and Jasper prevaricating about getting into bed, although since they can hear everything that's going on they don't feel so excluded. Mickgough has gone over to the pub for some tonics, when there is a hefty banging on the barn door.

'Who on earth ….?' Standing in the doorway with long, straggly black hair, flapping cloak, drunken eyes, is the man they call 'the witch'. He's straight out of *The Addams Family*.

'Does Michael Gough live here?'

'Yes, but …' he strides past me and chuckling at the delightful atmosphere before him, heads for the most comfy chair, saying,

'I'll have a glass of wine …' Well, we can't get rid of him. When Roddy and Jane arrive they look very surprised. Polly's whispering,

'Has he got a broomstick? Ask him if he's got a broomstick!'. Jasper says,

'Can he bend spoons?' I would like to hear about Paganism, but he just wants to talk movies with Mickgough, so he's quite boring. When he's too drunk he asks if he can crash in the house.

'No, it's a building site' says Mick, firmly.

'Well, maybe at yours?' he says hopefully to Roddy and Jane. 'I know your house of old. One time a group of us …' In the end, he's cross, and very pissed. He climbs into his huge old Citroen and roars off up the road into the pitch dark night. When Roddy and Jane get home there is a large toad on the doorstep.

'It's the witch!' Roddy giggles. The toad darts into the house ahead of them and Roddy follows it into the downstairs loo and closes the door. Next morning, it's gone.

'I bet he'll be back' says Jane. 'He really seemed to like this house.' Later that morning there is a toot from the yard.

'My God, he's back' says Roddy – the Citroen has drawn up outside, and out jumps the witch.

'I wanted you to meet my girlfriend'.

Polly and Jasper have settled in really well at school and have lots of little mates who all seem to like to come to ours at the weekends, so while they are playing I can get on working. We've taken all the 18th century doors off and I've got a grotty old bathtub in the yard, filled with caustic soda and I'm stripping them down to their lovely wood. Then I will sand them and wax them until they feel like silk. I'm hoping Mickgough will help me a bit this weekend, but a local couple have come to take him for a drink in the pub. They are all standing, staring at me in amazement. I've got a mask, heavy-duty rubber gloves, plastic apron, welly boots, and I'm scraping away.

'My wife is an energy phenomenon,' says Mick proudly. 'Are you coming with us darling?'

'I can't!' I say, in exasperation. They bugger off leaving me feeling angry and taking risks with the caustic soda.

At the beginning of the summer holidays, Nancy turns up in her Citroen 2CV.

'Come on Anneke – you work too much! I've got a picnic. Collect the kids, I'm going to take you to my favourite spot – it's a perfect day for it!' So we load up with rubber rings and towels, sweaters, binoculars and lemonade, and Nancy takes us to the Stiffkey marshes. We follow a path across little bridges – this place is vast. Carpets of pale blue sea lavender, winding creaks and marsh pools, the roar of the sea in the distance, the curlews crying in the salt-filled wind. We come to a place where the inlet is deep enough to swim. The banks are steep with mud. We lay amongst the lavender, the larks above us in the sky. The kids are swimming and sliding down the muddy banks, shrieking with delight. This magic place becomes our favourite spot for years to come. This is a place of timeless tranquillity. We often go to the beach after school. Nancy has taught us to look for stone-washed agate so we walk to the very end before it turns into the estuary – noses down, collecting treasure.

Now, we are waiting for the plasterer to come. The builders all have great respect for this man – he's an artist, so when he's working, they leave him to it.

'But *when* is he coming?'

'Ah, you can't rush 'im – 'e'll come when 'e's ready'. But I'm getting anxious because it's beginning to hold us up. The shower in the 'boot room' is finished. The walls are covered in our collection of Art Nouveau tiles. The attic rooms are finished and finally, here's the plasterer. He unloads all his equipment – he is a man of few words – we explain how we want him to follow the curves in the walls – no straight lines. He's got it. And while his little dog sits and watches patiently, he makes his mix and he's away, Mick and I watching surreptitiously in awe. It's a privilege to watch a master craftsman at work and he makes a beautiful job of it. We love the colour of the dried plaster so much we mix a flat oil in the same dusty pink and paint the kitchen with it, which looks beautiful.

The fireplace, which is surrounded by big cushions, has an old bread oven inside, and a shelf where I have a tiny oil lamp always lit. There is a Welsh dresser. Richard makes wonderful work surfaces in Ash along the back window. Two Belfast sinks. An eight-foot refectory table with six high-backed, antique country armchairs. A settle along the wall, a door to the larder and no beastly overhead cupboards! The front windows have their original wooden shutters. It is a huge, beautiful, comfortable room. The other wonderful room we've created is the main bathroom. We've built the bath up high against the chimney breast, with wooden steps leading up to it, with a huge guilt mirror behind, and potted palms and jungly plants in chardinieres. We have speakers so you can lie in the bath listening to music and looking out onto what will be the herbaceous border in the front garden. A huge French bow-fronted carved wardrobe is full of sheets and towels, and a little sign inside, 'Room to Let'! We have a bidet and an armchair and dressing table. It's a sociable bathroom, which becomes legendary.

By late September we have painted and sanded and polished and the rooms are finished. Wonderful country colours. I've recreated Mrs Craxton's larder, marble shelves, strings of onions and a rack for wine. Polly has flowery wallpaper and a brass bed. Jasper has terracotta walls and a ships bed. We have pale pink walls and a huge brass bed with a patchwork quilt. The 'boot room' is Gauloise blue and the drawing room is library green. We have a whole wall of books, with Staffordshire figures on the top. The room next to the kitchen is the kids' room with the TV and piano. The builders and I have a toast to each other and I am very proud that they call me a 'fellow craftsman'.

It's perfect timing – because Hurlingham Road – our house in London – has sold. Mickgough has been busy with the packers for a week or so and now they are arriving. I'm standing in the driveway when I see this huge furniture van edging its way into the yard and I have a distinct feeling of foreboding and doom. It's all been so wonderfully freeing to live *in the moment* in the barn with very little, and now, here comes all the furniture, boxes of possessions, all the objects to be dusted and polished and cared for. I want to decant it slowly from the barn, so we don't get overwhelmed and cluttered immediately, so just the essentials… but slowly, slowly, over the next few weeks, it begins to fill up and I'm resentfully allowing more and more.

Nancy and her family love the house and are full of praise for 'getting the decoration just right'. Now, everyone wants to come and see us. John Craxton is our first visitor. Here he is, with his friend Spud, in their leathers on a motorbike. He's ecstatic, loves what we've done. He waxes lyrical about the kitchen, paces out how many fruit trees we can get into the front garden and gives us excellent advice on the importance of the drainpipes. We go for a pint or two of Abbot Ale. Walking back from the pub I have my arms wrapped around my dearest uncle.

'If ever you need help,' he says quietly, 'My friends in Costessey will be there for you.' It sounds ominous. Does he know something I don't? But I love the feeling of someone looking out for me and I tuck the address of his friends in my pocket, just in case. We are left filled with his enthusiasm and inspiration – what a remarkable man he is.

Jasper announces that he wants to change his name to John, and he wants a pair of black lace up shoes (enough of his white Spanish loafers). So I have bought him and Polly new school uniforms, so they will fit in with the other children. They look adorable setting off for the autumn term. I take a photo of them standing in the front door of their new home.

We've been very firm, now that we have the TV back in our lives, the children are only allowed to watch two programmes a day. I hear then plotting,
'You watch this one, because that's an hour long, then I can have this one!' They are becoming politicians. Blackberry and Jasper snuggle up at the end of a day's adventures and watch *Thunderbirds* together.

Jasper has outgrown his tricycle and Mickgough is thinking of getting him a second-hand bicycle for his birthday (always the penniless actors). But it won't do – Jasper's friend, who's father is the local electrician – has bought his son the latest model – a Raleigh Chopper. So on his sixth birthday, we give him the smaller version - a Tomahawk - and he practices riding it up and down the driveway, with Blackberry trying to bite the wheels. I've got a secret for Mickgough's birthday – I'm busy designing it with Richard.

Polly on her rocking horse

My mother is coming for a visit. I'm longing to show her my new and beautiful home, but I'm also dreading her usual criticisms and wise, acerbic judgements. I pick her up from Norwich station. She's been travelling around Mexico for the last year and as always has many mad adventures to share, and we are laughing all the way home. Polly and Jasper are very happy to see her again and are on the doorstep jumping up and down.

'Oma!'

I'm playing Rodriguez for my mother in the bathroom, she loves flamenco and gypsy violins and the comfort of the large guest-room, lifting her skirt and warming her bum in front of the fire. Next day we take her to see the windmills. She always asks after Edward Fox – she was very fond of him. Now, she wants to smoke some fishes, so she and I have found a large metal drum and Richard's given us some oak kindling, and she's hanging herring inside it with wire coat hangers. She covers it all over with a damp sack, and starts on the wine. Mickgough is exasperated with her. As the fishes cook, they fall into the fire and are ruined. She loves to point out to Mick that they are the same age – which he hates. She is maddeningly bossy as usual. She has such a sense of humour, adores Tommy Cooper and collecting rude limericks... *There was a young lady from Woking...* Wanting to engage Mickgough in deep theological discussions, interrupting him with,

'Well, I don't believe in God, but when I die I know I'll go to heaven, because I'm so good!' She insists that I have been very stupid to give up my acting career just as it was beginning to flourish.

'From six years old you wanted to be an actress – you had such talent - all the teachers, the scholarships, the parts you got, and all of this ..' She gestures to the house as I put her bag in the boot of the car, 'It won't last, you're too much of a gypsy, like me. You'll be off soon, you'll see, it won't be enough for you!' I feel so angry and frustrated with her, and guilty for feeling it. Yet as I wave her off – she's going to Devon to visit Tilly - there are tears in my heart as well.

I worry about her. Since she has sold her Spanish flat, she has no home, very little money. She's not bothered too much, she's thinking of going to Canada to see her brother Hans. I love this brave, intelligent, energetic woman for ever, but there is a hole in our connecting, where the absence of my brother is, we mirror the pain we feel in each other. We always speak of him and toast him,

'To Robin, who's with us for ever...'
The well of grief. The well of grief.

When I get home, one of the Staffordshire figures has flown off the shelf and smashed. Mickgough grumbles,

'It's your mother's mad energy.'

Mickgough has often spoken of how much he loves 'tumbling doves'. They were specially bred by one particular monarch who was a lousy shot. So to keep up appearances they obligingly tumble through the air. Richard has made a dove coat, and I have bought a beautiful pair of white tumbling doves for Mick's surprise birthday present. He's very tickled by this; they are now prettily fluttering about and the sound of their gentle cooing becomes the background music of our rural life.

'Lino Cut' of Polly and Jasper

Mickgough has bought a little clockwork spit back from France, and this we place in front of the kitchen fire, winding it up with a little key, and it turns, slowly, as we baste the chicken and a little bell tinkles when it needs re-winding. It's very charming.

Our first Christmas in our new home. Simon, Mickgough's son, his wife Sharon and their baby, Tamasin are coming. A part of me is dreading it. Simon makes such a fuss about everything being 'right'. The timing of the cooking, the turkey, the gravy, it's all *such a performance, dahling*. And actually, I'm feeling quite tired, after eight months of hard work on the house, but Polly and I have found an antique cot for Tamasin, and the house is big enough for us all. The Christmas tree is the most beautiful ever, the fires are lit, the soft antique lights throughout, Mozart's Mass in B Minor plays in the bathroom. On Christmas Day the feast is successful (thank you Clement Freud). The sun shines and we walk along the beach finding agate. Even though the wind is biting cold, Sharon climbs out of her Afghan coat and leaps into the waves, naked. Her beautiful body, so feminine in the winter sea. This will become a Gough family tradition. We are all shrieking and rubbing her dry with our scarves and hats when she comes out. Looking out of our

16

bedroom window I see Mickgough standing in the patchwork dressing gown I made him, and his furry-topped Afghan slippers. He's scattering corn for our collection of bantams who are clucking around his feet. He looks like an illustration from a fairytale.

♫ *We were born before the wind* ... ♫
- Van Morrison

1972 has started with lots of projects and ideas to enhance and continue our good life. We read John Seymour's *Self Sufficiency* and all about leylines and Mick starts his next passion – the compost heap. Everything is carefully layered – the veg peelings, damp newspaper, seaweed from the beach, the childrens' nail and hair clippings – it's a science – we're learning. We feast on moules marinieres and afterwards he crushes the mussel shells – he is obsessed! We plant quinces, cherries, apples and damsons in the front garden so that in years to come the house will peep out over the top. Red and yellow roses climb up the walls at the back and I'm designing a herb garden, to go where the builders left all their rubble in the field. I'm dreaming of a hexagon shape with brick paths and beds of lavender and camomile. Jonathan and Linda have started work on their cottages. They'll take out the ceiling and open it all up with a wrought iron spiral staircase. They come to ours for baths and Linda bakes bread in our oven, until her Rayburn is put in. I want to like Linda, but somehow I just don't trust her. Nancy is away in Greece with David and Roger, but they will be back in March to start work on The Townshend Arms in Stiffkey.

Our dear friend Roy Broadbent has died suddenly. He was only 57, Mickgough's age. It is a big shock for us all. Mick has invited Roy's widow Dee to stay with us as she needs somewhere to get away for a while. I'm so mean. I think,
'I don't really want a grieving widow to look after, when there is so much work to do'. I couldn't have been more wrong. This wonderful, generous woman shares so much with us. She is quiet and sad, and present, and yet so interested in our new life and so full of wisdom. She and Roy had met at art school and on the onset of World War II had chosen to become farmers, growing food for the

nation in Lincolnshire. She has much knowledge to share. She loves the design of the herb garden.

'It's a fifteenth century French design. When their knights went to war, the ladies would be left to renovate the chateau and they made herb gardens.' How strange – because – I had been practicing some calligraphy. Mick had given me a book of ancient scripts and one evening I was copying one which I felt curiously drawn to, and all of a sudden I felt like my hand was possessed, and I completed the alphabet with a flourish, and all the while it felt like 'home'. When I checked, the script was fifteenth century French …

♫ *We have all been here before…* ♫
- Pink Floyd

So, with string and stakes, we mark out the hexagon, and drive to Heacham for the lavender. How can Dee be so encouraging and generous, in these, her darkest hours? Now her youngest son, James (Jim), has come to collect her. I need him to help me with moving some heavy furniture from the barn.

'James, are you feeling strong? Mick's hurt his back!'

'Yes – strong as a lion,' he replies. 'A dandelion!' Now, dandelions will always remind me of Jim Broadbent. This man, who is now one of Britain's best-loved actors! I am quite ashamed of my mean little mind when they drive away. I have learned a lesson about dealing with grief.

Mickgough came home late last night, and as usual he has to leave again tomorrow afternoon – he's rehearsing a play for The National Theatre. His time with us is so precious so this Saturday morning he's in his woodshed, script propped up, chopping kindling, when there is a knock at the door. A short, attractive woman in her forties, with an open and determined face.

'Does Michael Gough live here?' Oh shit, I think. Another request for Mick to open a fete, support a writer's group, attend a coffee morning. We've only been in the house a few months and already we've been inundated.

'My name is Persephone and my son William is in *The Winslow Boy*. We wondered if we could meet Michael and maybe he could give Will some tips on acting ….'

'Come in, sit by the fire, I'll go and find him.' She's taking in the beauty of the kitchen with great interest. I sneak to the woodshed to warn him, but no, he's endlessly generous to one and all.

'And anyway, it's time for a coffee and a Gauloise – how can I help?'

Persephone is an oboe player and has four children, two of whom are waiting in the car across the road. Jasper overhears this and jumps on his Tomahawk – Blackberry following – and bicycles across the road to the pub car park. Peter and Dickon see 'a beautiful white haired boy on his bike, curiously checking us out'. So begins a friendship which will last for years. Persephone's latest husband Brian, is a graphic artist. They live in a flint farmhouse on the coast. She and Brian are very involved with 'Community' – which is the first 'growth' centre in London. They have weekend groups in their home lead by the charismatic Michael Barnett, whose book 'People, not Psychiatry' I read with great interest. Peter and Dickon now become part of our family. While Persephone and Brian work in London 'the boys' are with us. Later they call themselves The Axe Gang and carve their name on one of our trees. Their adventures are very innocent. They always come in when it gets dark, for tea and *Blue Peter*. All the kids love to sprawl in front of the open fire with the dog. If you look inside the chimney you can see a piece of old tractor wedged across. In the winter, the snow tinkles down and sizzles on the embers. But sadly, the telly has replaced the bedtime story and they have to be hassled off to bed every night. Sometimes, I feel like an unsupported single parent.

Polly is learning piano. Her teacher Simone says she has a real feeling for music… of course! And Jasper wants to be a magician. He's always practicing card tricks.

'Where are my specs' Mickgough will wail.

'On your head, Dad!' comes the reply.

Mickgough has bought two goats and called them Maisie and Rose. At first we all love them – so small and cute – and so funny when they nibble everything in sight. Our clothes, our hair, my Golden Virginia. We keep them in the stable and let them out on tethers in the field so they can keep the grass down, but they are always getting off, and a wail will go up,

'The goats are loose!' And they'll be eating the lavender or the roses. Pretty soon they are huge and unmanageable. I'm often pulled off my feet when I'm putting them out. Now when Mick comes home, the first greeting is,

'Maaaaaiiiseeee! Roooose!' So I'm beginning to really resent them.

I've gone over to see how David and Roger are getting on with their place in Stiffkey. I find an enormous digger is busy gouging out deep swathes of the car park, David and Roger are up at the top of the hill, directing.

'Let's have a pond there!' Much waving of the arms.

'Yes soopah! And a gulley coming up here!' They are on acid.

Thursday is our market day. This has been going on since ancient times. All the country people gathering to meet and trade and shop and gossip. Oliver Cromwell had an office in this town and I can hear the market sounds reverberating over the centuries. It is the highlight of the week. We all meet up here. If you need to see someone, you're bound to bump into them on market day. The town centre is cluttered with stalls. Down the narrow street is the auction house, teaming with people. Our friend Patrick, the auctioneer, who is nicknamed OnePoundSurely, is on his podium, clipboard and gavel in his hands,

'How much for this sofa? OnePound Surely?'

David, Roger and I have found some great bargains. I've bought two large killums - Turkish carpets - and a wicker bathchair. It's so exciting and nerve-wracking to bid – my heart is pounding in my head so loud, I have to ask,

'Did I get it? Did I get it?'

Outside the auction is the fleamarket, tables filled with goodies. I'm collecting antique china, miniature chests of drawers, old tins and coronation mugs for the kitchen. The lady on the W.I. stall is knitting us mittens in rainbow colours, so they 'Go with aaaanything!' The thick Norfolk accent surrounds us.

Polly and Jasper make sure I don't buy them second-hand sweaters, because they won't wear them! Up in the town our baskets are filled with local veggies, supplies from the just-opened health food shop. Linda and I have bought ourselves some welly-boots which are called Hunters, and look like riding boots. I have stencilled silver stars up the side of mine, to let people know I'm not part of the huntin', shootin' and fishin' lot - I wear patchouli oil! At lunchtime we meet Richard Scott, our antique dealer friend in the pub for a pint and a sandwich. His nickname is *The Cracked Cup* – because he has a shop full of beautiful but cracked china. By the afternoon it's all closing down, it's like the end of a party, and we are away to our homes to have tea and un-wrap our bargains. Richard wonders if this little blue dish could be Ming. I put the butter in the Victorian butter dish. Will Mickgough like the carpets? David and Roger are pleased with their art deco lamps. Another market day is over.

I'm listening to such fantastic music – influenced by Jonathan. The Grateful Dead, Bob Dylan, Leonard Cohen... we love Bob Marley's *Natty Dread*. On one of the market stalls I've found a little musical clockwork figure with an umbrella which plays Mickgough's favourite...

♫ *Raindrops are falling on my head ...* ♫
- B.J. Thomas

An American friend of Mickgough's has sent his son to stay with us for a while, before he goes to university in Paris. He is a very bright young man and obsessively interested in the spiritual master, George Gurdjieff. Nancy knows a local man who apparently worked with a pupil of Gurdjieff. So we have boldly gone along to see Ronnie Stennet Wilson (RSW) and to ask if he would be interested in leading a group, if we were to gather a few people together. We are amazed and delighted when he agrees. A few people miraculously emerge and we are having fortnightly meetings in each other's houses. It's terribly serious, and continues to this day.

This morning, Mickgough was shouting and having a go at Jasper. Mick brings a bag of washing home with him so I try to send him back to work with enough ironed shirts to last him. As I am carting a huge pile through the kitchen I see a note on the table.

'Polly! Where's Jasper?'

'I don't know' she calls back. 'He took some chockie bikkies and his toothbrush and went out the back door'. I'm panicking.

'Mick! I think Jasper's left home!'

'What?!' Mick runs up the stairs to the first floor windows and as I join him we see a tiny figure stomping determinedly across a vast, distant field. When he reaches the gates to the next one, he falters, looks back at the great distance he's come, and after an agonising time, slowly begins to walk back. We welcome him with joy and relief.

'Sweetheart! Darling Jazz! What's troubling you?'

'Well,' says Jasper, cashing in on all this love and attention, 'I can't manage on 10p a week pocket money. That's a coke and a packet of crisps and I don't have any left over to save, and it's not fair!'

Chapter 3

The Search Begins

I've taken to sleeping upstairs in the attic with Polly and Jasper so we can be closer when Mick's away. I've put my bed right under the window and as the village lies on a ridge, the views are right across the fields to the Benedictine Priory.

One day Nancy and I set off with the children to the marshes. We are picking samphire which is a lovely sea vegetable, like asparagus. The children are splashing in the creeks.

'I can see that they are happy,' she says. 'And Mick loves it here too, but what about you?' She is the first person to ask me this.

'Yes, I'm busy and fulfilled. I just wish Mickgough could spend more time with us, because it feels a bit like being a single parent with him away so much of the time. What would be brilliant would be to find him some work up here. If only there was a local theatre …' We toss the idea around until it develops into,

'Perhaps what North Norfolk needs is an Arts centre? A place for theatre, film, art gallery space, workshops?' We are lit up with this idea.

We are at home, washing the samphire.

'We could find a building, get funding!' Nancy knows someone on the Eastern Arts Association Board, so she sets up a meeting with him, just to sound out the idea. Mickgough is supportive but not sure how much time he could give. We are asked to put forward a formal proposal and a petition, and we need a local official to give it credence. RSW – the Gurdjieff leader – agrees to support us. And overjoyed, Nancy and I spend the summer searching for a space or a building.

We have heard about a new Marlon Brando film – *Last Tango in Paris*. It has come to the cinema in Fakenham so David, Roger, Nancy and I go to a matinee. I am sitting with two gay guys and a grandmother watching Marlon Brando do rude things with a bar of butter. We come out into the warm late afternoon giggling, and yet we know this film is a milestone - much discussion on the way home. If we had an Arts centre we could show radical films. Would there be enough interested people to support it? Nancy and I continue our search for a building. We drive the length and breadth of the country over the next few months. An old grain store on the quay in Wells-Next-The-Sea becomes available and we think it's perfect. It will be called The Wells Centre.

When they show *The Go-Between* at the Fakenham cinema, Mickgough is running late so David and Roger ring the cinema and ask if they can delay the showing, because Michael Gough is coming. The cinema makes an announcement, and everyone waits for him to arrive.

We are in a gift shop in Wells. The children are looking at all the nice things. I've got the candles I came for so,
'Come on, kids!' Jasper is looking earnestly at a small china box with a rose on top. He picks it up and takes it to the counter. Looking up at the till lady,
'How much is this?' he says solemnly.
'£1.75' comes the reply. He looks at the money in his little hand.
'I haven't got that,' he mumbles sadly, and joins me and Polly in the doorway.
'What were you going to do with it Jazz?' says Polly. I can't speak, my heart is aching for him.
'I wos gonna give it to mum cos she likes things like that.'

Up the road out of our village there is an old pilgrims' path which leads across the fields to the priory. It's my private place. When things get on top of me, Blackberry and I go walking across the ancient meadows, that have never been cultivated. I'm always healed and nourished by the nature. These fields are full of magic mushrooms. Jonathan says the cows are all stoned because they eat them all day long. The hedgerows are full of wild flowers and barn owls hunt along the field edges.

Tragedy strikes. Blackberry has been shot by a farmer, because she was 'getting up' the pheasants which he wanted to shoot. The children can't understand this and we are all in shock and grieving the loss of one of our family. However, the goats are being given away, and I'm only relieved about this.

I'm talking to one of the little old ladies in the village shop. She's sitting down on the chair by the counter and complaining to Mrs Roberts about the money changing.

'Why couldn't they wait until all us old 'uns had left before they did this? I don't understand it all.' What she can see very clearly is that now the cabbage she is buying is twice as expensive. Honey, which used to be 4/6 is now 50p! The shop and Post Office is such a centre for all the villagers. The news is passed around, the pensions collected, the support given to the locals when needed. This is how village life has sustained itself since early times. There is one old dear who hobbles to the pub once a week with her jug for Charlie to fill up with beer. I tell her I'll bring it to her cottage.

'No, bless you,' she says 'but it's the only time I get to talk to anyone.'

The pub in the next village - The Bluebell Inn - has benches all around the central scrubbed pine table, and the old landlady climbs down the creaking wood steps to the cellar to fill her jugs with beer. Charlie has a night out at The Bluebell. When it's time to leave he can't manage to get his vintage Vauxhall into gear so he drives the two miles home in reverse.

Jonathan and Linda are settling in and they have a white rabbit called Enoch, who hops around indoors. Jonathan has built a floating bed on chains under a big skylight and he is converted his Morris van to run on methane. He has huge canisters in the back and it can only go 30 miles an hour, but he's determined.

I meet the wife of a local landowner, who's opened a posh second-hand clothes shop. I'm surprised she's doing this because she's so glamorous and outspoken.

'Well,' she says, 'once you've had everyone else's husband, what else is there to do in the country?'

Edward Fox has come for a visit. He has brought his new love, Joanna David. They love the house and the herb garden and commission me to find them a house here as well. My absolute favourite job! Very soon I've found a lovely old farmhouse in a nearby hamlet. It even has a ruined Abbey in its grounds, with 'Edward' on a shield above the door. But he misses the moment and Persephone and Brian buy it instead.

It's autumn and I'm making wines and jams and pickles. I've got 24 demijohns - parsley, strawberry and elderflower, bubbling away in the boot room, and a store cupboard full of marmalade and damson jam and pickles galore. Squirreling away my nuts for the winter seems so archetypically right. David and Roger come round for a game of Racing Demon, and I am decanting the parsnip wine – which is ready to bottle – and it's mighty powerful stuff. I've made my own labels - 'Church Farmhouse, Parsnip, 72'. Roger Lloyd Pack comes for supper. Although his rent is only ten bob a week, he is having trouble paying it, as his acting work is sporadic. David and Roger have a friend called Josephine – she's very eccentric and a marvellous illustrator. She's round and plump, with masses of curly hair and cherubim lips. Her parents are ex-colonials. She calls the children 'brat a moles'. As I'm scrubbing out the dustbins.

'Ah yes,' she says 'fragrant dustbins!'

I've been reading *The Female Eunuch* by Germaine Greer. I've now announced that the top room of the house shall be my own room, where if you wish to enter, you must knock. Mickgough says,

'You're sick.' Well, I'm standing up for my rights. And, as Germaine says, I'll still be attractive! I'm fed up with being the one who knows where everybody's socks are.

'To hell with this – find your own socks! And I'm tired of having to nag you children to get to school on time – here's the clock – you be ready to leave on time, and I'll drive you – I'm not writing anymore excuse notes!' I'm having a revolution.

'I'm always tidying up after you all – I shall go on strike.' But it's hopeless, because it simply gets worse. The kitchen table becomes cluttered with Lego and homework and birds eggs and empty cups. Clothes are dumped everywhere. After a few days I can't stand it, and I have a total blitz, and it all looks beautiful again. But now, I'm back into nagging mode, and they all resent me. What to do?

The Townshend Arms is transformed. They have taken out the floor of the main part of the pub, so it's open to the roof. What used to be the bar has become the kitchen, which is always warm and welcoming.

The Guardian is spread amongst the Golden Virginia packets, the milkman will sit with 80-year old Mrs Mann, sipping tea. David and Roger are the first gay men in the village. How will they be accepted? These are old country folk. As the brass bed is being hauled in through an upstairs window, Mrs Mann is chuckling to David,

'You'll 'ave to chuck Rog out of 'ee in the morning – ee'll be too *carmfortable.*'

We have given them our lovely pub mirror – 'Lower prices than we charge are impossible if satisfaction is to be guaranteed' – which will live in their future lamp shop. A wrought iron spiral staircase goes up to the bedrooms. A reclining Buddha, a ship, an elephant, a rocking horse on the ledge - every surface is smothered in antique objects. The walls with glass-fronted cupboards, stuffed with antique tin toys. They have built a conservatory at the back with vines and datura palms. The whole place is filled with lamps and paintings and collectibles. It's gorgeous and unique and we all love it.

On Guy Fawkes night, they build an eight foot guy – which straddles the bonfire in the car park. He is a dashing figure in Elizabethan garb with flowing paper hair. As the fire takes hold he is exploding with fireworks. His arms shoot up in the night sky, rockets firing from his fingers. He has burned to his core, which is now a grinning devil with Catherine wheels for eyes. We are all shrieking with excitement – and I have jumped up and down so much I've peed my jeans – it's the best bonfire night ever.

It's another big family Christmas. Tamasin is walking and Samuel is a baby. Polly is in heaven – she loves to mother Tamasin.

We've all gone to The Priory for Midnight Mass – this wonderful building is all lit up with candles. It's bitterly cold and frosty outside, and not much warmer inside. Simon and Sharon are singing loudly with beautiful descants. David and Roger's friend Roddy has taken acid and is sitting hunched up in his beaver coat, with a somewhat green pallor. He doesn't do religion and he resents being here. The priest mounts his lectern and starts his sermon in a plumy, monotonous voice,

'Now I know some of you never come to church, during the rest of the year, so I would like to say to those of you...' Roddy rises indignantly in his boots.

'Well, bugger this! I don't need this!' and stomps out growling.

Early on Christmas morning I go down to the kitchen before anyone else is up. I talk to the amaryllis on the table.

'Dear Amaryllis, What's wrong with me? I feel so utterly desolate.' Ever since Mickgough lost his temper totally with me, in the late sixties and beat me up, he's afraid of experiencing that deadly rage again, and he's never really forgiven me. So although it all looks rosy on the surface, deep down we've lost the trust. I've been doing everything I can to rebuild it, but I just feel unseen and exhausted. And there's this disturbing voice knocking on my psyche, to keep searching for something... which feels like a place that I remember... but I can't find the door.

Jonathan and Linda spent Christmas in Penang, Malaya. They're telling me all about it and how much I would love it. The sunsets, the colours, the people so exotic.

'Better go soon – it'll soon be ruined with tourism' says Jonathan. After the usual Gough Christmas I feel like I need something – a holiday, or better still, some therapy. I go over to Stiffkey to ask David the name of his brother's therapist.

'Why not come to London and do a group this weekend?' says Persephone. Funny how things somehow just fall into place.

Mickgough seems very keen for me to have a break. He has a play to direct at Fakenham Grammar school, so he's happy to be at home. The next thing I know, I'm off to London to do a 48 hour marathon encounter group! And then, I book myself a flight to Kuala Lumpur. But first, I have to get through this weekend. Richard (Cracked Cup) and Persephone are doing it with me. They know what they're in for – I don't.

'Encounter' is the latest therapeutic device and Denny Yuson and his wife Leda have extended it to a 48-hour marathon. The participants have very little sleep, it helps to break down the barriers, and makes us more vulnerable so that insights can emerge. There is something called the 'hot-seat'. When it's your turn to enter the circle and begin to share your issue, the group can tear you apart like a bunch of piranhas. They see your shit and call you on it, so it's pretty frightening. One of the participants has a withered arm. I smile kindly at him, I feel sorry for him. Leda, who is a beautiful, dynamic black American, starts by stepping straight into the centre and accosting the guy with a withered arm.

'I don't like this trip you've been laying on me – this guilt and shit – it makes me sick!' She proceeds to throw up in his lap. Goodness! What have I let myself in for? It's frightening and challenging and inspiring. I thought I was screwed up, but it seems I'm not alone. Suddenly my unhappiness seems so unimportant compared to other people's real problems. I see how we all have layers and layers of defences. There are tears, revelations, and much honesty. When it comes to my turn on the hot-seat I spill it all out. How Mickgough is angry with me all the time, all my feelings of guilt, because it seems as though I have everything – recipe for happiness – yet inside I feel this gaping hole. What's wrong with me? It feels very good to share it all and be heard. Leda says,

'I can see you are a good mother and a good wife but where does the *woman* get nourished?' I make excuses for Mickgough.

When it is over we are all gathered in the reception rooms of the centre. I meet the charismatic Doctor, Shyam Singer. He looks at me penetratingly and says,

'Your eyes are clear but you still need help. You will go to India.'

'Actually, I'm going to Malaya, to search for Buddhism.' I say. Such naivety. Taking Jonathan's advice I've packed insanely light – a swimsuit, a sketchbook and a toothbrush, and I'm flying off to South East Asia, determined but frightened – I feel that I'm going in search of myself.

♫ *She's a restless spirit on an endless flight …* ♫
- The Eagles

I'm sitting jetlagged, stunned, on the beach, looking out on the Mallaccan Straits, with my little bag, and the name of Jonathan's friends, who he's told me, I'll meet on the beach. So here I am – with this paradise before me. The beach is fairly empty apart from some Malay fishermen and a German or two. Before long, an American traveller comes up to me.

'Have you somewhere to stay?' I follow him into the jungle village and after some negotiation I have a bare room in a bamboo house in this kampong. I fall fast asleep on the floor, with my sweater rolled up for a pillow. I'm woken by sweeping sounds. In the early mornings, the women sweep the jungle floor. There are steep steps up to a communal shit-house. The poop falls many feet down a shaft, where the little jungle piggies happily gobble it up. I go into the village for some tea and buy myself some equipment – a straw mat, two sarongs, some flip-flops, and I'm ready for the beach. It's so beautiful and I'm working away in my sketchbook. The waters are still, like azure glass. The women in the village washing around the well. The palm trees. I've never seen anything like it. I meet an Australian woman who takes me under her wing, and we go to a local café and eat the hottest food I have ever tasted - nasi goring. My eyes are *watering*. And we eat it with our fingers, which pushes all my English buttons. She says,

'You use your right hand to eat with, because your left hand is to wipe your bum.'

I pull out my little piece of paper and explain that I'm looking for Jan and Malik.

'I'm Jan!' she says, laughing, 'What a coincidence, and here's Malik.' He is a beautiful Malayan man in a sarong. I tell them how much I would like to see a temple so we jump onto some bicycles and head off deep into the jungle. There, is this exquisite little decorated building. A monk is ringing bells and chanting inside. On our way back to the beach they ask me,

'Would you like to come to the opium den?'

'I'm up for anything!' Behind another temple is a small, low bamboo building. Malik is negotiating with the old Chinese man at the door.

'They don't like to let westerners in,' he explains. But I smile hopefully, and we are led into this very dark interior. There are platforms with recumbent men in vests. Tiny jade oil lights, a heavy smell of opium. I am directed to lie down, with my head on a small wooden headrest. Opposite me on the other side of our light is an emaciated Chinese man, with a glazed expression. I watch, fascinated, as he works the little knob of black goo with a pin, into the bowl of the opium pipe, which is decorated with ivory and mother of pearl. Offering it to me he indicates,

'Let out your breath, and suck slowly.' I do as he says and he looks pleased with me and starts to prepare another divine smoke. I am a euphoric puddle of water. After a few pipes we leave. But I feel completely melted – it's very hard to stay upright on the jungle path, following Jan and Malik who are hysterically giggling. I'm so ashamed, because I'm throwing up into the bushes.

'Don't worry,' says Malik. 'you just need to be still.' As soon as we reach the beach, I lay gratefully down into a hammock.

Well, now I can see why all those artists at the turn of the century were into opium. It's so visual. The body is melted and the mind is free to imagine anything. The colours, the stars and the water are utterly beautiful. It lasts about four hours.

I'm filling my sketchbook with drawings of everything around me. I'm fascinated by the mixture of cultures. Indian, Malay, Chinese. A day or two later,

'It's getting too full of travellers,' Say Jan and Malik. I'd only seen half a dozen or so. 'We're off to the east coast. Want to come?'

We sit on the wooden slatted seats of an exceptionally noisy and ancient bus which takes us up into the Cameron Highlands. The mountains are full of mist, and appear strangely Scottish. We rattle down to the wild, endless beaches of the east coast. There are very strong winds from the South China Seas creating massive waves. We find rooms in a Chinese fishing village. To my horror, I discover I'm sharing mine with a Black Widow spider, who likes to sleep in my cast off clothes. I'm drawing the water buffalo grazing by a creek. Little boys are catching carnivorous catfish. I'm sitting on a bench watching the sunset when these very young girls come, giggling and chattering up to me.

'They are curious to see your body,' says Jan. So shyly, I open my sarong and they peer in with interest. They are the village prostitutes. Kids. Next day, the girls want to take us through the river to a temple. We are wading into the murky waters, up to our waists and I'm feeling vulnerable because of those catfish, and I'm not wearing any knickers.

Now Jan and Malik are heading back to Penang, and I want to go on to Thailand and see Bangkok. Malik gives me the address of his friend Oot, who lives there. They help me onto a bus which heads along the coast, stopping off at villages and towns along the way. By the evening I'm getting very stiff. We travellers are given time to eat in a street café. I've gone in trepidation to the loos in the back. The filthy stinking shitholes are always a nightmare. No – I can't stand it. I step out into the fresh air and surreptitiously squat down behind a tree, only to see the bus taking off up the street. The next bus doesn't go until morning. I have no money. I was going to change some travellers' cheques in Bangkok. Feeling self-conscious and afraid, pretending to be totally cool, I walk off up the road like I know where I am going. I find a basic bus shelter a little way out in the fields. It has a bench, I prepare for a long night. Some little children come and give me some biscuits. I wrap myself up in my sarongs and frightened as hell I wait the night out. By dawn I'm smothered in mosquito bites. A young boy on his bike stops and looks surprised.

'No bus today. Today holiday! You stick out thumb, hitch lift!' After a while a car comes by, filled to the roof with Chinese passengers, chickens and laughing children. After half an hour, the next one is the same. Hell's bells. I'm just beginning to head back to the village to get help when a yellow sports car comes roaring along and stops for me, it's a couple of teachers on their way to Bangkok. They squash me in, feed me mangoes. They are playing Carole King.

♪ You've got a friend … ♪

In Bangkok, I give a taxi driver Oot's address. He looks surprised, shrugs and drives me to the edge of the Klongs – the slum villages on the edge of the city. A beautiful Thai girl says she knows where Oot lives and I follow her through the maze of walkways. I can't believe that people live in such poverty. Hovels made of plastic and rags, people everywhere, washing, cooking and surviving on scraps. We arrive at a sort of café. There are tables, and American music, a few G.I.s, and some gorgeous Thai girls drinking beer.

'Is this where Oot lives?'

'He's in the back.' They look amused to see me here. I step into the back room, through thick clouds of hashish smoke, I see this beautiful Thai man sitting on cushions like a Buddha, smiling. It's Oot, and this is his smack den. Amazingly, his father is the chief of police. I take a hit of a massive great joint which is being passed around the clientele, and sit back and watch this extraordinary scene. The den is filled with stoned G.I.s telling strange tales of the war they are in up north in Vietnam. Out in the front the beautiful girls – prostitutes of course – have learned to speak American. They wear high heels, which amazes me because of the wobbly wooden walkways.

'But they're so useful.' Says one, as she kicks a large brown animal under the table. It squeals and runs away. It's a rat, as big as a dog.

I can't stay here. I'm off to the north. On the way to the station I see the huge watts and very smart westernised streets, like in New York. But I'm away to Changmai in the mountains – I don't like cities. On the train I meet a German boy, Dieter. He's an

33

intellectual. We talk. He's been travelling in South East Asia for a few years yet he has no possessions, just a small cotton bag and a flute.

'So, are you a seeker?' he asks.

'Well … yes.'

'So what are you seeking?'

'Um… Nirvana?'

'What do you suppose that is?'

'Happiness I hope!'

Chiang Mai is gorgeous. Set in the mountains. The travellers' hotel is of course, a brothel. I notice holes drilled in the wooden walls. Peep holes which I fill with loo paper. I don't get much sleep because one Chinese client seems to have a few girls jumping on him, from what I can hear, and there are some stoned French travellers who talk all night. In the café, the travellers talk of Chiang Rai, further north. So I climb into another bone-shaker bus to see this exquisite Thai town, high in the mountains. I've heard about the hill tribes people. I've been told there are even more temples in Luang Prabang, so I keep travelling up into the remote mountains on the borders of Burma.

This is a magic hill-town. The Christian Missionary is making a good living, charging travellers an exorbitant amount to sleep on his roof, but it seems the only place to stay. The day I arrive is market day. It couldn't be more different from Norfolk! The Hill Tribe People gather from the mountains all around, in their embroidered clothes, the little children are exquisite. I buy as much fabric as I can manage. A beautiful jacket, some silver jewellery. That night I'm on the missionary's roof, I have smoked some excellent Thai grass, when BOOM! Big explosions, like massive fireworks.

'Ohh! Aah!' we travellers ecstatically cry.

Next day, an edict has gone out – all foreigners must leave – it's too dangerous. We are on the edge of the Vietnam war. Our fireworks were American bombs. We foreigners are piled into an aeroplane – Royal Thai Airlines – nicknamed AirScare. We are to be flown to Vientienne in Laos. It's is like a French town, covered in brown dust, waiting for the monsoons to wash it clean. I meet up with Dieter again. He's standing in the street, barefooted and without his bag.

'I've had my bag, money and passport stolen,'

'How awful for you,' I can't imagine how frightening that must be. But he just smiles – maybe *he* has found Nirvana.

I stay in an old wooden house on the banks of the Mekong river with some Canadian Peace Corps people. A vibrant Canadian woman called Colette sits cross-legged on her bed, in her Thai sarong and necklace of Buddhas, and tells us horror stories of what the Americans are doing in this ghastly war. I can't believe what I'm hearing. Such atrocities. It's inhuman, horrific. I'm beginning to feel homesick. I've been away six weeks now and it's been a hairy adventure, travelling on my own, but what answers have I found? I can now speak a bit of Thai, and negotiate the money. I've seen so many temples, talked to many monks. Mostly, they just asked if I had any western novels. I haven't yet managed to meet a wise priest, but now there is a possibility of having a meeting with a Tibetan monk. He lives a few hours march along the Mekong. I feel like I'm on a pilgrimage. Walking along the path behind Collete, beside the busy Mekong river life – the Sampans and Dhows, the punts and traders, people washing in the sepia swirling waters, groups of children follow us chattering,

'Hullo! Ok! You got dollar?'

When we finally arrive, it's just a wooden hut, where one or two monks are cooking and washing clothes, and he is sitting on a bench outside, smiling. We go up individually and sit at his feet. When it's my turn I feel so special. I sit down, and look up into his open face, present and laughing and kind.

'He asks if you have a question,' says a monk. I've been honing this question since Penang.

'What is the meaning of Buddha nature?' His reply is translated,

'That all beings are essentially pure.' He touches my head as I bow. The monks give us tea, in the dappled sunlight. The Tibetan Master has closed his eyes and hens are pecking at his feet.

When I get home to Norfolk, Mickgough isn't there. There is a big meeting in Wells. So I jump in my car, wearing my hill tribe jacket and rattling with silver beads and Buddhas. In the upstairs room of The Golden Fleece, a large crowd has gathered. I see Mickgough and sit down beside him. The Wells centre is going forward. Nancy is so pleased. I can see that Mick's friendship with 'G' – which I was so worried about before I left for South East Asia – has definitely developed while I've been away. So that was why he was so keen for me to go. I'm plunged back into my old insecurity once again. I've tried to accept that Mickgough needs to have affairs – I just hoped he would keep them separate from our family life, but now, it seems…

Next day, Jasper comes rattling around the corner of the yard, pretending he's got a machine gun.

'Da-da-da-da-da-da!' I'm very shocked, and I explain that I have seen young boys, not much older than him, recruited into the army and shooting people for real.

'Don't play these games around me!'

I place a Thai Buddha on the fireplace shrine.

Chapter 4

The Dark Side of the Moon

The *Doctor Who* production team want me to come to London for a photo shoot to celebrate the 10th anniversary of the show. They are suggesting Gatwick as a backdrop. I persuade them to come to Norfolk! To Charlie and Mrs Cox's amusement, the Cybermen stay in the pub. They are dressed in their cyber-suits while they have boiled eggs in the kitchen. I take them out to the marshes, where there is a pipeline, and we take pictures. I'm wearing a skirt from my favourite shop in Norwich, called 'Head in Clouds'. It's so good to be with my darling friend Michael Craze. We pick it up as though it were yesterday.

'How are you duchess?' Seeing him reminds me of my old acting days. Aah, the independence of days filled with rehearsals, sharing the fear and the fun with fellow actors.

'Do you regret having given it up?'

'I remember, as soon as I got back from rehearsals a child would be thrust in my arms. It was exhausting working on *Doctor Who*, and being the best mother and wife, and the hostess with the mostest! And yes, I do miss it. Never mind that I never have a bean anymore! Mickgough gives me fifteen pounds a week to manage on and that includes petrol, so I can't even pay my car tax, and I got nicked, and had to go to court and explain that I was broke. It was so humiliating ....' So Mike says,

'Why don't you call your agents?' When the crew leave I feel like I want to jump in the Tardis and follow. The photos we took will be used in the Radio Times Anniversary Special. I call my agents. They are delighted to take me up again.

'But you must get some new photos.'

But somehow, my heart's not in it – and it's not a profession that you can be half-arsed about. You have to really want to do it. It seems like another world now. I've got to get the veg garden dug over.

> ♪ *And if your head explodes with dark forebodings too, I'll see you on the dark side of the moon ...* ♪
> -   Pink Floyd

John Peel spends the whole of his programme totally dedicated to this astounding album – Pink Floyd's *Dark Side of the Moon*. We listen to it in stereo and Polly and Jasper are amazed to hear the sounds move from one side of the room to the other.

I take the gang of children round to David and Roger's to watch *Monty Python*. This ground-breaking comedy has grown out of the humour of *The Goons*, the madness of *The Alberts* with a healthy dose of Dud and Pete's satire. We all become great *Python* fans. Interestingly, they use the farting foot in their title sequence, which Bruce Lacey had originally created.

Roger Lloyd Pack and I have gone to see a Cornish community theatre company called The Footsbarn. They have come to Wells-Next-The-Sea and set up a marquee on the green with benches all around the edge. They perform *A Midsummer Night's Dream* in the centre. We locals all sit around, children and grannies. Dogs run in and out while these energetic actors create a magic happening. They can do it all – they juggle and swordfight, they sing and clown around, and dance with members of the audience. The set up reminds me of Sean Kenny's set for *Stop the World, I Want to Get Off*. We gather with the actors in the pub afterwards and Rog and I just want to pack our bags and join them on the road. *This* is what theatre is about – hands on, in your lap, in this moment – we make you laugh, we make you cry and we leave you wondering … the roving players, the troubadours. I'm so moved by them, I tell Mickgough. He relays it on to the people at The National Theatre and in a while they engage The Footsbarn to perform in the foyer, and this launches them on an illustrious career, touring the theatres of Europe.

Charlie has had a fruit machine installed in the pub. One lunchtime we are having a drink and Jasper is on the machine, when 'Ting! Ting! Ting!' – he has won – and all the change has spilled out over the floor. When he's picked it up, it amounts to seven pounds. He solemnly announces to all the old boys sitting on the bench that he will buy them all a drink, and for Mrs Cox, he buys a box of chocolates.

Tom Bantock and Antonia Fraser enter our lives. He comes from an Anglo-Irish family. His mother had travelled in India with Lady Betjeman. He is six foot and skinny with a crew cut and a flying jacket and cowboy boots. Antonia's mother is an archaeologist and explorer. Antonia is also six foot, skinny with a crew cut, and the same leather jacket, so they look like twins. Tom is a sort of eighteenth century poacher rogue. He arrives with a team of Irish Wolfhound lurchers at his heals and they want to stay while they are negotiating the buying of their farmhouse nearby. Tom is thick with the local gypsies and wants to put some of his wagons on our field. He drives a green Triumph TR2 and he lets me drive the children to school in it – we can reach 70 mph on the Morston road and we are all shrieking with excitement. This car now enters my dreams. When things get hairy I leap into my green machine and with my foot pressed down hard, I escape the ghastly nightmare. I dream that I can fly, but sometimes I can't get off the ground, and the baddies are coming to get me.

Antonia has been travelling in Afghanistan and is trading in ethnic clothing and jewellery. I love the dresses. Embroidered bodices and very full skirts, my hands smothered in antique rings and I wear Spanish riding boots. My other favourites are a red 1930s Fairisle cardigan and my wide flared jeans.

Now the nights are filled with much laughter and feasting. Jugged hare! The kitchen floor littered with huge, sleeping dogs. After supper, we go out across the frosty fields, coursing in the starlit nights.

Antonia has a friend in Scotland who has opened his Baronial home and is running it as a hotel. She's taking Polly with her for a holiday. Polly is ten now and is busy packing for her very own adventure.

'We're going to be staying in a castle mummy!'

After a week, Mickgough, Jasper and I go up by train to Oban and join them for a night and to bring Polly home. We are amazed to see Polly was right – it is an enormous old Scottish castle, now being run by the 'Monarch of the Glen'. As we climb out of Antonia's old Jeep, the Laird is coming to meet us. He's a dashing 40-year old with a thick beard and a big grin, dressed in a kilt and brogues. But unusually, it's my hand he is immediately shaking.

'*The Highlanders* was my favourite story....' He's a *Doctor Who* fan! So with a polite nod to Mickgough, he has tucked my hand under his arm and I can see by the look in his eye, he wants to whisk me away to his battlements.

'So how *was* it working with Patrick Troughton?' That night we are dressing for dinner. Antonia has lent a little black velvet jacket and a swirling tartan skirt. The very long dining table is laid in the big hall which has the ancestral armoury mounted on the walls. As we are taking our places, my Scottish hero collects me up and seats me next to him in the place of honour. I can see Mickgough is seething with fury, down 'below the salt'. When the feasting is finished, the tables are cleared. The fiddlers tune up, the dancing begins, and I'm drunkenly capering up and down with the Laird, his face is shining and his kilt is swinging. Mickgough is eaten up with rage, and won't speak to me for a week.

It's Christmas 1973. After the pub we are all gathered around the piano. Roger Lloyd Pack is playing and we are singing carols. Robert is part of our group – he's Marilyn's brother, and Marilyn is married to David's brother (do keep up!). He has long blond hair, a velvet jacket, plays the viola and he's flirting with me and I like it, even though I know it's a very dangerous game - the last time I had a lover Mickgough came close to killing me – but I'm feeling starved.

Marilyn and I have hatched a plan to start a flea market stall at the market on Thursdays. We both have so much clutter and so we hope to be able to make a little money for ourselves. We set it up with much care and attention. I've bought a Dutch postman's left-hand drive VW Bus, and we pack up all our goodies on Wednesday evening and are unpacking at 6:30 next morning with all the other stallholders. Our stall becomes very popular. We have an Edwardian mannequin draped in hats, feather boas, antique clothes and beads, the table is crammed with lovely china – Clarice Cliffe, Royal

Doulton tobacco jars, tin toys, antique clothes and books. Marilyn is very proud of her father, who was a miner in Stoke-on-Trent. She grew up in The Potteries and has an astute eye for 20s and 30s china. During the day friends will come and park their dogs and babies. The van is open at the back of us so I'm making coffee on the stove and we play music to enhance the atmosphere. We are selling and trading and we love it.

♪ *Woo hoo, witchy woman, she's got the moon in her eyes…* ♪
- The Eagles

When I've made enough money - £100 - I buy one of Tom's wagons. It's genuine Irish. I strip it down, repaint it and get a new canvas roof. It's months of work, and in the end it is gorgeously restored.

Etching of the wagon

We've worked very hard in the veg patch, clearing out the deep horseradish roots, nettles and docks, but finally it's pretty clear, and I've planted peas and beans and beetroot.

42

My mother is coming for another visit. Mickgough is very clear.

'I shall be in the drawing room – you can bring me my meals there, and tell me when she's gone.' Very supportive! Roger Lloyd Pack says she can stay in his cottage. So Tom trailers the wagon over there too, and the children and I can stay there with her. I say to Linda,

'We are away for a week, so do help yourself to some peas,' I'm so proud that my efforts can be shared. When I get back, she has stripped the plants, eaten what she could and put the rest in her freezer – obviously this community spirit has to be worked on! This time my mother's stories are of California. She's been staying with friends in Oakland, enjoying meeting and hanging out with the university students. She loves young and open modern minds. She loves Robert – I've taken the risk and I'm now getting it on with him when Mickgough's not at home – well, I have a need to love and to be loved. Mickgough still withholds his love from me – always judging, criticising; and here is beautiful young Robert, adoring me – attentive and romantic and a great lover. Mind you, I always make sure Mickgough's rice pudding is in the oven when he comes home. My mother gets Robert to play *The Foggy, Foggy Dew* on his viola in the garden. We all go to the Hastings Arms pub where we sit with all the gypsies – my mother is right at home. One old lady has a face like oak bark and is smothered in gold jewellery and teeth. We ask her how old she is. She adds up scores of years on her fingers, we reckon she's over 100. She pins us with a bright look,

'It's not the body, it's the spirit that stays young!' My mother is 57 – her spirit is eternally young, but I feel her age and her frailty this time. She's planning to stay with friends in the south. But now I must take her to our doctor as she hasn't been feeling very well lately. He dismisses her with,

'Well, you look healthy enough,'

'That's just because I'm tanned!' She's exasperated. Her cancer is not diagnosed. Oh, Moe, I wish I could make you safe, give you a home, make sure you have what you need, but I'm only hanging on by a thread as it is.

♪ *Hanging on in quiet desperation is the English Way…* ♪
-        Pink Floyd

43

Since Mickgough is the only one left who hasn't taken acid, he's decided he wants to try it. He's read Aldous Huxley's book, *The Doors of Perception and Heaven and Hell,* and he's intrigued. Jonathan will supply the dosage. Polly and Jasper are away with their friends, the phone is off the hook, the house is beautiful with flowers and sweet food ready in the larder for later. I will be with him to take care. He's beautiful. He starts around the garden, on his knees.

'Aah, it's so – so – yes it's – aah!' We walk across the fields and he has become my knight. Pushing back the hedges to let me pass, he's talking to the herd of cows, lying on his stomach watching the insects and tiny flowers, stretched out amongst the tall grasses and laughing. Many hours later we are walking back down our lane. An old local goes by on his bike.

'Artanoon!'

'HALLOOOOO!' Says Mickgough, as if he's on Dury Lane Stage. 'How aaaah you?!' The old boy falls off his bike, into the hedge. Mickgough is mortified. In that single moment he understood what I had always said. How when you are using the full force of your personality, it bombards the other person. It's actually a sort of violence.

Late that night, sitting beside the embers of the fire, the candles are lit and we are drinking tea, and we talk. Real talk. This is the Mickgough that I love, inside all the actor bluff, just ordinary, beautiful him. We both have lovers. As long as the two of us are solid in our marriage, then isn't it possible to love other people too? If he's going to have lovers, I want the same freedom. He has become so real that he can empathise and he seems open to the possibility. A few days later I overhear him on the phone to a friend.

'Load of old balls, dear. Give me a pork chop and a cigar over acid anytime.' He has reverted to his old self. I'm going to have to be very careful with Robert, who I'm beginning to really love.

Polly is going to the local secondary modern school. She's failed her 11 plus, she's not academic. She doesn't care because all her close friends go with her. She's good at music, painting and sewing, and she loves little children. Jasper gets a proper big bike, and cycles to his school every day. Mick is very busy at the National Theatre and doesn't seem to get home much.

Persephone tells me about a group of 'seekers' who have been out in India with a spiritual Master. They need somewhere peaceful where they can spend a weekend meditating. We clear out the barn, lay more carpets and set up some simple cooking facilities. About 15 of them arrive in various cars and vans. They are all dressed in red or orange, and wear a beaded wooden necklace around their necks, with a photo of their 'Guru'. They are very friendly, laugh a lot, play footie with Jasper, and they invite me to participate in their Dynamic Meditation. Blindfolded – I puff and breathe, and then everybody is shouting and screaming, so I join in. We have to jump up and down with our arms up in the air, and shout.

'Hoo! Hoo! Hoo! Hoo!'

Then we are still, and we soften and dance. When it is over they play a tape of Bhagwan, their Guru, talking – but I can't understand his Indian accent and I don't want to be indoctrinated, so I walk out into the garden on my own, and I feel like a new born lamb, all soft and innocent. I feel sorry for these people, who are so full of life and laughter, having to wear a uniform and a badge. There's no way I would do that – just another form of slavery – *I'm an individual!*

Mickgough's previous wives want money, so the bailiffs are coming to check out our home. Just like back in Barkston Garden days, I'm left to deal with them. I ask them if they would mind taking their shoes off,

'As it's my religion,'

They seem to leave their bailiff's attitudes at the door with their shoes. I make them coffee and show them around in their socksies. One of them complains that he has gout.

'Ah, you must pee on your feet – it's supposed to really help,' By the time they leave we are all best friends, and as they put on their shoes, they tell me that they have noted that this home contains 'nothing of any value'. We are off the hook again.

Roddy, Jane and their daughters Hannah and Alice live in such a beautiful house in the next village. It's huge, with an Elizabethan staircase and doors, large barns and walled gardens full of figs. Jane is an inspired gardener and she is busy planting beech hedges and herbs amongst the flag-stoned terraces. She has a kitchen from *heaven*. Next to the Aga, is a single daybed, to rest and read. A ten-foot Welsh dresser is smothered in early country china. There is a long refectory table, a pantry and an enormous larder with marble shelves full of antique country dishes. Next door to that is a room to make pastry, as she is a renowned cook. While she is finishing off her delicious supper for us, we watch Roddy's slides in the drawing room at the end of the house. He has such a good eye, his shots are masterpieces. What a unique and talented man he is. He sits at the kitchen table with his black covered art book, and a small stylo pen, and draws as he talks. Wonderful Zen-type doodly pieces of magic. Roddy collects round stones, so the shelves and tables begin to get covered in more and more round stones. Jane is worried she's going to get 'buried in stones'. The yard is full of bantams clucking about.

Pastel of Jane's garden

Chapter 5

On the Edge of the Unknown

I'm over at David and Roger's making some old velour hangings into curtains to go across their front windows, when Persephone bangs on the door.

'Oh my God! You've done it!' She's dressed from head to toe in orange and with a big grin she announces,

'I've become a disciple,' Well, you could have knocked me down with a feather. I had no idea she would do that, and I want to hear all about it. It seems that all the people she most admires in her 'Community' circle, Paul and Clare Lowe, Denny Yuson and Michael Barnett, the group leaders of the day have been to India, had meetings with The Master and have become disciples. So she has written her letter and received a new name – Ma Veetasmi.

'It means *beyond ego*.'

Well, I think she's lost the plot altogether, but still, each to their own. There's no way I would do that!

Tom and Antonia have moved into their somewhat remote farmhouse. They have given a sumptuous feast as a housewarming party. It's all very gothic. A massive carved wooden screen as a headboard for a treble-sized bed (he's hoping for many wenches). Long refectory tables are strewn with pewter plates piled high with game. When David and Roger go over a week or so later they find the tables as we had left them, empty wine glasses and leftovers rotting in the dishes. Tom and Antonia have gone to Scotland – back later.

Michael Craze calls me with the sad news that William Hartnell's died. I wish Mike lived nearer, so that we could have a drink together. He's not been getting any work. No work? He's so beautiful and talented! He's thinking of working as a pub landlord. I have to wonder if it's a wise choice – he might drown his disappointment. Acting can be the meanest profession of them all.

Roger Lloyd Pack has met the love of his life. Her name is Jehane Markham and together they've managed to buy his little cottage. He and Jonathan are busy retiling the roof, and renovating, and while the work goes on, Jehane and Roger are staying with us, having baths and suppers after the dirty day's work. One day we drive to a derelict Victorian workhouse and fill my VW with black and tan tiles, which will be laid in their kitchen, and we give them our old ship's table. I always like to spread myself around my friends' homes.

Jasper, Jehane and Roger

The Stiffkey village hall is falling down. Money is needed to build a new one. David and Roger are on the fete committee. They throw themselves into it with enthusiasm - a perfect canvas for their ingenuity and sense of fun. It will be held on the field above the

48

village. Mickgough has promised to open it, and Roger Lloyd Pack dresses as a vampire, which makes a huge impression on Jasper. David and Roger make a finely balanced platform, with a brass bed attached. When the bean bag hits the target, the fat lady will fall out of the bed. It's Josephine, who's dressed in Victorian lace. Richard has offered to be in the stocks – he dresses in a First World War military jacket. There is a fancy dress competition and Roger Lloyd Pack's daughter Emily looks sweet in her ethnic clothes.

Jehane

Emily

Linda looks luscious as an 18th century Bo Peep in a very low cut bodice and blonde curls under a large straw hat. She has their new pet lamb – 'Lambert' – on the end of a blue satin ribbon. It's a beautiful warm August day. Josephine is obligingly falling out of the bed with loud shrieks, and flashing of breasts and suspenders. The local old boys can't get enough! Poor Richard is receiving all the negativity of the crowd as they hurl eggs, tomatoes and abuse at him. At the end of the day, he's very shaken. Marilyn and I have our stall set up with a wind-up gramophone playing 78s. Mickgough and Jehane award the first prize for the fancy dress to an 84 year-old man from the village who is in an authentic Victorian Crinoline and bonnet, and has even made his face up!

Mickgough with the winner

A local comes up to our stall.

'Aren't you the girl from *Doctor Who*?'

'Yes! No! Not anymore. Excuse me!' And Marilyn is surprised to see me dive behind the table.

'I thought if you were in the acting profession you would love the attention!'

'Mickgough does – I don't – it's different for everyone. Anyway, it was another life. Now – what price shall we put on this Spelta figure?' Back in the sixties I hated the publicity that went with the job and went to ridiculous lengths to avoid it. The day ends with two local teams playing football, and an over excited David filming their bums. We have raised enough money for a new village hall, with a bar for the locals, which will be built next year.

Our white doves have been hanging out with the local pigeons up on the church tower. They've long since packed in all that tumbling lark and are happily breeding! The children and I love to walk across the sands when the tide is out. This time we've gone with an old local man who digs for the famous 'Stewkey Blues' – wonderful cockles. We are very far out from the land and suddenly he holds his weather-beaten old hand up.

'Ah – there 'tis!' His face is lit up with pleasure.

'What? What?!' We can't see what he's alluding to.

'The turn of the tide. We need to get back now, cause that'll be comin' in now, and fast … you have to respect the tide,' These sand flats are notorious for cutting people off. Polly is squealing with fear.

'Quick mummy, quick!' At the same time she's very excited. Polly has a favourite story, *The Little Wooden Doll*. When we get to the sad bit she sobs and howls and loves it, even though we've read it so many times.

'Read it again!'

Jasper is passionate about Elvis Presley. He stomps around the house, singing.

♫ *Return to sender… address unknown…* ♫

He also spends hours up in his room, his fine hands painting his little model armies – he's just like his Dad. Mickgough spends his evenings meticulously making models and doing jigsaws. And I hate him! I want his attention!   There is a lot of ghostly activity on our main stairs. You can hear people going up and down. One night I'm in our bedroom, sitting cross-legged, practising my guitar – Jonathan has taught me the 12-bar blues – but I can't concentrate because the ghosts are disturbing me.

'Shut up you lot!' I roar. And they do! Many visitors hear 'an old man stoking the fire' in an upstairs room, and hauntingly, there is the sound of a young girl sobbing – sobbing her heart out – it comes from the end of the house where the dairy used to be. When you get closer, it stops, and so you forget and go back to what you were doing. And suddenly, there it is again. We all hear it. I think it's Polly in another time, endlessly breaking her heart.

My periods have become outrageous, so we are off to see a specialist, Dame Josephine Barnes in Harley Street. Because of the ghastly abortion, back in the early sixties, my insides aren't working as they should, which is why the heavens open and I bleed profusely for two weeks of every month, so now I am chronically anaemic. Ever since that terrible time, I dream I'm looking down and seeing myself on a bed. There is so much blood, and some small thing that I want to rescue and love and feed. My spirit *saw* what was happening to me during that cruel operation, which was such a violation. The spirit *never forgets*.

Mickgough and I both agree that we won't have any more children, so I am to have a hysterectomy. We go to see the surgeon who will perform the operation at the Norfolk and Norwich Hospital. He is talking to Mickgough about 'leaving the playground, just removing the nursery'. I'm outraged and I take an instant dislike to him. I'm also very frightened, because this is major surgery. I've never had any faith in doctors – I've had too many traumatic experiences with them. I mostly find them really arrogant, so I don't trust the buggers. There is a Californian Doctor nicknamed Doctor Jellybeans, because he advocates eating a pound of sugar before major surgery, to keep the blood sugar up. So I have bought myself a box of chocolates. I've told the hospital I'm vegetarian and when it's all over they feed me tinned peas and carrots and ancient fluffy apples. David and Roger come with supplies – home baked bread, veggies from their garden. I'm taking massive doses of supplements and vitamins. I'm listening to Janis Joplin on my headphones and doing Yoga exercises as soon as I am able. The nurses are intrigued by me but grumble because there is always a trail of mud around my bed after my visitors have left. Six weeks later, I'm well enough to go horse riding with Polly. I go to have a check up with the surgeon. He's very pleased with himself.

'A model recovery,' he preens.

'No thanks to you!' I retort. 'The nutrition in this hospital is hopeless. If I hadn't been supplied with fresh food and supplements…'

'Oh well, if you believe it does you any good …' he says, indulgently. I'm glad it's all over, and I am utterly relieved to be finally done with this monthly moon draining. When I had a period in Thailand the packs of wild dogs that roamed the streets of the Thai villages would follow me home, sniffing. And at last, I'm free of the worry of contraception.

Marilyn and I are travelling around to the local auctions and visiting junk yards to collect items for our market stall. We put in a lot of work, but seem to be just ticking over. Robert is becoming quite needy – I've got to wriggle out of this relationship somehow.

The Wells Centre plan is going from strength to strength. It's really happening. But now Mick has become the star of the show, so Nancy and I feel it's been rather taken out of our hands, but we are happy that it's got a life of its own. She has bought the most wonderful ticket booth. It's an Edwardian mahogany bow-fronted cash desk, with bevelled glass and a glass-sided door, and she wants to put it in the building when they move in. For now, it's parked in our barn. Mickgough and I and RSW and his wife go to visit an arts centre in Suffolk. Ronnie has immaculate manners, opening doors, taking great loving care of his wife. Driving home, I lay into Mick.

'Did you notice? That's how I would like to be treated!'

'Middle class bullshit.' He sneers. 'You want equality – you can't have it both ways.'

Roger and Jehane and I go to Wembley Stadium to see a Crosby, Stills and Nash concert. A wonderful feeling of being bonded in the warm sunshine, with a few thousand like-minded souls, all singing.

♪ *Yes, only love can break your heart* ... ♪
-    Crosby, Stills and Nash

It's Friday night and Mickgough is due home from London. I put his supper in the oven, I'm tired and I can't wait up. I wake up, it's 2:30 and he hasn't come home. I know he is seeing a local woman and now I'm in the madness of jealousy. I just know he's with her. We women always know. I drive angrily to the next village. Sure enough, there is his car in front of her cottage. I knew it, damn him. I don't want to be at home when he gets back. I let myself into Jonathan and Linda's. I cry and fall asleep in front of the Rayburn. In the morning, Jasper wakes me up,

'I can't find the marmite, and I like your hat mum,' I had got cold, and put the tea cosy on my head.

Mickgough announces that Simon and Sharon are going to move in with us while they renovate the beautiful farmhouse they've just bought. It's the last straw. I can't cope with this. Simon is not easy at the best of times, and Sharon has two demanding, wild children. I shall drown in domesticity.

'May I take a break?'

'As long as you like,' comes the answer. 'We won't miss you. Polly adores Sharon, Simon can run them to school, I'll be at home a lot this winter – go and sort yourself out, do!' It makes me feel redundant.

♪ *Let your soul and spirit fly into the mystic …* ♪
- Van Morrison

I might go and find Alan Watts in California (I've been reading his book, *The Wisdom of Insecurity*), or I might do a meditation course. I take my meagre market stall savings and drive the VW to London. I'm hoping that if I do that meditation course Veetasmi speaks of, I may become clearer, and see in what direction I want to go for my *save my soul* break. I enrol at Kalptaru in Lonsdale Square and afterwards, as I drive away, I wonder where I'm going to stay while I'm doing this course. Since I'm up in North London, I have a brain wave. I'll go and see Mrs Craxton. I'm feeling elated, as I walk up the steps to Kidderpore Avenue, my old home, once again. I ring the bell. Mrs Craxton opens the door.

'My dear!' She's exactly the same. Untidy hair in a bun, many pairs of specs dangling down her front, the flat shoes. We are both overjoyed to see each other again.

'Come in, come in. *Have you eaten?*' When I tell her what I'm doing, she says,

'Well, you know where your room is. I'll just pop some soup on and I'm sure I have some pie left over from lunch. John will be home later, he'll be so happy to see you …'

In the next moment, I'm standing once again in my old room, looking at my reflection in the same mirrored Victorian wardrobe that I used to practice my speeches in when I was at drama school, 20 years earlier. And today, it's my birthday – I'm 34, and I feel I'm on the edge of the unknown...

In the basement of the centre, we do the Dynamic Meditation – this time with intention. After the hefty ten-minute breathing, we let loose into a ten-minute catharsis. At first I'm a little shy but before long I'm joining the others yelling and howling and letting it all out. Then we freeze and stay utterly still for ten minutes. The sweat pours down my face and I 'watch' my energy pounding away. Then we are into the *Hoo! Hoo! Hoo!* – jumping up and down with our arms in the air, and then we celebrate, dance, lie down. All this is done blindfolded, so we stay in our own space. We have a wash and a pee break, a cup of tea, and making ourselves comfortable we close our eyes and open our hearts, and listen – to one of Bhagwan's discourses, recorded recently in Poona, India. The discourse is called *The Way of the White Clouds*.

He is talking about spirituality, aloneness, relationships, love and sex ... the words are like drops of rain on the parched desert of my soul. At last. These words. My heart knows this is truth because I have always known. I am dissolving into tears of relief. These are the words I have been longing to hear, my whole life.

'Good to stay in silence when you come home,' says Mrs Craxton. I pour myself some soup and sit at the kitchen table. I know that something profound has happened to me but I'm trying not to bring my mind into it, with all its fears and worries. Bhagwan is telling us to be loose, and natural.

Meanwhile I'm busy running this household. It's really wonderful to be back here at the Craxtons'. Mrs Craxton is so understanding and encouraging about the meditation course. I will help her during the day. Mr Craxton died some years ago. She tells me with pride of the memorial concert that was held at the Festival Hall with royalty and her son Anthony filming it for the BBC. A sad loss to the music world. The house now runs as a music studio. Stella the cook is no longer there, so I take over, making lunches for the household and teas for the visiting orchestras. Today, Mrs Craxton is listening to a French orchestra playing Vivaldi.

'Too fast, two fast!' she says, shaking her head as she pours the china tea on the trolley. When they come out of the studio and into the dining room, they eat everything in sight, even the nuts on the marble sideboard, and leave crumbs all over the floor. These musicians! It's a gift for me to be able to give something back to this wonderful woman, Essie Craxton. She's now very elderly, and I am now the one loading up the trolley and making treacle tart. One afternoon she's asleep in the study. She makes a whispering sound,

'Harold? Harold?'

I'm afraid she might be dying.

'Anything I can get you?'

'No, no dear, thank you. The space I have to get through at the end is very small...' Neither she nor John have any criticisms or judgements, because they love me.

I read some of the blurb about Rajneesh. The emphasis in this meditation is moving from the head back to the heart, letting go of tension, and allowing your inner volcano to erupt.

'The calmness, the serenity, the Nirvana, comes not by stilling the mind, but by explosion'

I have made two friends on the course. One is a GP, and his girlfriend is an artist. They have become disciples. Their names have been changed to Asanga and Samapatti. I ask them loads of questions.

'But is it a religion?'

'No, Bhagwan is the source of the truth. That's why it's so potent. Like being with Buddha before the teaching became known as Buddhism.'

'But why the new name, and the necklace?'

'To make a break with your past. The mala has 108 beads, signifying the 108 ways of meditation.'

'Are there any rules?'

'The main requirement is to 'wake up'.' That's interesting... Gurdjieff always said we were fast asleep.

At the end of the ten days, I feel light and clear and full of energy, and I know that I want to become a disciple. Nothing else is as important. Before I write my letter to Bhagwan. I'm told,

'You must tell him what's in your heart. You must enclose a photo with your eyes clear. Then you will receive your new name.'

I'm writing to one of the most important spiritual teachers of our times, so I try to be concise and clear. I tell him about my guilt, after all I have the total recipe for happiness -a good life, a successful hubby, two gorgeous kids and a beautiful home. So how come I feel so confused and hurt and miserable? I tell him how Mickgough thinks I'm basically a bad person, but how I don't feel bad inside. And, why is it ok for the man to have lovers, but if the woman does, she's a whore? How I know, that when I love someone, it feels like a holy state. I want so much to go beyond this emotional pain and confusion. I've had glimpses of other states of being. I want to know who I am.

On a beautiful autumn day, I walk up Kidderpore Avenue to the post box at the top of the hill, and kissing the envelope, I post the letter which will probably change my life forever.

'I'm off to Whitechapel Market,' calls John. 'Anything you want?' I'm lying in the bath under his beautiful mural of figures in a Greek landscape.

'Yeah! An inlaid ivory picture frame for my Guroooo!' That evening when I get home, lying on my bed is a beautiful Indian, inlaid, ivory picture frame, and when I slot in the photo I have of Bhagwan, it fits exactly … now I have him laughing at me, as I brush my hair and worry about the future. He's laughing, as I cry, and miss my children. I'm being drawn into his world.

My reply from Poona is sitting in the letter rack in the hall. I take it to my room so I can read it in private.

'Beloved, your beautiful letter reached us and Bhagwan has given you a new name. Ma Prem Anita. It means Love Beyond Morality. It would be good if you could come soon, much is happening here. Love, Ma Yoga Laxmi.'

I'm overjoyed, and also, I must admit, a bit disappointed. Other people's names were so exotic. I, who always loved the name Anneke, will be known as Anita, but also, it's good. The whole point is to dis-identify with your past, so now, I'm not attached to any name and I'm given my wooden beaded necklace, with a picture of Bhagwan. When Asanga and Sammapati tell me they have booked their flights to India, I feel an instant stab in my guts. Oh wow. They're going. If only ... if only. But I can't, I have no money. That night, I have a dream. Bhagwan is there, in his white robes, laughing, and I hear him say,

'Nothing to be worried. Sell your van!' When I wake in the morning, there are his eyes, laughing away at me. I tell Mrs Craxton. She knows someone who'll buy it for £300. Mickgough is doing *Flea in Her Ear* at The National Theatre, and comes to have tea. I tell him my new name and its meaning.

'Hmph!' he says. 'Well you've found the Guru for you!' In front of Mrs Craxton, I ask him for permission to go to Poona. He agrees.

'I'm hoping it will change me enough,' I say, 'that I can return to Norfolk happier and more content.' Polly and Jasper have written to me, which makes me very sad because it accentuates the distance between us. But I have come so far, I can't turn back. And so, in the beginning of December 1975, I fly on my own to Bombay, to go to the Ashram of Bhagwan Shree Rajneesh.

Chapter 6

Ma Prem Anita

In the tiny Himalayan Kingdom of Sikkim, His Holiness Lama Karmapa has said of Bhagwan,

'He is the Greatest Incarnation since Buddha in India. He was *realised* in previous births and was one of the 99 Tibetan Avatars. His Golden Statue of two lifetimes ago is still in existence and being carefully preserved in the Halls of Incarnation, a secret cave in Tibet.'

As soon as I step off the plane, I'm struck at once by a feeling of déjà vu.

'I know this place.' Crossing the city to the train station, to catch the 'Deccan Queen' train to Poona, 'I know these sights and sounds.' They are so ancient. It's biblical. The train rattles for hours through the landscape, where once proud elephants strode, I see dirty thirties bungalows, and roads full of people and potholes. I take a room at The Railway Hotel. The bed is clean, a boy brings me a tray of tea, I'm exhausted. I'm woken by the sound of the street wallahs and the traffic chaos. I've slept long, and I'm hot. In the corner of the room is a stall with a tap and a plastic bucket and jug so I wash, drink more tea, and take a rickshaw.

'Where to?'

'Umm ... 17, Koregaon Park?'

'The ashram! Yes baba!' They all seem to know it. We rattle down a wide residential road. Huge mansions behind pillared porticoes, shabby plastered gateways and overgrown gardens. The road is shaded with banyan trees. All along the way are orange-clad disciples, strolling arm in arm. There are beggars and peddlers with their wares spread out in the street. What a scene! I feel overwhelmed and self-conscious, and very English. There are many bicycles parked outside the small wrought iron gate. A jolly Sikh is the guard and I'm waved in.

'Go to the office,' I sign in. I fill in forms. What is your occupation? I don't know what to say, so I put *housewife*. Everyone seems very kind in the office.

'She's just arrived – she can join in the celebration. Go with Mungala, she will give you soap and a towel – you must wash. She'll give you a robe and then you can join in the Darshan queue.' I explain that I have washed, but apparently Bagwhan has allergies, and so we must all wash our hair and clothes in special non-smelling soap. The ashram is very clean. I'm enviously watching these extraordinarily beautiful people floating past in robes and smiles. I'm going to see one of the most spiritual beings on the planet and I'm fussing because my fringe has gone curly in the heat. We are moving along the marble paths, through gates and suddenly, the rose-pink evening has turned to dusk. Night falls so quickly in India. We are edging slowly around 'His' luscious, overgrown garden. There is an over-powering smell of roses, marigolds, frangipani, and little twinkling lights in the trees. I hear distant music and laughter, excitement in the crowd is rising, and now we are entering a large hall, with pillars all around. It is called Chuang Tzu, and there are a few hundred people gathered in a circle, musicians and dancers. And then, there he is, in the distance, quite small, all in white, sitting in his chair on his podium, smiling, smiling, nodding. People are filing by and kissing his foot. I go into panic. Kissing his foot?! Can I do that? Bow down and kiss his foot?! The music and the mood intensify. As I'm getting closer, I feel like I'm melting, and then I'm down on my knees and happily kissing this divine foot, and I feel his hand placed on my head. Now I'm stumbling and being supported, by laughing, smiling, kind people. A little Prasad (cake), and soon the crowds are swelling back out into the night. Tears of joy are flowing. Later, I take a rickshaw back to my room, filled with love.

The next day we are filed into the garden for a special birthday meditation. Behind his house is a large lawn. His chair is placed under the trees. We gather round and sit. When we are all still, he enters. I'm watching. He is in a long white gown, with a small towel over his arm, his hands in *Namasté*, as he bows to us all.

Gently, he sits, and closes his eyes. The garden is filled with birdsong. In the distance the trains are shunting in the station, the sounds of India are floating away... Suddenly, I'm awake. I've opened my eyes to see that the garden is nearly empty. He's gone, and many people have left.

'But I thought we were to be here for an hour!' I say to my neighbour, stunned.

'We were,' she says, with an understanding smile. Now *that* was meditation!

It's very cold in the early mornings. At the end of the Dynamic Meditation I take off my blindfold and see the brilliant Indian dawn, clamorous with birdsong, and the ashram garden glittering with dew. Breakfast is bread, bananas and tea, and I am in the queue for the morning's discourse. I am sitting cross-legged on the cold marble floor in Chaung Tzu. Apart from the birds and the distant sounds of the trains shunting, the hall is utterly still and silent. The door opens and he's floating in and 'namasté-ing' all around. As his glance comes to me he looks directly at me for a moment. It's like an electric shock. A look of utter recognition. He sits in his white chair, crosses one leg over the other, places one beautiful hand on top of the other, and closes his eyes. The microphone is placed exactly where he will speak, so he won't move his body for the next hour and a half. When he opens his eyes he begins to speak quietly. The series of talks this month is called 'Come Follow Me', and he now starts talking about Jesus. He is speaking from the source. This is not the Jesus I was taught about in my village school; this is a vital and fiery man full of laughter and celebration; a master who brings revolutionary eastern teachings to an orthodox Judaic world. He's talking about 'love thy neighbour – as thyself' but we don't love ourselves, down the ages we've been condemned as 'sinners' and this has led to a deep division in humanity. If we cannot learn to love and respect ourselves, how can we love another?

'Enough for today,' and he's on his feet, 'namasté-ing' to us all. We are all sitting in stunned silence, small groups of people are hugging each other, many are weeping. Some are bowed forward, their head touching the ground. He will not emerge again till the evening, when he gives Darshan. He lives in seclusion, seldom leaving his room. He is a prodigious reader, with a permanent library staff keeping him stocked up with books on psychology and human growth.

We emerge back into the business of the ashram. It is six acres, a few houses. Bhagwan's quarters are at the back. He has guards at his gates. His family and a few Indian disciples live in one house, the rest are offices and accommodation for the disciples who run the place – the ashram is run by women because 'I want it to be run by the heart, not the intellect.' It's expanding very fast, because, he says, thousands will be coming. We are blessed to be here at the beginning. So the rest of us, we are called 'Sannyasins', have found accommodation in and around Koregaon Park. I can't imagine what the local residents feel about this invasion of westerners, all catharting away in the early hours, their peaceful, shady neighbourhood teaming with people and street-vendors and beggars. They have guards at their gateways, some have moved away, and the ashram has bought some of their houses in the back streets, which have become dormitories. Many people have built bamboo huts in the gardens. I have to leave my hotel and I am given a mattress and a mosquito net on one of the balconies. It's all I need, I spend my days at the ashram.

First things first. I look like I've just 'come from the west', so I must buy some clothes. We are encouraged to wear a robe so that there is nothing tight around our middles, as meditation is all about the flow of energy. I need a shawl for the cold mornings and cool evenings, some sandals – no need for knickers – what freedom! I sit outside the gates and smoke a beedie, which is a leaf rolled up with a smattering of tobacco inside –very delicious - and let the sun turn my skin brown. I see the beggars all around the gate, the little children are so bright eyed, and learning English. We play with them, give them 'baksheesh' and bananas. I sign up for the meditation camp. In the middle of the morning we do the 'Nataraj' – a dancing meditation.

'When the dancer disappears, only the dance remains.'

I dance and cry for everyone I love. I feel Robin is with me in this very moment, and he's happy for me. I dance for Mickgough, because it hurts so much. I dance for Polly and Jasper, because I want them to be proud of me. I dance for myself, because I've been brave enough to take the giant step into this reality.

A group of very haunted looking people go by. Some of them are hugging babies' bottles and one of them is wearing an orange, unmistakably Saville Row suit, carrying a teddy bear.
'Goodness! Who are they?' I ask.
'They are doing the Primal Group, and that guy is an English aristocrat who's dropped his title and has taken sannyas and his name is Devesh.

After the simple vegetarian lunch, eaten on our mats in the front garden, we lay in the meditation tent. It's the very hot part of the day, and everything slows down. We are listening to taped discourses. This time it's questions and answers. You can write in a question and he will answer you. I haven't even asked, but he is saying,

'When I look into your eyes, you will be shocked, because seeing is there. I love you, unconditionally.' People seem to ask questions about soul-mates and past lives. I hear Him say that all relationships come from the past, but not to get caught up with it - this present moment is so precious. As the heat softens into the mellow afternoon, we do the 'Nadabrahma', a Tibetan humming meditation. The music is utterly haunting. I wander back outside to the beedie temple in a daze. Now it is 'kundalini' time. This time we are all shaking our bodies and dancing wildly. At the end we lie down and the stillness is very deep. Lights are lit amongst the tropical lushness of the garden. It's time for supper. People are chatting and laughing, but much is happening within me, and I will stay quiet during these days. There is another meditation in the evening, while Bhagwan is giving his Darshan to a few invited followers, but I'm wiped, I need sleep. It's a build up. At the end of ten days I have touched places inside myself I never knew, and I feel quite empty and light, like a child.

Christmas is not celebrated at the ashram – it is just another working day. I've gone with Asanga and Samapatti to sit beside the river. I'm really missing my family on this day. Will Polly and Jasper remember they have a mum? I'm not missing the fuss that's made about the turkey, 'Getting the gravy right, *Dahling*', the whole song and dance. My Christmas supper is a potato pancake down at the station – one rupee!

I want to ask the Swami, who runs the meditations a question. He is sitting on a wall, with someone talking to him. I sit beside him and when he's free, he turns to me. I look into his eyes. They are like clear turquoise pools – I can dive into them. He is completely open. I mumble, and giggle. I want that – I want to be that clear. I check out the groups. Normally you must ask Bhagwan what groups he thinks you should do, but I'm not yet that surrendered – I still think I know best. Also, I'm in a hurry to become enlightened …

'So what are the most effective groups to do?'

'Well, Primal … but that takes three weeks. Encounter, definitely – Teertha goes for the jugular – there's nowhere to hide – that's a week long, and then there is Rolfing, which is the next best thing to Bhagwan, so I sign up for both. I will do whatever it takes. I mean business.

The rolfing is a form of extremely deep massage, and is very painful, but at the end of twelve sessions many of the ancient painful holding patterns are gone. The Encounter is terrifying - nowhere to hide – totally exposed. Teertha sees right into you and you see your 'stuff' very clearly. At one point, I have to stand up to a man in the group. I have to tell him to,

'Fuck off and get out of my way!' He is not to move. He is holding a cushion. I keep going. Suddenly he has morphed into Mickgough and I'm pounding the cushion with rage.

'FUCK OFF AND GET OUT OF MY WAY! I'M NOT HERE TO LIVE UP TO YOUR EXPECTATIONS!' I feel my roots spreading into the ground. My voice has deepened into a primal, female, thunderous outcry. I sit down, shaking. A woman sits behind me and places her hands on the base of my spine. My energy is racing. Later, another man is there, this time he has dark looks. I have to tell him not to hurt me.

'Don't hurt me. Don't hurt me!' I've suddenly become very little. 'Don't hurt me!' And there is my old childhood enemy, Roy, before me. 'Don't hurt me, you beast!' I scream and yell. 'Don't hurt me, I hate you!' I'm beating and punching him. Eventually I collapse in tears and the women in the group put their arms around me. Now we all have to stand naked in front of each other and share what we don't like about our bodies. *My bum's too big, my chest is too puny.* We all seem to share the same judgements and fears. When we share what we love about our bodies, I say,

'My hands, the tools of my creativity.' By the end of the group I feel like I have offloaded lifetimes of burdens.

Now I have two weeks before I have to go home, so I have decided to go to Goa. I'm told by the office,

'No, you have to ask Bhagwan if you can go.' I'm still not used to this idea that I can't do whatever I want, that now, someone other than Mickgough is in charge. When I get the reply, to go to Goa with his blessings, I immediately think it's because I'm such a hopeless case ... he's sending me away.

I take the boat along the coast to Goa. I'm looking out onto this magical Arabian sea. The boats we pass haven't changed their ropes since Jesus's time. The brown sails, the creaking decks, ancient visions. I'm taking 'Tantra – the Supreme Understanding' with me. It's the book that fell into my hand at the bookshop. I sleep on the deck, under the stars. I'm dressed in my robes, with a small badge which, in Hindi, says 'In Silence'. I'm respectfully left alone. This is an amazing freedom for me. I usually attract a lot of interest, especially from the males, but now, I'm a Sannyasin, and in this country, I'm respected, and given space to be.

I'm reflecting on my time in Poona. There is a synthesis of east meets west. Many of the meditations are eastern techniques that are thousands of years old which Bhagwan has adapted for our 20th century understanding. The groups are being led by the best from the west, so your onion is being well and truly peeled. There is a sign by the meditation tent - 'Leave your minds and your shoes here'. You have to open yourself up, let go, and trust.' After two days, the boat has arrived in Panjim harbour and I make my way through the labyrinthine market to the bus, squashing in with the chattering Indians, the chickens and fruit, we are off along the coast. I get out at Chapura. The bus rattles away and I am alone on a sandy ledge, just trees and bushes. I can hear the sea, so I make my way towards it, and in that moment I'm standing on the edge of paradise - an aqua-marine bay, blond sands, palm trees and rocks. I don't see any people. I make my way down. There are a few bodies up the beach, and they are naked, so I step out of my clothes, stuff them in my bag, and head out onto the rocks.

I find Asanga cleaning a fish on a rock. They have been here for a while. I'm swimming and meditating. At night the heavens are vast with stars. I'm in my sleeping bag on the beach and I have a candle in a coconut shell for a light …

'Good morning Baba! You like chillum?' A little brown cheeky face is smiling at me. Well, I must be in paradise.

There are people here. Not many, all westerners, although some of them look like they are natives of another planet. Very brown, skinny, naked people with bells round their ankles, carrying bundles of wood on their heads, a tea kettle hanging from their shoulder bags. They have lived here for years. When we see them walking south in the late afternoon, we know there is a party tonight, further down the beach. The drums are beginning to beat. There is a large gathering under the palms. The Portuguese travellers are partying, each person sitting on their mat, arms waving as the chantings become more resonant. We are stoned and tripping and dancing. There is no alcohol. Fires are lit and the drumming escalates. I'm playing in the fluorescent seas. I'm even managing to be ok with sitting in the chai shop on the beach, naked. Well, everyone else is, still …

All over India there are Holy Men – Saddhus – living naked. They are very far-out beings, with matted dreadlocks, glassy stares, orange stripes painted on their foreheads. Sometimes they are covered in ashes. They have no homes other than India itself. They are revered and respected, as are the sacred cows. At first it's weird because you can be buying material in a cloth shop, as you are waiting for your robe to be finished, drinking tea on the floor of the tailors, when a cow walks in. Or there is a raucous sound of instruments and drums banging, and a dead body covered in marigolds being carried by a crowd, down to the burning ghats by the river, or a holy procession with men with many needles or spikes sticking through their cheeks. They don't feel the pain; it's like walking on hot coals.

We take a bus to Anjuna market. What a vast and colourful scene. People from all over India with their wares spread out on the ground. Kashmiris with saffron, and carvings, and embroidered shawls. Tibetans with jewels and beads and silver. Rajastanis with drums and musical instruments. The smells of sandalwood and spices, smoke from the dung fires and water sprinkled on the dry ground. Bulls are wandering in and out of the crowd, garlanded with jasmine buds. There are astounding looking hippies, travellers from all over India. The sounds of flutes and tablas. This has happened this way for centuries, it is a timeless scene.

Back on our beach they are talking about Arumbol. It's very remote. I prick up my ears.
'Remote?'
'Yeah, it's where only the very far out hermits go,'
'Where is it?'
'Ten miles up the coast, you have to walk along the beach for a day, there's no bus, there's no town, nothing but a sweet lake next to the ocean, and a few bushes for the meditators to live in.' Right – that's it – I'm off. I get supplies, a kettle, a pot, some rice, onions and tea. I take the boat across the river very early in the morning. I will have to be walking in the high heat of the day to get there by nightfall. I'm feeling very apprehensive but I'm doing it anyway. I have enough water for today, but tonight I must find some sweet water to drink. I'm most worried about this. By midday I'm exhausted and hot – they were right – it's completely wild. The only people I've seen all day are fishermen. I find a tree with lovely dense shade and I lay down for a rest with my head on my pack.
'Baba, you must move!'
'What? What?' I'm waking up after a hot sleep. A fisherman is standing over me.

'What are you saying?'

'Baba this is not good to be under a cashew tree – the nuts can cause you much pain when they fall.'

'Thank you, thank you,' but he's marching away. I've eaten my glucose biscuits and my mango, and now the sky is turning lavender, and I truly hope those big trees up ahead are Arumbol Lake. They didn't exaggerate – it's a magic spot – completely wild. A large lake that I gratefully plunge into. Trees all around full of monkeys and parrots, and not a soul. It's very daunting but this is what, in a way, I have always craved, to be alone, on the planet, and to be at home in myself. Well, I must find a bush, some sweet water, and make my camp. I collect some twigs and make a fire. Asanga has shown me how to support the pot with stones. I make rice and tea and as the moon rises, I'm in my sleeping bag, and I'm pretty afraid.

'Oo-er, I'm all alone, in the jungle. What are all these sounds? What if ... what if ... no, don't go there ...trust!'

After a few days, I've got used to it. I swim and read and meditate and explore. I cook and sweep out my little camp. I clean my teeth in a sweet water stream. The crows are a nuisance because they want to eat my toothpaste. I've made myself a coconut cup, a coconut scrubby for washing up, a coconut light with my precious candle. I'm a happy hermit. *Tantra the Supreme Understanding*, washing over me, reaching down into my core, saying 'Yes' to everything. Happiness comes, you celebrate. Sadness comes, you say 'Yes'... But, one night I'm in my bag and I'm a bit anxious because the zip has broken, leaving me exposed. Suddenly, I feel a weight moving across me. My heart stops beating. I'm praying fast and furiously.

'Hello snake. Yes, it's me, lying here minding my own business. I won't hurt you, please don't hurt me...' As it slithers away in the moonlight I see it is a great big python.

Another morning, I'm in my camp, as naked as Eve, when a deep Hindi voice is babbling behind me. I turn to see a jungle man with a twelve inch knife at his waist, and he's shouting and gesturing towards me. Shit. This is it. Here I am, blonde, naked and alone. Just when I think my number is up, I manage to hear the word 'beedie'.

'Beedie? You want a beedie? Yes, yes, take!' And I give him my last packet. He grunts, nods and blessedly leaves. Phew, that was a close call. Maybe someone is looking after me? I mean, trust is all very well in the ashram, but out here in the world…?

I'm standing in my sweet stream cleaning my teeth when a huge tropical butterfly lands on my toothpaste. I'm gazing in wonder at the translucent colours of its wings, when it happens. I slip into the Absolute. The 'I' has dissolved. There is just this pulsating, perfect existence. I have no words or mind to describe it. Later, immersing the body in the soft sweet water of the lake, that old painful sense of separation has melted away. I am the water. The experience lasts for many hours. All is, and I am, in this perfect moment, a satori.

I haven't seen another hermit for the whole time I've been here, but I know I have lice, and I'm out of rice. Last night I dreamt of me in another life, standing at the counter of Larners ordering wine and brie. So now my time is up. I will make the journey back to the west carrying with me all the insights which I have gained. It's been a painful process, remembering who I am. My identity having become so enmeshed with Mickgough – the wife, the actress, the mother – but where was I? Everything will be alright. I can take on the roles assigned to me because I have touched that place inside where I have always been free, and no-one can take that away.

I have a farewell Darshan with Bhagwan. It's an intimate gathering on his back porch. He gives us a beautiful little box when we leave Him. Sitting at his feet is the most exquisite and alive moment I have ever experienced. He asks me if I have something to say. It's hard to say anything but I manage to mumble,

'I'm learning about trust.' And he gives me this beautiful answer.

'People say God is Love. But I say, God is Trust. Never lose trust in trust. And people will deceive you, and people will hurt you, but you keep trusting, because in the end, they are only hurting themselves. You stay open, and go on trusting. Very good, Anita. Come back soon.'

My farewell Darshan

Chapter 7

Tree of Love

I'm overjoyed to be back home, hugging Polly and Jasper, and telling Mickgough all about it. After all, it was he who introduced me to meditation in the early sixties, although he no longer practices. My body is in shock because it seems so cold, with the arctic winds whipping around the barns. The lovely apple green stair carpet is all stained with Simon's 'dish of tea'. The Victorian coronation cups are smashed, the plants haven't been watered and there's piles of ironing. But I don't mind – my beloved home seems so large and comfortable, and hot water comes out of the tap – what a luxury.

Simon and Sharon have moved into their farmhouse with their babies and dogs, and I'm buying orange coats, and dyeing sweaters. But did I really think I would slip back into my life and carry on as though nothing had happened? I certainly wasn't prepared for the judgements and criticisms I would receive from so many. Some people won't speak to me for years. Others are angry that I took such a risk … being in wobbly marriages themselves …how dare I! And now I want them to call me Anita – it's preposterous! Even Veetasmi is fed up because I keep talking about bliss, emptiness, let go etc..

'But they are the words that Bhagwan uses, so it's the language of the Sannyas world.'

I think that the Gurdjieff group will be so interested, but they dismiss me (their Guru is better than mine!). But Polly and Jasper are sticking up for me. People wonder if I've been brainwashed.

'Oh yeah,' says Jasper. 'She says her brain needs a good washing!' People ask whether it is all about free love.

'No!' says Polly, firmly. 'She's been to a mystery school.'

Jasper also defends me. One day, the vicar drives into our yard. Jasper greets him.

'Is your father in?'

'No ...'

'May I speak with your mother?'

'Well,' says Jasper, looking important. 'She's in retreat, meditating, and mustn't be disturbed.' The vicar looks nonplussed and drives off his Rover.

We have to go and have dinner with two of Mick's friends. I'm wearing my orange robes and expecting to be asked some good questions. These people are intelligent teachers. For the entire meal, there is no mention of the fact I've been in an ashram with an enlightened Master, listening to the unfolding mysteries of Zen and Taoism. Just at the end, the wife is playing footsie with Mickgough under the table and the husband is leering at me. The British press are calling Bhagwan 'the sex guru'. They are not interested in the wisdom and spirituality, or the insights I've had, they just think I'll be up for a bit of wife-swapping.

Jonathan takes me to Kings Lynn to buy an old Morris Minor Traveller. £150. I love it, and when I get it home, I sand and re-varnish the wood. It needs new brakes, but Mickgough says we can't afford them right now, so I must drive carefully.

Mick wants me to go with him to a first night at the National Theatre. Now, this is a big test for me – back into the world of the theatre. First nights always make me shy. So many of Mickgough's friends, great actors of the day. And here I am in my orange robes, and a fresh face. No lovely make up to hide behind – just me. But Mickgough says,

'Darling, you're beautiful. I'm so proud of you.' These are the very words I've wanted to hear for so long, yet somehow, now, I don't seem to need them as much. The evening is quite an ordeal for me but I try and stay true to myself. Bhagwan says,

'Be true, absolutely true – naked!'

A friend of Antonia's arrives. He opens the back door of his van and a few lurcher puppies jump out, grinning and yelping and licking our hands. Antonia is always trying to persuade me to have a lurcher.

'But they're so huge!'

'They do fold up!' Now here are these whippet-cross puppies – much smaller. I do love lurchers, and this one in particular, with a pointy nose and moustaches. We'll keep her, and call her Acha, which is Hindi for 'Good'. The children love her at once and are fetching her feeding bowls and a pillow by the fire. Our cat Gemini stalks off in utter disgust, nose in the air, and sulks on my bed for days.

Now Nancy is standing in the kitchen, she wants to know all about Bhagwan.

'What does he say about sex?' She always gets straight to the point.

'He says it's a journey, from sex to super-consciousness. It starts with sex, moves into love, ends in prayer. He's teaching us about love'.

She's hooked.

'What *else* does he say?'

'He says that we are given all that we need.'

'Well,' says Polly, who is sitting in the fireplace playing with Acha, 'Can I have a pony?'

When I was in Poona, I met a guy in the encounter group who said he'd come and visit me, as he had relatives in Norwich. Now, he's on his way, for lunch. His name is Akul, so I call him *Ah! Cool!* I overhear Mickgough on the phone in the hall.

'Some hippy-dippy friend of Anita's coming for lunch, so we'll talk later.'

This tall, good-looking man, in his mid-thirties jumps out of his Mercedes sports, wearing orange jeans and a mala. We hug. As we sit down to lunch, Mickgough asks suspiciously,

'So what do you do, Akul?'

'I'm on the Executive Council of the UN, so I live in Geneva …' Mickgough's going to grill him.

'What about this adulation you all seem to adopt?'

'It's not adulation of a man, it's a respect and a veneration for the highest level which a human being can reach. Being with him, we begin to feel the Godliness within ourselves…and of course, we all love him.'

'But isn't the ashram making shit loads of money?'

'Actually, the prices of the groups in the ashram are the cheapest in the world, and the best. For a five-day group with one of the top therapists, you pay less than £20. The main thing is to hear Bhagwan's lectures, which cost about 30p. And the evening Darshan costs no money at all, just commitment.'

Mickgough is washing up. The plummy voice on the radio announces,

'This is the BBC Home Service. Here is the news …'

I feel like an alien in this world. Where is my tribe?! There is a banging on the front door. I go to see who it is, Asanga and Samapatti, with backpacks and big grins.

With Mickgough's permission they move into the showman's wagon on the field – they love their new home – all mahogany and cut glass. We sweep out the barn so we can meditate in there. This is so brilliant for me, to keep the Poona energy going. Mickgough and Asanga have late night discussions about health and education. Samapatti and I are combing all the local second-hand shops for clothes and dyeing them 'autumn gold' in the washing machine. Nancy wants to come early in the morning to do the Dynamic, so does Richard and his wife Judy, so at 6:30 the barn resounds with what will be nicknamed 'the huff and puff'. Afterwards, we make porridge and listen to a discourse. It's all leaning towards the next natural step. First, we must run it past Mickgough.

'We would like to run a meditation centre for Bhagwan in the barn,' we say.

'As long as it is kept strictly in the barn, and not so full on as to be overwhelming.' I'm blown away at his generosity. But later, I hear him on the phone to Rex Harrison saying,

'No old dear, I'm just giving her enough rope to hang herself on.'

We write to Bhagwan to ask permission, and after a while we receive the Blessing and a name - Premtaru – which means 'tree of love'. Samapatti makes a beautiful sign, and we hang it on the gate. We need some funds to make the barn beautiful, a fitting place for our Master's work. Asanga has some savings, and I sell all the rings and antique jeweller I wore in the sixties – we don't wear jewellery any more. We clear out and repaint the barn, put down fresh carpets. We buy foam mattresses which Samapatti covers, we make huge pillows, upgrade the kitchen with big cooking pots and bread tins, we build a partition – one part for the meditations, the other for the library of Bhagwan's books, tapes and music. We have to make a hole in the door because the swallows fly 6000 miles back from Africa every year, and they were here first. We love to see their little beaks chirping for food. We are ready for our first mediation weekend.

There is quite a bit of interest. One woman pitches her tent on the field, meditates, and then retires to her tent to guzzle her home-made wine. She brings a friend who is an Australian lawyer, she will take Sannyas soon, and be called Anando. Some people come from London but the main support group is local, including Roddy Maude Roxby and Nancy. It's a great success and we are encouraged to extend into a four day retreat.

Meanwhile, I've been invited by the BBC to join the *Doctor Who* cast and crew for a party at White City. Once again I'm feeling very self-conscious in my robes and scrubbed face. Mike Craze is with me in the lift as we ascend to the party, and he's typically non-judgemental, but it's strange for me to step back into what used to be my life. It's astoundingly loud, everyone is knocking back free booze. Jon Pertwee comes up to me and gestures towards my mala.

'So Anneke, what's all this about?'

'Well, um…' Where to begin! 'Basically, it's about finding out who you are…'

'Who you are?! What do you want to know that for?! Why do you think I'm an actor? I don't want to know who I am! Give me another double!'

I had heard Bhagwan say how acting can be a deeply spiritual experience, as you get into lots of different roles, you get loose of the one that you think is you… all the world's a stage.

Afterwards, Roger Lloyd Pack and I go to a Rolling Stones concert. I am apprehensive of the large Earls Court crowd, but it is an amazing energy. The audience is ecstatic with anticipation, as this huge beautiful flower opens on the stage and Mick Jagger comes dancing out onto the edge of a big petal, and starts singing …

♫ *I can't get no… satisfaction…* ♫

We are standing on each other's shoulders by the end. The crowd has transformed into a whole and Jagger is baptising us all with buckets of water!

'The cow barn is on fire!' announces Jasper, running in from the yard.

'What? What happened? We'll call the fire brigade!' Jasper is looking sheepish. We rush into the old barn on the other side of the driveway. The cows are roaring and smoke is emerging. Mickgough is letting them out into the pen at the back, as the firemen arrive, and start pulling their hoses out. The farmer has been alerted, and there is a lot of damp straw and cow dung. When it's over, we bring the firemen a drink as they are packing up. Most of them are the dads of Polly and Jasper's friends at school. We are back in the kitchen, when the Fire Chief says,

'The police will come to find out what happened'.

'It wasn't Jasper,' says Polly, loyally. 'He was only practising a trick, then he came to play badminton with me and then it started.'

'But I put out the fire I made,' says Jasper, 'I did!' What a drama. When the Police come, we persuade them that it was just an accident. They want Mickgough's autograph for their wives.

Mickgough and I are getting on well. There's more love between us. Polly and Jasper are happy at their schools, although Jasper is going to miss Peter and Dickon this autumn because they are going to live in London, as Veetasmi is going to be running the London centre Kalptaru, which has a big new place in Camden Town. I've promised that the boys can come and stay with us for the holidays.

Simon has opened an antique book shop in Holt and Samapatti has made a beautiful sign for him to hang outside, and I have painted a sandwich board to stand in the street – BOOKS – OPEN!

Their farmhouse is very pretty and Sharon will have her mother Rachel Gurney to stay with them over Christmas, so at last we will have a mellow Christmas to ourselves, no big deal. Polly wants clothes and I give Jasper an Elvis LP. Mickgough has a few days off and it's so good to be together.

Premtaru is keeping busy. Many people are interested to know more about Bhagwan. We charge a reasonable rate, most of which goes back into the house fund, to cover expenses. But when we have one of the established leaders coming, then we are given a fee for accommodation and food, so all in all, it is working out really well. We don't expect to be paid anything for our work, it's our meditation, and hard work it certainly is. Keeping it all 'sannyas clean', cooking for 20 – 30 people sometimes, huge vegetable soups, nut roasts, home-made bread, sending out flyers and organising. We are a great team. Asanga runs the meditations, I do the shopping, cooking and cleaning, and Samapatti the art and office work. And it's unbelievably rewarding to see people change and grow, and drop their burdens and their neuroses, and get into their hearts and their playfulness. We are taking bookings well into the next year, everyone wants to come.

Veeresh, who used to be Denny Yuson, is coming in the spring, to do an 'aum' marathon. VEERESH?! He's a huge star in the Sannyas world, and his groups are legendary, so this one is totally booked up as soon as it's advertised.

We have a beautiful photo of Bhagwan on our 'Puja table' in the barn. It is the focus for the meditations. This day, I have decided that I want to have a Darshan with him, so I have washed and put on a robe, and sitting on a cushion I put on the Nadabrahma meditation tape. It's the most haunting music. As I am humming I am transported back to the ashram in the afternoons. I open my eyes and your eyes, Bhagwan, are beaming into mine. It makes me gasp with shock.

'Now you have no need for me to be in my body,' I hear you say.
'But ... but ...'

'Good, Anita.' With a chuckle, you've gone. I write to him in Poona to tell him of my experience and wonderfully, he answers my letter in a discourse.

'Anita has written to say that she can be with me when she looks into my eyes in a photograph, and this will be happening to many of you...' They send us the tape, and I couldn't be more overjoyed. Asanga cuts me down to size.

'Don't give it to the ego.'

Some money for repeats has come in, and I'm going to use it to get on with building a conservatory on the side of the house. The 'dairy doors' will open into it. I design it with Charlie's son Rodney, and we order up the wood and glass, dig beds for fig trees and lay pammets on the floor. It's so exciting, watching a building grow, I love it. We find some second-hand French doors. Rodney's up ladders with a friend, puttying in the glass. After many weekends, it's finally done. I paint the woodwork and plant a vine and a fig, install some wicker chairs and an iron table, and it's the most beautiful space, fulfilling a dream; I always wanted a conservatory.

Chapter 8

Zorba the Buddha

We are preparing for this big weekend. Luckily, Mickgough is away filming, so I don't have to worry about his needs. Veeresh runs a centre in Holland, and does his groups all over the world, and now he's coming to our little home-made Premtaru. I've cleaned and made over my room in the attic, especially for him. There are 23 participants who will eat and sleep in the barn, and two assistants, who we've put in the showman's wagon. The dairy is bursting with food and many loaves have already been made. The pillows are ready for bashing and the heaters are on so the place is welcoming. By early Friday evening, everyone has turned up, except Veeresh, who's coming from Holland. They've had their tea, and they are settling into a circle to wait, most of them are extremely anxious. Marathons are what they are!

Now he's arrived. Big hugs and smiles. He's completely captivating, small but dynamic. He enters the group room, goes to his place in the circle, sits down and closes his eyes. The moments pass. Then he speaks.

'Bhagwan loves Zorba the Greek. His passion, his wildness, his dance. He would like us to become Zorba the Buddhas – passionate and meditative. Drunk on the Divine. So tonight's session is called 'The Jolly Farmer''

Whispers go around the circle.

'The Jolly Farmer?' They are wondering if this is some new and terrible device.

'No,' I say. 'It's the pub!'

'The PUB?!'

'Yes!' says Veeresh. 'You are all to go to the pub, and enjoy.'

Well, we didn't need to be told twice, so 30 happy, orange people descend on our little village pub. The drinks flow, the jukebox is turned up, dancing is happening, it's a party. Charlie and the locals just love it. By 11:00, the dancing is becoming too wild. They are beginning to rip their clothes off. I'm desperately trying to stop them, when Veeresh announces,

'It's time to go back to the barn.' And it's straight into the Dynamic Meditation. Wow! This is how Veeresh works, right on the edge. We work most of the night and only have four hours sleep. Anam is one of his assistants. He's gorgeous, and has an exquisite Danish girlfriend who's a model. They have their breakfast in the kitchen. Polly is fascinated by this beautiful woman. I'm taking a tray up to Veeresh in his attic room.

'Stay with me Anita,' he says.

'Yes please!' We become bonded. I'm at his side for the entire weekend.

I am to book a table for dinner at the Blakeney Hotel for the last night. It is one of Veeresh's habits. After all the shouting and yelling, the extremities of emotions, he likes to sit with his assistants – I have become one – having dinner, with silver and twinkling glasses, and be served in a quiet atmosphere. Veeresh has donated a considerable sum of money to Premtaru, and he promises to be back soon. He has given me a little silver box, which I keep for ever.

Over the next months we are hosting continual groups. The next teacher to come is a Chinese Tai Chi Master, Gia Fu Feng. We are out on the field doing Tai Chi in the spring sunlight. He's inscrutable, and also very humble. We feel very privileged to work with him. It's amazing how the local village people accept this influx of orange people. They like our laughter and our lightness of being. One weekend, it's a full moon, and we all go to the Binham priory and hum in the ruins of the high altar. Polly and Jasper and Acha come too, all are included.

Mickgough and I are having very passionate sex these days, and I am feeling hopeful that our marriage will survive.

Roddy Maude Roxby is filming a piece of inspired madness for the local TV. They follow him as he puts his wonderful face into one leg of some white boxer shorts, places a dark shawl over his head – instantly – he has become a nun. He's leaning over the gate talking to the camera about 'we sisters....' Cows come up to the gate.

'Come along there.' He says 'Don't be shy!' he's communing with the cows. He also does an act in a local village hall, which every one of us remembers to this day. He's dressed as a mature woman with a large bust and a haughty voice, giving a lecture behind a table.

'What do to with your pets when they pass over. Place between a folder, place some weights on the top,' He demonstrates. 'I have one I finished earlier, and here we have it ...' Out falls something furry and flattened. 'Pressed pets – thank you so much.' He bows, and turns away, and reveals his bare bum, as his busty dress is only the front!

Polly has taken to wearing four or five different outfits a day.

'I'm not doing your washing for you Polly. You know how to use the machine!' She's into clothes. She's very fussy. She likes antique shirts, and men's jackets, and she's ordered a pair of boots behind my back. They arrive, and are now on the kitchen table.

'Polly! I won't allow you to wear them. They are much too high – they'll damage your back!'

'I'm going to wear them!' she says, defiantly.

'You'll send them back,' I insist.

'I won't, I won't!'

'Come with me!' I need some support here. I march her over to the pub where Jehane and Roger are having a drink. The boots are placed on the counter.

'Now, I ask you, can I let Polly wear these?'

'Mmm,' says Jehane. 'Nice boots Polly. If you can't keep them, I'll have them.'

'No Jehane, don't encourage her!' Polly and I end our fight in tears and,

'I'm sorry, I'm sorry, I love you,'

'No, I'm sorry, I'll send them back.'

Asanga and Samapatti like to walk about the place naked, and I have remonstrated with them, because it's not appropriate. I'm concerned about the locals. So we have fallen out and Samapatti is pregnant so they have gone to live in Wales. Now I'm running the centre on my own – but not for long.

An old friend from Poona, Sandesh, comes up from London and helps me run some weekends. Zen happenings. We all go riding on the beach, and the horses run away with us. We are playing Zen badminton – no rules. We make music at night, playing tablas and guitars. During the day, he sits on the doorstep of the house, in the sunshine, reading the racing results, smoking beedies. He's an entrepreneur, and in the sixties, ran a club in the Fulham Road called The Teddy Bear's Picnic, where people regularly danced on the tables.

During some of the meditation weekends, the participants will be put on a restricted diet, so the joke is that when they have to go off for a solitary walk, they are actually in the hedgerows madly stuffing their faces with blackberries and mushrooms, and sometimes they sneak into the pub, darling old Charlie loving the joke.

'Oooo, Argh! Couldn't resist it eh? Blast. You're alright. I won't say a thing mind, blast no!'

Poonam, who is one of the most respected group leaders, is running a Sartori group. We have to ask each other, every fifteen minutes,

'Tell me who you are,' It's a Zen device. After a few days, I'm in the zone,

'I'm the hoot of the owl! I'm the light in your eye! I'm … I'm not! Hahahaha!' I've seen the cosmic joke. I'm rolling around in laughter and tears. I'm removed from the group room, and one of the other participants leaves, most upset.

Mick is playing John the Baptist at The National Theatre. He's invited an actress friend for the weekend. She is very bright and attractive and I'm feeling suspicious. He wants to take her to an iron-age camp nearby,

'Are you sure you're not talking about yourself?' she says, as she grins at me, doing the washing up. I like her.

♫ *You can't build your dreams with suspicious minds …* ♫
- Elvis

Polly is now 14, and has a very sweet boyfriend called David. We all love him. He's handsome with dark eyes and dark hair, and is the son of a local farmer. Polly adores him. It's so sweet to see them together. They have a little gang of friends, all older than she is, so they like to go to the pub, and then come back to ours to crash.

'Can they stay in the barn Mummy?'

'Only if they are prepared to do the meditation in the morning,' And surprisingly, they do. And even more surprising, they really enjoy it. Polly has met the love of her life. Of course, she is very young, but for her, David is it.

Jasper has terrible asthma. This has been going on for quite a while on and off. So when I can, I have taken him to have acupuncture treatments, with an excellent Sannyasi doctor. But now, he's heaving, and unable to breathe, and I'm very frightened. I'm trying to get hold of Mickgough. He usually stays with Roddy when he's working in London, but Roddy says he hasn't been there for months. I call Mick's mother in Windsor because sometimes he stays with her.

'No, not for months,' The same reply. I am beside myself. Here is Jasper in dire straits and I don't know where his father is. Luckily the crisis passes, and he is able to breathe again, Polly and I are very relieved. But where is Mickgough?

Finally he calls me.

'WHERE WERE YOU WHEN WE NEEDED YOU?!'

He sounds very sheepish.

'Umm, staying with a friend,'

'What friend? I need to know where you are!'

'Umm, a girlfriend.'

'A GIRLFRIEND? What do you mean? Who is she? How long has this been going on?'

'Umm, three months,'

I'm devastated.

'But you've been home and making love to me!' In that moment I have a ghastly premonition that we are finished. 'I need you to come home so we can talk about it!'

'No. Henrietta says she doesn't want me to see you again.'

It's like a death. One minute, I have a life, a marriage – such as it is – and the next, it's all changed. I'm in shock. Who is this woman? How am I going to tell Polly and Jasper? I have so much fear. Mickgough has always said,

'You can leave any time you like, but you'll get no money, and you won't keep the children,' So what now? I have no real income. What job could I do? I was trained and had worked as an actress for eighteen years, I can't type or add up – it's very scary. What will happen to our beautiful home? Will it all be taken away? Must I lose everything? And now, I can't even talk to him. I suppose the writing had been on the wall for quite a while, I just hadn't wanted to read it. Now here we are, and dreadful decisions will have to be made, but oh, not yet. When I think of all the tears I cried, the love, the care, all that I put into the relationship, the shirts I ironed, the rice puddings I cooked, my hopes and my worries, my jealousy, my PAIN. I could cry and cry and never stop. And what of our beautiful children? What of them? This is going to devastate them. My heart is breaking. My marriage has been my entire adult life. For fifteen years my identity has been wrapped up in being Mrs Gough. Now all my dreams are shattered.

Polly and Jasper and I have all got into bed together up in the attic, under the stars. I've told them Mickgough has a girlfriend, and we cry, and hug.

'What does it mean, mum?'

'I don't know. I don't know.' Eventually he does come home - to 'fetch some things'. We go up to our lovely pink bedroom in the middle of the afternoon, and get into bed, and cling on to each other and cry our eyes out. Then we go down into the kitchen and drink a couple of bottles of wine. We don't quite know where we go now, except that she is in his life. She is ten years younger than me, the same age as Emma, his daughter. I feel very mixed emotions as I wave him goodbye.

♫ *Your eyes are soft with sorrow, Hey, that's no way to say goodbye* ... ♫
- Leonard Cohen

Chapter 9

Overland to India

'Never before was there such a search, because never before was Man in such a crisis. We are on the threshold of something new. Either humanity will die and disappear, or we will take a leap, and a new being will be formed. Before that happens a great Buddhafield is needed, where we can create the future.'

- Bhagwan, 1977

It's late September, and round the corner of the barns comes a huge bus, followed by another. They pull up in the yard and a bunch of Sannyasins jump out headed by Sandesh.

'Hello Beloved Anita! We're going to take these buses over land to Poona. We want to stay here while we rip out the seats and get them ready for the trip. Do you want to come with us?' Without hesitation,

'YES!'

I want to get the hell out of it all, after the weeks of agony, tortured with jealousy and days of tears, helplessness and fear, and everyone giving me their advice and opinions. I couldn't afford to stay on here and the thought of moving into a room in London is hell. The children won't want to live in a bedsit with me. What am I going to do? Go to Poona, have a reality check. Mickgough and 'she' can get on with it. Emma and family and all the cousins can use the house when they need.

For two weeks, this highly energised group of people camp in the barn as we get to work on the buses. Sandesh and his girlfriend Daya, who is a six-foot ex-Dior model with red hair down to her bum, and her two-year old boy, an American professor, a German musician, two mothers with kids, Nancy is the oldest, as she is in her sixties, and a four month old baby. Sujan, who is a dance teacher, and Vismaya, a therapist, an Australian woman with her child, and a few more to make the numbers up to 30.We eat and dance and make music together. We are getting to know each other, which is important for the epic journey ahead of us.

Polly definitely doesn't want to come.
'I'll stay with Dad and go to school in London. Have fun!' And Jasper definitely does.
'It's going to be an adventure!'

We rip out the insides of the buses, make kitchens in the back, each of us will have an overhead space for our personal belongings, the size of a small carry-on case, which is obviously not going to be enough, as we'll be travelling through the winter. Jazz fills his space with his collection of Tintin and Asterix comics. Then we are studying the route that we'll take, pouring over maps and atlases. We must cross the Turkish mountains before the passes are closed because of the snow. Prageet will drive the Bedford Bus, Pranam will drive the Volvo. We will mount a tepee on the Bedford roof, so when we stay for a few days somewhere we can set up our tent and spread out and do our washing. We are all putting in as much money as we can, and this will go into a pot to fund the trip. We have side-stepped Jasper's schools because he is 11 now and should start his secondary education. Good. Because it's in the next stage that the real conditioning begins, when they fill you up with all that you'll need to keep the rotten society going. They're not nurturing unique individuals who might think for themselves and then become rebels, wanting to ask questions. As Jasper wisely says,
'Doing this trip will be the best education I can have.' Polly and I have been curled up together in her darling little bedroom, sobbing our eyes out. We hate goodbyes. I'm in the back window of the bus in floods of tears as we leave the village. Goodbye, goodbye my lovely home. Who knows when I'll see you again.

In London, we fill the buses with supplies. We have a grinding machine so we can grind our own flour to make bread as we travel across the continents. Shinosaki, a Japanese monk, is hitching a ride with us back to his monastery in India. We all have cameras and tape machines, and musical instruments and pillows. The day we finally start, we break down between London and Dover, first one bus and then the other. Interminable waiting, while Prageet and Pranam sort out the engines. Eventually we are on the ferry and crossing the channel. We are ecstatic, making music and dancing on the deck. The other passengers are amused at this group of laughing people in orange.

'Where are you going?'

'Overland to India, to join our ashram.'

We have a few hours of daylight left when we arrive in France, so we press on for a while, eventually finding a large field off the main road, where a farmer says we can camp. Our first night. We set up the tepee, light a big fire, cook supper, and gratefully crash, some in the tepee and some in the buses. That night there is a tremendous storm. The water pours through the gap in the top of the tepee, and we are all drenched, our sleeping bags, our clothes, and we never really dry out until we reach Germany. In Munich, we play music in the main square, make enough Deutchmarks to go to the famous Bierhaus and drink. On the ceiling, we can see where the swastikas have been painted over with flowers. The German member of our family is reacting very strongly to 'all zis zat I left behind'. The rest stops in Germany are ultra modern and efficient. We women have showers, wash the children, our clothes, and drink the good coffee. We stay in a Sannyas commune. These Germans are very serious. They live and work in this large rural farmhouse. They don't speak – 'except for necessities.' Prageet and Jasper sneak off to a local bar to play pool.

The Volvo bus is broken down and needs a very expensive new part. We must stay here for two weeks. We help the community with the cleaning, cooking, and gardening, and we all meditate and listen to Bhagwan's discourses, we make music, dance and drink wine. By the time we leave, the Germans are laughing and gossiping and have loosened up.

'Good luck, good luck!' They hug us as we leave.

When we get to Greece, we stay in a campsite on the edge of the beach, in Thessaloniki. I'm in heaven. Greece! I'm remembering John Craxton's lovely paintings and stories. The Mediterranean light does something special to my soul. Prageet and I go to a local bar. I'm drawing the old Greek peasants who are playing chess and drinking ouzo. Prageet leaves me 'playing happily in the sea'. I was pissed, and I had all my clothes on. Jasper sees me being carried into the campsite. I had fallen flat on my face on the path, and passed out.

'I thought you were dead. Cool!'

Every morning, wherever we are, the day begins with the sound of Shinosaki playing his drum. He has become one of the family. He is particularly sweet with the children, and he is very centred. One time, in the night, in a very busy Turkish city, we are on foot and trying to cross a busy and chaotic main road, when suddenly, Shinosaki steps out into the middle, holds out his arms – he's in his power – he shouts something in Japanese. The traffic miraculously skids to a halt, and we all scuttle across.

Istanbul is a revelation to us all. We make camp within the city. We sling washing lines across the trees and orange clothes glow in the firelight as we cook. We must press on – no time to see the mosques or visit the Whirling Dervishes. We hear the muezzin chanting prayers in the minarets – I love this sound. With all our breakdowns and delays, we are very far behind our schedule, and the winter is upon us. It's getting very cold and we're running out of funds. High up in the Turkish mountains in the thick snow, driving is becoming hazardous. We have hung our wet clothes around a huge old iron stove in a roadside café, and we are huddled around it having a serious meeting. Should we play it safe? Go back to Germany and spend the winter in that commune and start again in the spring? Or do we press on and risk it? We are of one accord.

'We go on! Risk it!'

Now, comes the most dangerous part of the journey so far. The high mountain roads are icy death traps. We keep getting stuck in the snow or we slide right off the road. We are rescued by huge T.I.R trucks, which winch us out or tow us across the passes. It's frightening and dangerous and seems to take for ever. We sleep in the buses on the side of the road, icicles forming on the inside of the windows. Only Shinosaki doesn't lose it.

Eventually we arrive at the Iranian border. It's late at night, in deep snow. The buses are waved through, but we passengers must line up and have our passports checked in this very dismal office. It takes ages, and just when we are hoping we can join Prageet and Pranam in the buses, and get some supper on, we are told that the border is closed and we will have to wait till the morning. We are loudly protesting.

'But that's our home! The children need food!' We are at the barrier, explaining with frustration that we are stuck. Prageet and Pranam and the Iranian guards on one side, us and the Turkish guards on the other. Shinosaki throws a snowball. Moments later we are having an amazing snowball fight, which ends in much laugher all round, and the guards shrug and let us go through to the buses.

Iran is the most desolate place so far. We pass villages made of mud. It's becoming more eastern. When we stop for petrol and a meal in a roadside station, they refuse to serve us, looking at us with deep suspicion.

'But we have children, and they are thirsty!' We have to manage till we get to the border, where the guards climb officiously onto the buses, seize our cameras, take the films out, and crush them with their boots in the dusty gravel. Now, we pass across the border into Afghanistan, where immediately chirpy little boys climb on.

'Hello Sahib! You want hasheesh?' They are waving huge lumps of golden Afghan hash.

We stay in Herat, a mud town. We've been taken to a special shrine and darkness has fallen very fast, so we hitch a ride back to town with a wild Afghani with his horse and cart. In the pitch dark night we are galloping along the deserted tracks, with him cracking his whip, his wild eyes flashing under his turban.

As we drive through the Khyber Pass, I remember how I felt when I was nine and how much I loved the film *Kim*. An early déjà vu. There are camels, and huge old lorries, all decorated. What a scene! Jasper is enthralled. And at last, as we get towards Pakistan, it becomes warmer. Pakistan feels weirdly menacing, so although it seems familiar, we are relieved when we cross the border into India. We spend Christmas at the Golden temple in Amritsar. This is the first time in our entire journey that we sleep on mattresses in rooms. All travellers are given free accommodation for a week. At night, we sit on mats, in long lines, and they come with rice and dahl, and fill up our bowls in the Dickensian candlelight. We are happy to have a nourishing meal because by now we are almost out of funds. We stand in the haunted square, where so many Indians were slaughtered by that infamous English Major (later played by Edward Fox in a film). The temple is truly golden in the evening light and filled with Holy Men of all kinds. Driving through India is almost the best part of the trip, although the roads and the Indian traffic are impossible. It is so warm, we take it in turns to sit up on the roof. Jasper and I love this, we can really see the land we are passing through. Way out in the countryside, we see the primitive villages, people washing in the rivers, the bullock carts, the naked Sadhus striding along. The towns at night, the shops and cafes lit by oil lights, teaming with people. Terrible poverty and lots of beggars. The monkeys leap in the trees, scaring the chattering parrots, the smell of spices and incense. Everywhere there are temples and shrines. Indian women in fantastically coloured saris, their wrists and arms and ankles smothered in tinkling silver, carrying heavy loads of building materials on their heads.

We visit the Taj Mahal, and we all sit in the round shrine underneath, and do a powerful, humming meditation. When we come out it's dark and a thin sliver of moon hangs over the minarets and is reflected in the fountains.

And now, our goal is in sight. We stop off at a river, a few miles north of Poona, and we scrub the buses and ourselves and we make flags and banners. Three months more than we had planned for. During the journey, as we began to run out of money, we had sold what we could, so that by the time we reach Poona we really only have what we stand up in. All cameras, tape recorders and tools long since sold to buy petrol and food. Now, at last, the moment we have all been waiting for. We are drumming and singing ecstatically as we drive slowly down the shady tree-lined roads of Koregaon Park.

'We made it! We made it! Here we are!' A tall, bearded, American guard in robes steps out into the road, looks at us with definite disdain.

91

'You can't park here, you're blocking the road.' And he waves us on. It's an anti-climax, but actually, we have become quite famous. Our voyage was being followed with interest.

'The people on the buses are here! They made it!'

Bhagwan's secretary Laxmi gives us all free meditation and discourse passes for a month.

The first person I see is Patrick Maxwell, that painter friend of ours who worked with Mickgough and Roddy at the drug addiction centre in Chelsea in the sixties.

He's now called Rashid and he's here with his wife and two young boys. He helps me and Jasper build a bamboo hut in the grounds of 'Prems', a restaurant set in a large park, which is filled with other huts. I'm very proud of our hut. It has two rooms – one for me and one for Jasper, who is happily settling into the ashram way of life. He has joined the ashram school and as he's the eldest he is helping with the younger kids. The teachers are Montessori trained, and Bhagwan reminds them that the children can't be 'taught' anything, only encouraged to be free, so they are an unruly bunch. Bhagwan says,

'We must all love and be responsible for them.' There's one little boy, Siddartha, who marches along to the discourse. Children are not allowed in the discourse so the guards stop him at the gate, but when Bhagwan hears this he says,

'No, no, he is allowed. He is an old disciple of mine from many lifetimes ago, hmm?' So he rolls out his mat in the front and curls up and goes to sleep on it. Jasper hangs out with a twelve year-old Californian boy called Jim. Their sport is to leap off the sides of a hill, 40 feet, into a deep well.

It's wonderful to be back here with all the familiar faces and many new ones. The ashram has expanded. A vast seven-foot teak structure - the 'Gateless Gate' - has replaced the wrought-iron gates. Now there are weaving workshops making the cloth for the robes and a pottery making teapots and cups. There is a German bakery which turns out massive amounts of bread and woodworkers making musical instruments. Bhagwan has put a beautiful silver-haired Greek woman in charge of the gardens but he doesn't like anything to be cut down so she is always trying to do a little surreptitious pruning. Her team of carefully picked Swamis grow all the vegetables to feed Bhagwan. He eats the same simple meal each day and each day he says,

'Delicious.' Because he's left yesterday behind – he's so in the now that he's forgotten.

At the Gateless Gate

Lack of money is a big problem, and one night Jasper comes,

'Can I have some rupees for supper?'

'I'm sorry, I haven't any.' He looks absolutely pissed off with me. Sannyasins are very generous, and we all help each other out, but I've come to a bleak place, where I don't want to ask anyone for any more. Later, when Jasper comes back into our hut,

'Jazz, are you alright?'

'Yeah. I traded one of my Asterix comics with one of the guards so I've had supper in Prem's.' The guards all like to read Tintin and Asterix.

I've carefully forged myself a meditation pass for this second month. I'm sure that Bhagwan would approve! I'm pretty nervous when I first show it to the guard but I am waved inside. In the sari shops they sell cotton underskirts which are very cheap and we get them in orange. Up the side is printed 'medium rags'. I love it – from Mary Quant to medium rags! Another Swami I've met is Devesh, the English aristocrat. He lives in a house behind the ashram and plays opera. He is cultured and intelligent, and I like him a lot. He asks if I would make him a robe-type dressing gown. A commission! I choose some beautiful soft silk and make him a sort of kimono. He is pleased, and I am grateful for the rupees.

In a rickshaw   Jasper's mates

A laughing Sikh has asked me to cut his hair. He whips off his orange turban, and his long greasy locks hang loose. As I'm cutting I ask him how it is for him as a Sikh, to be embracing Bhagwan's revolutionary teaching.

'Oh no darling,' he roars with laughter. 'I'm just here for the girls.'

Monsoon season is upon us, and the hut isn't water-tight. So Jazz and I move into a room with a beautiful English woman. We have mattresses and mosquito nets and we manage once again. I'm doing the Dynamic every morning, and I'm venting all my rage and sadness over Mickgough and the end of my marriage. How many tears can I cry? This is a massive 'let-go'. I sit on a wall with the tears falling, but in this place, this is so natural, no-one comes to stop you. We have the freedom to be, and soon I am hugging and dancing again.

Being here is like being in a hothouse. We are growing so quickly, listening to Bhagwan's discourses; such profound understandings set the mood of the day. So many spaces we move through. We all support each other to 'let go', and stop taking ourselves so seriously. We do our work with focus and awareness, and hug each other a lot. The music of the meditations in Buddha Hall permeates the atmosphere and each day finishes with the singing and dancing of the music group.

♬ *Let the way of the heart…* ♬
- Anubhava

Sandesh has teamed up with a wealthy American and they have had a bamboo restaurant built down by the river. Daya and I are cooking in the kitchens. It's horribly hot and sweaty, but it becomes a hit with the many disciples, who are arriving in their droves from the west. It provides me and Jasper with enough rupees to get by. Alanka, my English friend has given me the money to do the re-birthing group. Bhagwan says that we all carry the birth trauma, so in this group we breathe ourselves back to that moment. I can feel myself upside down, squeezing through a tight space, and pain – such pain - then gasping for breath. Bhagwan says that death will not be as devastating. I touch my spirit before conception. I'M VAST…

I am brought down to earth when Jasper leaves a note for me. 'I'll meet you at the front gate when you're finished. Your son.'

Chapter 10

Swami Dyhana Yogi

One day, Jasper announces that he's traded his day's food money in, bought himself a photo of Bhagwan, and he's booked himself a Darshan with the Master. I had made an absolute point not to persuade him, in fact I may even have been encouraging him to simply be himself – no need – and now, he has made his own decision, and I'm going to go with him. We are all washed and scrubbed, and lining up to go past the 'sniffers' – the women who smell you - into Chuang Tzu for the evening darshan. We are up close so we can be called out. We are all gathered in silence, with the singing of the music group in Buddha Hall, resonating in the background.

♫ Nothing ever happens… what is… just is… ♫

Bhagwan enters, 'Namaste', and as soon as he is seated with Vivek and Laxmi on his left, and Shiva, his bodyguard, on his right, Laxmi is calling out the names of the people taking Sannyas. After a while, it's our turn.

'Ma Prem Anita and Jasper?' Jasper kneels down in front of Bhagwan, I'm in the background, beaming with joy. Bhagwan writes Jasper's new name, and says,

'Swami Dhyana Yogi. It means 'path of meditation." As he puts the mala over his head,

'Hold your arms up in the air. Feel like a tree in the wind. Hmmm. Very good, Yogi.' We go back to our room and celebrate with tea and toast. A few days later, Yogi announces he's moving out. Jim's parents are wealthy Californians and they are living in a large, comfortable, air-conditioned house, so I am abandoned, and I miss him dreadfully, and only see him around the ashram during the day. But I'm also proud of him, that he wants to be independent, and quite understand that he'd rather live in luxury. I feel sad and guilty because I am unable to provide more than a mattress and a mosquito net in a shared room.

Jasper becomes Yogi

I'm always on a diet and I like the clarity that comes with fasting. I do a ten-day watermelon fast. On the eighth day, in the music group, I'm not dancing, I'm floating. *Dancing lightly on the edge of the time.* And this morning during the discourse, Bhagwan is dissolving before my eyes and turning into a sort of Chinese man and in this moment I know he is Lao Tzu, and here I am with him again.

We take rickshaws to the city centre. Mahatma Gandhi Road is known as MG Road. In the back street is a café called Greenfields. It sells great buffalo curd and has a proud sign outside saying 'We serve Nescafe.' This street is full of tailors and jewellers and Ayurvedic medicine shops, and leads into the market. One day Yogi and I are shopping for the restaurant, baskets of onions and vegetables to be loaded up in a rickshaw.

'Hallo, yes?' We see this old grey-haired Indian in a crumpled striped suit, wearing round red plastic-framed specs. 'Yes, hallo, I am a beggar, here are my credentials,' and he waves his certificate under our noses. We give him baksheesh. The road to the ashram is lined with street beggars and vendors.

'Backcrack? Neckcrack? Wholebodycrack? One Rupee baba!' There is one old being, on a small platform on wheels. He has no legs, and stumps for arms, and he's blind. He holds out his stump to you,

'Blind, one pasea?' And yet his face is beaming with joy. Blind, One pasea, I will never forget you. Under the arches of the main highway live the tent people. This is a vast complex of dwellings made out of rags, cardboard and tin. Little homes where people build fires and cook, and children run around among the chickens and rabid dogs. At night it is lit with tiny candles and oil lamps. I love this light. This is how nights were before we had electricity. One thing is very curious. When you look in any of these beggars' eyes, what you see is LIFE! Here they are, now, and they are throbbing with vitality.

Before the very hot weather comes, we must go back to England, we have many things to sort out. I send Bhagwan a letter. I tell him how sad and torn I feel. The husband, the children, the home. How to stop holding on. I enclose a photo of Mickgough. I am secretly hoping that Bhagwan will recognise him as an old disciple. I'm holding my breath for my answer. I go to the box in the main office. Laxmi is behind her desk, Sheila is talking very loudly. Arup is organising. These are the big heavy Mamas. The energy is highly charged in the office. I sift through the folded bits of paper. There it is – Ma Prem Anita. I retreat to a quiet part of the garden beside Buddha Hall. I'm very anxious. I unfold the page and in Laxmi's writing I read,

'Divorce the husband.
Sell the house.
And come and be here for ever.
His Blessings.'

Devesh gives us the fares home, and in May, we arrive back in London wearing orange pyjamas. We are on the train from Gatwick to Victoria. The commuters are crowded in, reading novels, yawning, tired, dandruff on their donkey jackets. In their eyes, boredom, sleep. They are absolutely not here. They dream endlessly of somewhere else. Winning the pools. I have this curious feeling that they are the beggars, not the ones under the arches in Poona.

We stay with Veetasmi, in Mornington Crescent. Mickgough is going to give us some money to tide us over the next few months. He is at Roddy's. So very excitedly, Yogi and I set off to see him. I have by now worked through some of my rage and disappointment, and have accepted that he is together with Henrietta, and so I have wrapped a beautiful present for the two of them, with a note saying, 'For Mick and Henrietta, with love to you both.' It's an olive branch. It seems after all the rage and pain, the most important thing is to remain friends. I shan't ask for any money. I know that has always been the stumbling block with his past wives, and he can keep all the possessions – I'm not attached to any of them – not really. When we get to the door, my heart is pounding. I'm longing to see him. And Jasper wants to tell him all about Poona. The door is opened by an ordinary looking woman, with a scowling face. It's Henrietta.

'There's your money! Count it!' she snaps, throwing £50 down the front steps and she slams the door in our faces. We are shocked. What extraordinary behaviour. We are ashamed for her.

We meet up with Polly, and travel sadly back up to Norfolk.
'What's she like?' says Yogi.
'Posh and bossy.'
'Poor Dad.' I don't comment. I've promised myself I will never say a bad word about their father – my problems with him are my own, but my spirit is shrieking.
'Hah! I'm glad she's difficult! Let him suffer!'
Our darling home looks sad and neglected. Someone's broken one of the conservatory windows, and it has blue plastic taped over it. All the white woodwork is chipped and the herb garden is overgrown with weeds.
'How has it been for you, Polly?'
'Ghastly. Dad said he didn't have room for me to stay with him, so I was farmed out with a friend of theirs, who had a house full of bedwetting misfits. I hated the school in Putney so much, I got

caught nicking clothes in the High Street. Dad had to come to the police station and bail me out.'

'Why didn't you tell me?'

'Because I knew you'd just come home, and I wanted you and Jasper to have a grand adventure. Anyway, we are here now. Can David come for supper?'

My mother has been staying with some Quaker friends in Devon while she's been having chemo-therapy, but the cancer continues to spread. She's lost her hair, and she wears a frightful red wig when she arrives. The children are shy and embarrassed, which I can see, really hurts her. Her courage tears me apart.

'You know me,' she says. 'I thought I would just get a donkey and a flagon of wine, and disappear into the Spanish hills. No-one would know. But actually, the pain was so intense, I had to go into beastly hospital.'

'I'm dying you know,' she says, matter-of-factly. 'but show me your herb garden.' It's now hopelessly overgrown. 'Give me a hoe.'

'There's no need, we're selling up anyway.'

'So? The plants still need tending, and you want to leave it looking nice.' And with that, she is out in the afternoon sun, in her Spanish apron. She's dying and she's doing the weeding.

'The worst bit about the chemo is that I don't like my wine anymore, and I can't sit in the sun.' she says, sadly, as I wrap her in a lounger chair, with pillows, and her book. 'Tell me more about the ashram. I wish I could go there. I know I would love it. Orange is my favourite colour.' The drugs have affected her negatively. She's either very wired, or very wiped. I long for the visit to be over. She's going to Devon to be looked after by Tilly. I feel so sad and so guilty.

Two Sannyasi friends come to stay with us. Geet and Iti. They are both teachers, and we strike a deal. They can stay, if they will tutor Yogi. So we get all the maths and English books that Yogi should be doing, and we get a microscope, and Yogi and Geet are off on the 'path of knowledge'. It's rewarding to see what fun they are having, and how quickly Yogi progresses. He has soon done the set curriculum and is rattling into the following year's work. They are peering at bugs and sperm with the microscope!

It's a beautiful summer day. I'm driving down to London in my friend Puro's Mercedes sports, Jehane and Roger have tickets to a Bob Dylan concert tonight.

'Would you like to try some cocaine?' says Puro.

'Oh, go on then.' I instantly become an impossibly expanded version of myself, so wildly passionate, so much to share. I talk non-stop for four hours, as we bowl along through the ripened wheat fields.

The concert is momentous. Dylan looks kind of ravaged and his songs more edgy and poignant than ever. At one point, everyone lights their lighters, the auditorium is lit up with thousands of souls in harmony. At breakfast, next day, we are reading the reviews, one mentions that Dylan's staying at the Kensington Palace Hotel. Jehane and I take a bus to Kensington – I want to give him a Sannyas magazine and Jehane is clutching a slim volume of her latest poems. By the time we arrive at the hotel our bold plan is not looking quite so rosy.

'Oh God, they'll have security all around him, we'll never get through!' says a nervous Jehane. Sometimes I'm blessed with my mother's chutzpah.

'Come on Jehane! Let's see what happens!' As we approach the entrance, Dylan magically emerges from the revolving door, in a black leather jacket and shades. 'Ah!' I say. 'There you are!'

'We loved your concert!' coos Jehane. 'May I give you this?' She hands him her poems. He takes our offerings and heads over to the large 'Dylan on Tour' bus, climbs into the front seat, and we are delighted to see him opening the envelopes... we are wrapped around a lamppost, dissolved in rapture, our knees have turned to water.

I've decided to go and see a psychic. Ann Seveson is the most renowned at this time. I visit her in a flat in Hyde Park. She lays out my horoscope.

'Ah, you are a lone spirit.' The non-trusting part of me quickly says,

'Well I've got a husband and two children.'

'Let me see. Yes, you will marry two more times ...' *Non-trust* interrupts with,

'I can't believe I will want more of this pain!'

'Let me have your children's dates.' She casts Polly's – not a word – now she casts Yogi's.

'Well, what I see here, is that your son is your husband's brother.'

'Mick's brother was called Peter, and he died in the war.'

'Ah yes, that's him. So he's back.' I reel out into the sunshine of Hyde Park. Two more marriages? And Yogi is a returned Pete? Should I tell him?

Our beautiful home must be put on the market. I hate the For Sale sign outside in the road. It makes me so sad that it will all dissolve. All that we had created. What changes have occurred in the years that we have lived here. This wonderful kitchen that had seen such an array of interesting friends, loving, laughing and feasting. Beautiful children having their birthdays and Christmases. The fires in the winter, the dogs that had sprawled, the music we had played, the love we shared. The thought of having a sale of the furniture, strangers in the house, bidding for our possessions, is too disturbing to contemplate, so Simon wants to take it all.

'Keep it in the family, dahling!'

Mickgough and Henrietta are away in South America on tour, so I have to get on with it alone. Firstly, we have to find Polly a boarding school. We send off for various prospectuses, but both agree that none of them look like she could be happy there.

'Much too straight mummy. What would the other girls be like? I'd never fit in there.' Jehane suggests Michael Hall, the Steiner school in Forest Row. So one summer afternoon I drive us down to Sussex for her interview. We are very lucky to be offered this place for her, as the school is always booked to capacity. It's a beautiful 18th century mansion, with a complex of buildings, vegetable gardens, pottery studios, a theatre. Polly and I are a bit over-awed, but put a brave face on it. First, she has to spend time with the movement teacher. Then we meet some of the other teachers, who are all very friendly, and finally we are sitting on the front terrace on a bench with her main teacher. He's chatting easily to Polly about what she will be required to do. I'm thinking it's going very well, when suddenly, Polly bursts into tears.

'Shush, Polly, not now!'

'No, no,' says the teacher, taking her hands kindly. 'What's up Polly? Can you tell me about it?' Polly spills out all her doubts and fears, and ends up with,

'And when am I going to see David?' This understanding man then comforts her,

'David can come and see you whenever he can, and we will be your family Polly'. Now I'm in floods of tears.

'The thing is, I've got to go back to the ashram.'

'Of course. It's most important that you do. We have quite a few pupils whose parents are with Bhagwan, and meanwhile, we'll nourish and teach your daughter.' What a wonderful place!

'But how can we afford the fees, mummy?'

'We'll try for a scholarship, or we'll find the money somehow.' Meanwhile, the teachers of the school all agree that Polly should definitely become a pupil. She will start in September, and David is so sweetly proud of her.

By the late summer, the house has sold, and the contents are being moved out to Simon's and Roger Lloyd Pack's. I sell all my books to Simon. I've collected first editions, art books, antique flower books – it's such a wrench. I entrust Simon with the trunk full of all the large sixties photos taken by John Cole and Michael Wallis. Huge grainy studio shots of me in black leather, lovely images of the children and our family life, the birthdays, the Christmases, all my journals and sketches of the children since the very beginning. I pack the kitchen stuff to go to Roddy's barn, for Polly to have later. Everything of Mickgough's, his books and antiques, I pack carefully, label, and place in the drawing room, because he will come at the very end. I have rented a flat in Maida Vale, where we can stay while Polly settles into Michael Hall. Yogi and Polly have gone ahead to Emma's - she lives around the corner - and I am left at the end to love and mourn this house which I love so much. I say my sad goodbyes to all my friends, they wish me luck. Goodbye darling trees – they are now bearing fruit – damsons and quinces. Acha has gone to some friends. Each parting seems so final I am destroyed. I've cleaned all the rooms, polished the taps, cleaned the windows. On the last night ever I light the candles and the fires, and walk around with a bottle of wine, and sob and howl. I go down on my knees and give thanks. I am driven to London the next day, a basket-case of grief. I'm hanging on to a pillow for dear life. I don't let it go for three days. I never get over leaving this house, I haunt it still. I never get to talk to Mickgough again. It is so unbelievably hard, not to express to him any of what I am going through, and I see very clearly that Henrietta is certainly not going to allow any contact, let alone friendship. Although Mickgough doesn't want to give me any money, of course, the law is on my side. So very soon, I'm given £15,000, half of the selling price. I'm rich! For the first time. I celebrate by buying Yogi a Pentax camera, and Polly a sliver flute, and two tickets to India for Geet and Iti.

We will stay on in Maida Vale while Polly spends her first term at Michael Hall. She will board with Jehane's mother, Olive, in her beautiful farm which is nearby. It all works out very well, she makes some very good friends. Wendy Cook lives nearby, and her two daughters, Daisy and Lucy, also go to the school. Polly calls me on her first night.

'We had supper in the main hall of the mansion. A roaring fire in the fireplace. Candles. And we had brie for afters! I love it here mummy!'

By the end of that first term, she's got a scholarship and she's happy and settled, and moves into the main schoolhouse. So Yogi and I get our flights booked for India and in the spring of 1979, we fly back to Poona.

Chapter 11

The Buddhafield

The ashram has expanded still further. Many more people are here. Buddha Hall has a drive all around it because a rich Sannyasin has given Bhagwan a Rolls Royce, and he just loves to be driven from his house to the hall, even though it's only a few yards. Of course he loves his Rolls! When he was a child, a bullock cart was the mode of transport! There are special steps at the back where he steps out, and it's a prized job to open the door for him. There is a boutique, press office, book and tape shop, restaurants and bars. Rashid has sold his Welsh farm and returned. Sandesh, Daya and I rent a large modern flat. We have enough room for other friends to stay. Veeresh is doing groups, and Somendra, who used to be Michael Barnett, is the most famous of the therapists. He is running a group called Leela, which means 'play' in Hindi. We pass under the windows of his group room and we hear really good music blasting forth. Fleetwood Mac, Vangelis, David Bowie.

There is a book department, from where hundreds of books are sent all over the world. Every word that Bhagwan utters is recorded for posterity. We watch people arriving with all their hang-ups and fears. In a while they are glowing, dancing and in love. I love seeing an old lady in a wheelchair, happily waving her arms in a dancing meditation. Sometimes I choose to sit on the outer edge during discourse, and when it's over we turn and bow to him as he is driven by, and he will look me in the eye and the look is one of such love. Unconditional love is very rare and very potent. We are so very blessed. The most qualified people will be cleaning the toilets, the least confident will be in charge of a team of masseurs. It's all designed to help each individual to break through his defences and touch into his innate emptiness. People are becoming very soft and beautiful. In fact, it's becoming a complaint among the horny women,

'Where are all the hunks? They've all grown their hair long, become soft and skinny, wear dresses and meditate!'

The disciples who guard Bhagwan are trained in Kung-Fu. There have been many threats on his life. He's notorious in India. He's lambasting all their religions and their politicians, advocating freedom and love. The orthodox society is outraged by his scathing tongue. His favourite targets are the priests and the politicians. He's ruthlessly exposing their corrupt power games. The guards practice in their robes, with huge staffs, and they are on the alert at all times. One time during a discourse some mad visitor had thrown a knife. It missed Bhagwan by inches, yet he didn't even blink. When a bird landed on his microphone, he also didn't flinch. Journalists from all over the world are arriving constantly - Germans, Japanese and Russians - sent by their newspapers, to find out what's happening here. Alan Whicker makes a film, Stern magazine comes, and the Daily Express sends Bernard Levin. I always liked Bernard Levin, because he once gave me a good review – actors never forget! He is marvellously perceptive, joining in with the Sufi dancing, listening to a discourse, hanging out with the Sannyasins. He writes a brilliant article called 'Dying for Enlightenment'. Others would write negative stuff that their editors wanted, mostly focussed on the sex but many of them take Sannyas and never go back to their desks.

The striking thing about the ashram community is the abundance of love and sex. Normally 'out there in the world' we live with a kind of rationing mentality. It seems so hard to find a lover and keep him or her, so when we do, we cling, we get jealous, and it's all very painful. Bhagwan says that man thinks of sex for three quarters of his life, and women dream of love. But here, we are encouraged to enjoy each other and not to cling. It's really not possible to do anything else, because we are all free. So if you've had a great night with one person, you can't expect they'll be there the next, but someone else might! I seem to have four or five gorgeous lover friends. It means we have all relaxed our desperation, and the sex can actually move into a more meditative place. The energies melting, dissolving into each other. We explore the valleys rather than the peaks, then there is no end to it. Tantric lovers go on all night! Bhagwan is no longer listening to all our endless 'stuff'. He is now giving energy darshans', where he simply zaps us. He tells outrageous jokes. We have a brilliant artist who draws cartoons for the Sannyas magazine.

'The more profound the truth, the worse joke I choose for it, because otherwise you all fall asleep.' This also upsets all the serious people, who don't think a spiritual master should tell jokes. His discourse on the word 'fuck' is one of the most hilarious ever. He says he has to be unpredictable because the truth cannot be spoken. Last night I had an energy darshan. I sat in front of him and closed my eyes and felt this tightness in my chest, bursting open and energy was flowing upwards – when it was over I could hardly stand up. This morning I had my eyes closed during the discourse and I was drifting. When I opened them I was amazed to see an empty chair. Now I know he is just… a presence.

I sleep with my mosquito net tucked underneath my mattress which is spread on the tiled floor of my room. One night, I'm woken by a movement at the bottom of the bed. Something scuttling over me. It's dark and yet it's unmistakably – aagh! – it's a rat! I'm heaving the mosquito net free, I'm naked,
'Argh! Get off! Get off!' It's a primal moment of absolute fear. The whole block of flats is having a rat infestation. It takes about a week to get rid of them. They scamper down the passageways when we get home.

Bhagwan's family are 'Jains'. Because they believe that all life is sacred, they even have the ground swept before them so that they do not inadvertently tread on an insect. The disciples who look after Bhagwan are distraught, because there is a cockroach living in his room and they can't get rid of it. Finally, in exasperation, they tell him of their dilemma.
'No problem,' he replies calmly. 'Release him from his body.'

We have a maid, an aya. We all chip in to pay Josephine (she's an Indian Christian) to wash the floors and do our laundry. Since we all change our clothes two or three times a day because of the heat, the washing and ironing is a priority for us all. She squats in the shower and scrubs with soap, and bashes the clothes, and there are many plastic buckets for rinsing. She hangs them out on the balconies and by the time she has finished the cleaning they are dry and she sits cross-legged with an ironing blanket and sheet on the living room floor. So when we come home they are all on hangers on the large rail by the door. I draw her working. I love her body shape, squatting, so loose and natural. She is very sweet and also stupid and sly. She likes to steal things – our face creams, tapes, my hair-cutting scissors.

'Josephine, you've taken my scissors!'

'No, No, Anita,' she whines. 'I not take your things, I am a good Christian! I have five children. My mother is old and ill, baba.'

I'm laying low with a terrible ear infection and I read *Shogun* from cover to cover. It coincides with my spending time with a new and beautiful lover. His name is Prabuddha and he is the most exquisite Japanese man. I'm remembering a past life of mine, in 9th century Japan. He was there – again. He's very sweet, fine and gentle, and his beautiful body is translucent. He has a friend who teaches me Zen bamboo painting. First we mix our ink, grinding fine powder and adding water. The rice paper is laid out on the floor, huge Japanese water brushes are carefully loaded,

'You must use whole *bodeh*,' And with that, he leans over and like a dance he places the brush on the paper and paints without a falter, a beautiful group of bamboos. When it is complete, he sits back and closes his eyes.

Our dear friend Devesh is working on the tills in the canteen. He takes me and Yogi out to the Blue Diamond which is a modern hotel where a lot of wealthy American Sannyasins stay. It has a swimming pool, and now we can become members and swim. Living in Poona with money is much more comfortable, except, everyone always asks you for money, and I do love helping people. I bought Prabuddha's friend a sitar, because he is such a good musician.

When the moment is right I tell Yogi about what Ann Seveson said about him being Mickgough's brother. His eyes expand.

'I have a recurring dream,' he says. 'I'm being shot down. I see all the dials in front of me. I'm going down over Luxembourg. But we won't tell dad, because he wouldn't believe it anyway.' So we never do. But later, I have the opportunity of asking Mickgough's sister where Pete was shot down, which we never knew.

'Over Luxembourg,' she says. He was very handsome, had lots of girlfriends, was mad about photography, and became a hero in his mother's eye. When we show photos of Yogi as a baby to Mick's mother, she exclaims,

'Ah, there's my darling Pete.'

'No Gran Gran, that's Jasper.'

'Oh, oh, they look so alike...'

'If you want to know the Buddha's whereabouts – in the sound of your own voice, there is he.' - Zen

I have signed up to do the Vipassana. This is an ancient Buddhist meditation. Ten days, blindfolded, sitting on a stool, watching your breath in silence. Surely I shall go mad with boredom. There will be no escape from myself. The Vipassana group room is on the roof of one of the ashram houses, right on the crossroads. So, rather than peace and quiet, we are meditating amidst the daily mayhem of the Indian traffic. We start at 4:00am, sit for an hour, get up and walk very slowly round the hall, eyes on the ground, for half an hour, and then we sit again till breakfast. Then walking, sitting, walking, sitting till lunch. A rest, more of the same till supper, and bed at 9:00, up again at 4:00. The first few days are torturous. I get pins and needles and an aching body, and insane dreams and mad, mad thoughts. But all the time, you just have to watch your breath. There is a sign over the doorway which says 'Make friends with yourself'. After six or seven days, it all goes slow, and by the eighth day, I'm in heaven. So empty. Such transparency. I can see it all. Ah! This breeze! This banana! Well, I think, I must be enlightened. *This is it!* Yet on the last day, I can't believe it. Here's that mad old mind busy again. *We're out soon. We must go to that nice tailor and pick up the new robe. And go and show Devesh how beautiful and surrendered we are now. And …* So, It wasn't as easy as that. I can see that to become truly empty may take years. And meanwhile, chastened, I go to the office and apply to start work in the ashram.

My first job is sticking labels on newsletters. Then, I graduate to washing the floors in the cellar of the book department. Deadly dull work and although I'm making the best of it, my spirit feels imprisoned. *I've given it all up to do this?* Yogi's got fed up with smoking dope and playing poker with Jim, and has started work. He's upstairs in the book department, packing. So he can leave his snippings all over the floor, and I have to sweep them up.

'Surrender Ma!' says Yogi, with glee.

Deeksha is a tyrannical Italian woman who runs the kitchens. She is notorious. Bhagwan sends the hardest cases to work under Deeksha. She is huge and vicious and loud. The kitchens are super-clean and well-organised. The swamis are stirring massive steel pots full of dhal, perched precariously on gas stoves. There are teams of people sitting at tables chopping veggies into plastic tubs. There are ovens making chapattis. After a meal there are shifts of workers wearing wellies and gloves, much laughter as they scour the pots clean. It's late in the night when the last floor has been mopped.

I've become a member of 'Girl Fridays'. We move around the ashram helping out where needed. I join the cleaners and I'm washing the showers of Anubhava and Aneeta. I've got a crush on Anubhava. We sing in the music group with him every night.

♫ ... *let the way of the heart...* ♫

He's a fantastic German musician and poet. Aneeta runs the Sufi Dancing in the morning. These two are the stars of the ashram, so I love making their room beautiful and spotless. Then, I am sent to the kitchen, which is what I had really dreaded so I'm being as unobtrusive as possible, when suddenly, there is the big Italian Ma, pointing at me.

'You! Get-a the butter from the fridge!'

'Yes Ma!' I jump to my feet. I have no idea where the fridges are, but I move. Someone indicates down the side of one of the work areas. A whole row of fridges. Shit. Which one? I hear Deeksha yelling,

'Where's the fucking butter, Ma?' I must be quick. I open one at random. Wow. It's absolutely stuffed with expensive western chocolate bars. Rows of Swiss vitamins. Cheeses. Champagne.

'What are you doing?' She pushes me out of the way and slams the door shut. 'How dare you! Take the butter! Move, move! Take it to Rupesh. You've wasted so much time already.' This was her private fridge. These ashram mamas made sure they had what they needed. Bhagwan says there is nothing that goes on in the ashram he doesn't know about... I wonder...

Anubhava composes these beautiful songs, with different parts for the men and the women, so we are rocking away, every night, in the immense Buddha Hall, which has a tent roof and white marble floor.

♫ *Even though you have broken your heart a thousand times...* ♫

One day, someone comes up to me in the Beedie Temple – Bhagwan says we can smoke as long as we make it a meditation.

'Psst ... Ma ...weren't you in *Doctor Who*?'

A few days later, I'm called out of my basement to go and meet Anutosh, an English theatre director.

'Bhagwan wants us to start a theatre group. Would you like to join? We are going to do *A Midsummer Night's Dream*.' So now, my work is with a group of actors from all over the world, and we are getting to grips with Shakespeare. This is an entirely different way of working, because there is no commercial pressure. This work is our meditation, so we have the time and freedom to really explore both the play and ourselves as actors. We all feel that the depth of Shakespeare's insight must come from somewhere else. We begin to delve into his timeless understanding.

We actresses can't wait to buy some mascara. Padma, an inspired American artist, is doing the costumes. I'm playing Titania, the Queen of the Fairies, and I love my medieval costume. Sidhena, a brilliant designer, is doing the sets. Chaitanya Hari, a renowned musician known in Germany as Deuter makes magic music for the production. The children, one of whom is a German Princess and related to our Royal Family, are the most divine fairies, and after a few months of working, we have a really good production, and a theatre booked in ten days. Our director's assistant comes into the rehearsal room,

'Message from Bhagwan. I shall read out the alterations, there will be no discussion, we will then go straight into Prayer meditation!' The actors playing the major parts are now playing tiny walk-ons, and vice-versa. Then, stunned, we are all flat on our faces, spread-eagled on the floor! You could hear the static.

'Shit, I'll never learn the lines! The costume will never fit me!' But this is Bhagwan's theatre, it's not to decorate our egos.

112

On my throne as Hippolyta

The first night is unbelievable. We are all consumed with fear. I am now playing Hippolyta, who is a Queen and a huntress. I jump up on my mossy bank, with my armour and my hunting bow, and I dry utterly. I don't even know who I am, never mind what my lines are. It's a terrifying moment which seems to last for ever. But then, I am miraculously speaking again, and no-one seems to have noticed. We have a standing ovation, and we are a big hit. We will now play for a week before going on tour to Bombay.

One of the people I most admire in the ashram is Chaitanya Hari. When we are in Bombay, we the cast spend a day in a swimming pool.

'Come!' says Chaitanya to me, invitingly, as he starts to climb to the top board.

'Up there? Are you kidding? I don't even jump in from the side!'

'Come on Anita,' he insists, and since I can't resist him, I follow him up to the very top board.

'Now you have to jump,'

'Jump?' I'm clinging to the rails, my knees are shaking and I'm feeling sick. 'No way!'

'If you can't make this jump,' he says, 'How can you jump into the unknown?' And with a charming smile, he jumps. Shit! One second later, I follow. I hit the water feet first and I am sinking fast, amidst a rushing sound and turquoise bubbles. This is it. I've had it. I'm going to drown. But miraculously, I begin to rise. Will I get to the surface in time. I'm gasping and spluttering, and he swims over and gives me a hug.

Later that night, after the performance which has taken place in an enormous Indian theatre, all made in marble, I join Chaitanya up on the roof. We have put our mattresses up there as it's cooler. I lie in his arms looking up at the luminous night sky filled with stars and he talks to me about our destinies, about Bhagwan and truth.

Before we leave Bombay, some of the bad lads in the company are going to the opium den. I like hanging out with the bad lads. But what's this? I don't like what's happened to me. Now I'm all stoned, and I've lost my lovely meditation clarity. Drugs no longer hold any fascination for me.

Yogi and I have been making tapes – all our chats and gossips - and sending them to Polly. I have received a curt note from Mickgough – Polly arriving at such and such hour, Bombay, and the date. Well of course, it would have been kind if he'd asked us, but we don't really care – Polly's coming! We go to Bombay to meet her and I book us all into a hotel for the night. She arrives, wearing little white lace gloves. We are all so happy to see each other, and she has Yogi and me in hysterics when she does her version of

'Well, how d'you-ah – I thought you were my handyman' – from The Rocky Horror Picture Show. She is so captivating. When we get back to our flat I expect her to need a few days settling in time – but no.

'Lend me a robe mummy, I want to come to a discourse, I want to hear him.' Afterwards she comes to me with tears in her eyes. 'I'm glad you're both here, and can I have a dress made?' We walk about the ashram hand in hand and Chaitanya says we look like sisters. She's bought her flute with her so she props her music on the window ledge, stands up straight, her darling face serious and concentrated, and plays some delightful Mozart. I am in tears.

It's Christmas time and I want to make it special, so Sandesh has an old Indian gentleman friend who has a house by a lake. We go and stay there for a few days. Yogi and Jim swimming, while Polly and I cook a turkey and Brussels sprouts.

Polly and Yogi at the lake

The theatre group are now going to do a production of *Twelfth Night* and they want me to play Maria, which is a lovely part. But I surprise myself by saying,

'No. I have to go back to the west now.'

'What? What is there for you?'

'I don't know. I just feel very sure that I must go back.'

'What about the flat?'

'We'll be back – we'll leave everything here – we'll just take small bags.'

Polly and I each have a darshan booked. I am a worker, so I will be in a different queue. I see her go up to the sniffers and get rejected. I'm distraught. What will she do now? But no – here she is again – this time her hair is wrapped in a turban and she's in. Now the darshan begins, and I'm called up. Bhagwan motions for me to sit beside him and others, he places in front. As he places his hand on my head and the music plays, I've melted into his lap. There is nothing I can do, and yet there is a voice inside me saying,

'You've got your head in his lap!' I had noticed that after these 'connections', disciples would have to be carried off and laid out on the edges of the hall. Well there's no way I'm going to do that...

And here I am, a puddle of joy, being scooped up by a large bearded Swami, and gently laid, sighing on the edge of the marble floor. Polly is above me with a shining look in her eyes.

'Polly, could you hear alright? Did the mosquitoes bite?'

'Ssh mummy,' she says. 'He's beautiful. He's so beautiful.' And when we reach the gate, Yogi is waiting for us, and arm in arm we wander back to the flat, and I know that they have both received the most precious gift.

Chapter 12

A Constant Vagabond

Back in London we stay at Veetasmi's. Polly must go back to school, Yogi is so happy to see Peter and Dickon, and I think I'd better call the nursing home, to see how my mother is doing.

'Good that you called. She nearly died in the night. Better get down here as soon as you can.'

I get the train to Devon and a taxi to the Marie Curie nursing home. Her bed is next to large French windows which look out over a huge tree in the garden. She seems smaller than I remembered. Bald, with a face like a puffed up child.

'I knew you'd come. Can you stay? I'm so afraid of these nurses. You know I saw Robin last night?' It's hard to be brave and hold back the tears.

'I have to find somewhere to stay Moe, but I'll be back – I won't leave you, I promise.'

There is a Sannyas community a few miles away. An obsessive German in a vast 18th century mansion, which he is busy converting into a centre. I can have a room in return for helping with the improvements. I rent a cheap car and I'm back in the home with my mother. She's on a very high dosage of morphine, so she's kind of crazy. In between bursts of great clarity,

'So it all fell to pieces with you and Mickgough? I knew it would. He was punishing you for being you. This woman – is she younger than you? Of course.' She asks after Polly and Jasper, and then she's into some crazy rant in Dutch, and from what I can gather, we are back in her childhood in Holland.

I'm exhausted when I finally leave, and on the way home there is a pub called The Black Dog. It's a great comfort to sit in a quiet corner and have a nip. Back in the 'centre', Nirup shows me what he wants doing. I have to clean miles of parquet flooring with a toothbrush.

So the weeks go by, having me nursing her every day, my mother improves somewhat, although her fear of the nurses remains. What I see in this Marie Curie home is unbelievable. The neglect, the bullying, the poor old people left crying on their pots. The nurse, with high black boots, who my mother calls 'the Nazi', comes breezing in.

'Now Anna, upsi-daisy! Here's your supper. Eat it up like a good girl.'

'Oh thank you nurse.' Very obsequious. 'Fish fingers, how lovely!' As soon as she's out of the room, 'Bloody old bag. I hate fish fingers.' She gives me a shopping list. For a moment I can see her spirit of old, her wicked almond eyes light up. 'Get me rollmops! Ah, how I'd love some smoked eels and a bottle of wine! We'll have a drink, you and me.' But when I bring it, she can't really manage it, and once again, we are back in Holland in her childhood,

'Ik wil geen zwarte paarden!' She's doesn't want black horses?! In my mind I see an Edwardian funeral carriage with black plumed horses. I stay until she settles down for the night, drive home, and clean a few yards of parquet floor before bed.

'Tell me more about the ashram,' she says. 'What does Bhagwan say? I always loved orange – it was my favourite colour you know.'

'He says that a Sannyasin is one who goes on wandering. A constant vagabond. A gypsy who makes no household anywhere. Even if he lives in a house, he knows it is only an overnight stay, and in the morning, he has to go.'

'Ah,' she says. 'He's quite right.'

In London, Yogi is living with Veetasmi and going to the Sannyas School in Muswell Hill. Polly is back at Michael Hall, so I'm left to get on with it.

'I wanted so much to see Nicholas.' Says my mother. 'But he won't come. He didn't know that I never married beastly Roy. So technically, you know …' She can't bring herself to say the word 'bastard', so meaningless in her world. Her pain destroys me.

'Give me his number!' I say, enraged. I haven't seen my younger half-brother since the sixties. I call him.

'Nicholas. She wants to see you.' But he refuses to come. 'If you don't come, I'll never speak to you again.' and so I never do.

Now, she's begging me to raid the drug cupboards, to get a lethal dose, to end it all.

'I can't, Moe, I can't.' Her eyes light up in fierce accusation.

'I'd do it for you!' We have a blazing row. I go out and sit under the lime tree. When I come back, she's asleep.

Apparently I have cousins living in Norfolk. She had kept up correspondence with my father's sister, Charmain. She gives me my father's address in South Africa. It transpires that she had kept in touch with him all the time, telling him about Robin and me. I have had no contact with him since I was three. Now I'm 38, and I'm writing to him for the first time. It's a difficult letter.

One sunny morning I'm weeding the raspberry canes in the walled garden of the centre, when Nirup comes, waving an airmail letter, and I know it's from him. I sit down and read my father's handwriting for the first time in my life. He is full of commiserations, and a request that when it's all over, I should come to visit him and his family.

'I've still got some orange nail polish.' Says my mother. 'Would you paint my toenails for me?' It had been fashionable in St Tropez in the 1930s and she had worn it ever since. I shrug. I don't see the point. She looks utterly hurt. I quickly get the polish and paint the nails of her swollen feet, and that hurt look will haunt me forever. I haven't yet forgiven myself.

Nirup is very demanding and is always whining.

'Ah, you are so un-surrendered Anita,' when I don't want to work into the early hours. I see that it's so easy to abuse these words of Bhagwan's. These are very deep understandings which may take a few lifetimes to really get. You can't just use them when someone doesn't do what you want.

119

In the spring holidays Polly and Yogi come and stay with me, it will be their last visit to see their grandmother. She's been very fussed about it.

'Will you do my hair?' She's only got a few white wisps left. 'The nurses can get me in a chair, and wheel me out in the garden, and wrap me in a blanket.' It's a poignant and difficult few hours. She has so much love for the children. They know they won't see her again, and they are embarrassed by their emotions.

When we get back to the centre, Polly says,

'You can't stay here.' Sometimes, she's like my big sister.

'That Nirup is a bully. You've got to move, mummy.' So a few days later I'm driving to the nursing home for the day when I see a woman hitching along the country road. I give her a lift.

'My truck is at the garage,' Sally explains. When she hears my story she's sympathetic. She asks if I would like to come and stay with her and her partner on their farm. They are a lesbian couple, living in a delightful old farmhouse with calves, pigs, chickens and ducks, a lot of land and a tractor, and I love it. It's so nourishing, and they are very kind and supportive.

'Mmm,' says my mother. 'You're just like me. I lived with two gay ladies in a school during the war, where I dug the vegetable garden.'

'Well I'm going to dig vegetables for these two!'

'There'll be trouble. You'll see. Lesbians always get jealous!'

I really like Sally, and curiously, she looks like a female version of Mickgough, so she's kind of familiar. My Aunt Tilly has come over for the day, with Uncle Hans from California. We are all sitting around my mother's bed. She wakes up.

'What time is it?'

'Half past four, Anna.'

'Oh well, I'm not dead yet, so let's have a cup of tea!'

On the farm the days begin with all the animals shouting for their breakfast. I help out, feeding the calves. They have a wondrously huge old pig, and enclosures full of chickens. I use their tractor and plough up a veg patch, and I plant beans. My mother wants to hear all about it, and loves to give advice.

'Plant your carrots in July to avoid the fly.' She is reminiscing about the Sun Rising School where we lived during the war.

'You were such a magic child. You used to wake Robin and I up at some ungodly hour to see the colours in the dawn sky. You were only four. Quite unusual, just like me!'

Sally's partner has gone on a trip which has left us together, and she and I have shared a bath. Afterwards, we get into bed and have a soft and loving time. My first same sex experience. It's so sweet and nurturing, and just what I need during these long, difficult and heart-rending days. But one night, we are curled up together upstairs when the window of the bedroom bursts open. Her partner has climbed a yard ladder carrying a 12-bore shotgun, and with a cry of,

'You bitches!' she is ready to blow my head off. I leap up with a pillow in front of me, like a shield, when my mala breaks, spilling wooden beads all over the floor. Somehow that defuses the angry moment slightly, and we manage to calm the offended woman down. But it's obvious I must leave, so Sally finds me a converted shed, high up on a hill above another farm. I love this place. All alone. If I leave the door of the outhouse open I have this wonderful view.

My mother is very bad again. Now she is very afraid.

'Where am I going to, Anneke? I've always denied the existence of God, so now what?'

'But Moe, existence is God. Didn't you always tell me, if you want to talk to God, go into a field, not a church. How you love the sound of the wind in the tree outside – it's all God.

'Ah,' she says, with a little sigh, 'I always knew that.' I sing her *You are My Sunshine* and *The Foggy, Foggy, Dew* until she drifts off to sleep.

I have been in Devon now for six months and I'm exhausted. I have taken a couple of days off and Sally has taken over the nursing. There is no phone in my barn, and when she comes up the hill in her jeep, I know what she will say before she steps out.

'She went in the night.'

So your anguish is over. You who loved me the most, who taught me to always be true to myself, to smell the roses after the rain.

Her Quaker friends help me to organise her funeral. On that morning, I go into the woods and pick wild foxgloves and daisies to lay on her coffin, which is so small, it's like a child's. She was 72. She has no possessions, just a small briefcase containing my father's love letters. One of which begins, 'Darling, do you remember the Lagonda?'

Chapter 13

Alchemy

'If the gold is to be purified it has to pass through fire.'
- Bhagwan

On the way back up to my little barn, I'm thinking that I deserve a tiny holiday. I'll go on a pilgrimage to St Mawes, where we lived after the war, and I'll paint and rest. I'm tired. But here's Veetasmi, standing in the drive, looking very pleased with herself. And here's Somendra!

'I've just buried my mother!'

'I'll put the kettle on,' says Veetasmi. Somendra hugs me for a while,

'We need you to come back to London with us because we are going to set up a house and an office for Somendra, as a base for his European groups, and you are to be one of his assistants.'

'I was going to have a holiday!' I say, lamely.

'No time for holidays, there's Bhagwan's work to be done.'

We rent a very large house in Hampstead, there's room for us all, and I am to make it aesthetically pleasing. I can't believe it actually backs onto the Craxtons' garden. I can see the studio. I know that Mrs Craxton has died, and I couldn't bear it if the house has been sold, so I never walk around the corner to see if John still lives there. I just find myself looking over the wall at my childhood and wondering.

♬ *Simple twist of fate ...* ♬
-        Bob Dylan

My father has invited me to visit him in South Africa, and I know I must do this for my mother, as well as myself.

I'm wearing my new pink, silk suit from Wallis, and I'm anxiously looking out for him when I arrive in Johannesburg. This is such a great big moment for me. He left in 1944, it's now 1979. I'm worried that I may not recognise him, but here he is, walking towards me, and he's cross because the flight was delayed, or something, so he's kind of off-hand. This isn't how I'd played the scene in *The Railway Children*, at the end, when Bobby sees the familiar figure, his face full of love, emerging out of the steam.

'Daddy, my daddy,' and then the ecstatic hug.

We drive to the residential area where he and his family have a large bungalow, spread around a pool. I meet his wife, Elsie. She's just had a face-lift, so her eyes are puffy and she's pretty uptight. The house is spacious and filled with his paintings. He's good. Some very striking landscapes, good portraits – so – it's in me genes! We have dinner in their very English dining room – red walls and a chandelier over the oak dining table. I've drunk gin, and I'm lit up, and talking about Bhagwan. My father is smitten with me, and Elsie hates it. When she goes into the kitchen to get the coffee he says,

'You're just like your mother,'

'Well, she was an amazing and wonderful woman, so I hope so!' Her spirit is swinging triumphantly from the chandelier.

We spend two weeks together. He asks about Robin and how he died. He looks so old and sad.

'He would have been a brilliant writer. Someone to be proud of.' He is very taken with me and takes me to all their boring old English drinking clubs. They have a maid called Elizabeth. After breakfast I help her with the washing up. Elsie protests that I don't need to. But I get talking to Elizabeth – she is wonderful and huge and black.

'But where do you live?' She shows me her tiny room at the back, it's the size of a broom cupboard. 'And what about your family?'

'They live in the townships.'

'When do you get to see them?'

'Rarely.' I had seen the townships as we flew over – like Indian slums – no electricity, dirt roads.

Elsie and my father have a son called Richard, who is a journalist. But I can't open my heart to him, because Robin is growling on my shoulder. They are too keen to persuade me what a good life it is here in South Africa. The streets of Johannesburg are empty on Friday nights – they are all watching *Dallas*. They have a little 'getaway' bungalow in the parched countryside. The walls are thin and I can hear him snoring. I'm sleeping next to my father. I never called anyone Daddy. I had seen photos as a child and I worshipped him. He was my David Niven, and I missed him. My daddy. I cry softly into my pillow.

In the afternoons, I'm in his studio while he paints a portrait of me. We don't talk much. He curses a lot when it doesn't go well. It reminds me of my Dutch Grandfather, flying into a rage when I wouldn't sit still as a five year-old, while he painted a portrait of me in St Mawes. My father's is a very large canvas, and I'm sitting cross-legged in my pink robe.

They have arranged for me to spend a few days on a safari camp. It's very kind of them, because it's expensive. I have a fantastic time. I'm hoping to see some elephants. There's something about them which always resonates for me. Our guide is a knowledgeable and yummy young man. He takes us through the bush. I see the colours in my father's landscapes. We see the grazing herds of springbok and giraffes, a lioness eating her kill up a tree, and at night he takes us black rhino spotting. Very scary. This huge snorting animal emerging in the dusty headlights. I get drunk and get it on with the guide, listening to the sounds of the African jungle all around us. We don't see any elephants but then, from the little four-seater plane that flies me back to Johannesburg, I see a herd traipsing through the bush.

My father and Elsie drink a lot and one day my stomach is suffering.

'I'll just have some tea,' but my father is insisting I take a spoon of medicine. 'No, no, I don't want it!' I flash back to my highchair, and he is angrily making me drink my milk; the child is empowered.

'No!' I say, and swipe the spoon out of his hand, glass and sticky medicine goes everywhere. Elsie is clucking in the background.

'Tut, tut, you two should never live together!' (She hopes!). I storm off past the pool to my room. After a while he comes in to apologise. I need to jump into his lap and be hugged, but instead, I get into my head,

'No need, it's fine, it's too late to tell me what to do. I'm not three anymore.' In that moment I miss the opportunity to forgive him.

He wants to set me up with a rich friend of his.

'It's a good life here.' But I can't wait to leave and get back to my people. I promise to let him know when Polly gets married, he thinks he'd like to come. I feel a huge sense of relief as the plane takes off.

Back at Alchemy, I'm very worried about being an assistant to Somendra.

'What, me? I don't know nuffing!'

'Not true. You have worked for five years with the very best therapeutic leaders there are, you've done most of the groups at the ashram, and you are a disciple of a Buddha. This absolutely qualifies you as my assistant!'

Alchemy consists of eight women, three teenage boys – Yogi, Somendra's son Deresh and Veetasmi's son, Dickon – and Somendra. Veetasmi is his secretary and I am cook and illustrator. We are a closed community. We are all working on ourselves so we don't go out, apart from the groups, and we don't have friends over. Somendra has insisted that the boys must go to Tavistock school. They are very resistant to this, and after a couple of terms, it doesn't work. These ashram lads have grown up, as they say, the other boys are all larking about, playing truant and getting drunk while they want to get the knowledge, so it's a drag. One night we are sitting having supper, and Somendra asks.

'Have you guys done your jobs? The dustbins, the logs?'

'Uh … no.'

'In the monasteries,' says Somendra, 'Those that didn't work, didn't eat. Anita, take their plates away.' The boys jump up, empty the bins and fill the wood baskets, we never have a problem with them after that.

That's Veetasmi, on the right

When Somendra goes off to do a group, he takes two of us with him as his assistants, which means we organise the tickets, the travelling, and the group fees with the centre leader. We take care of his every need, his room, his clothes, and we are there to play the music he wants, and to support him in the group. We have to be absolutely on the ball, all the time, and it's incredible. We travel all over Germany doing groups in schlosses, and centres in Berlin and Hamburg – sometimes there are hundreds of people. We women become known as the Alchemy Babes, and I learn more from working with Somendra than I have ever done. What an experience, what a gift. But he can be a tyrant too, if things are not exactly so. One day, he's been angry with me, and as we step out of his Mercedes, he bashes me over the head with an umbrella.

'Wake up Anita!' It's supposed to be a Zen stick. Zen masters were notorious for beating their disciples to wake them up.

Now Polly turns up. She's breaking our 'no visitor' rule.

'Stuff that! Where is he?' she says. Somendra has a red and green light over his study. When it's red, as it is now, you mustn't enter.

'Polly! You can't go in!' She takes no notice and storms in.

'Oi! I don't care who you are – you don't hit my mother!' Somendra loves her at once, and she is allowed to come whenever she likes. She puts on my 'celebration' dress, we have tea and take Polaroid photos of each other.

Our washing machine has broken down so I've parked the Mercedes near the launderette in Hampstead High Street, when I bump into my darling old friend, Peter Cook. I haven't seen him since the sixties.

Oh Peter. It's early morning and he is staggering out of a booze shop. His arms full of vodka and newspapers. His beautiful face old and haggard, and darkly ugly. It's what alcoholism does to you. I'm shocked and saddened, and trying not to show it.

'Ah,' he says, pointing to my mala. 'You did that! Did it help, Anneke? You must come and tell me all about it.' And he stumbles off up the street. Peter Cook, the funniest man in the world, on a path to destruction.

Yogi and I go down to Michael Hall School to see Polly in her end of year production of 'The Playboy of the Western World'. It's a very professional production in the theatre, with a lovely set and costumes. But it all fades into the background because Polly is the star. In her apron and with her broom, she shines. She's also, sort of, just like herself – bossy and practical and vulnerable. She cries and laughs and is wonderfully wicked. She steals the show. Afterwards, all her friends are hugging her. The teachers tell me she's quite a rebel, but she is much loved by her fellow students.

She and David are moving into a darling little old cottage on David's father's farm in Norfolk. We go to the Maude-Roxbys' barn and get the boxes we'd stowed away together, so she can have all our plates on her dresser. She wants to recreate our old home. David's working on the farm with his father and will take over when he retires. They plan to get married once they are settled. I couldn't be more content with all of this. She's so happy, and they are so much in love with each other. All is well.

It's very intense living and working with Somendra. Nothing escapes him. We have to be one hundred percent awake, all the time. Just when I've been cooking for a group, really stretched, that's when he will choose to come to inspect the cleanliness of the larder shelves. I have a board in the kitchen, where I put the photos and postcards of our friends. Nothing must last longer than a week. I share a room with Girisha. My day starts at 7:00, preparing Somendra's breakfast, which he takes in the drawing room, overlooking the garden. At 10:00 we all file into his room. The meeting starts with eyes closed in meditation. Any issues that are present – living so closely together brings up a lot of stuff for us all at various times so we have to deal with our issues. I have endless trouble with one of the German girls. She's such a bully, and argues with me all the time.

'Ja, aber ...' is her habitual expression.

We discuss plans for the next group,

'Berlin – 150 participants – 3-day group – and I'll take Anita and Barbara with me as assistants, so book the flights and make sure my accommodation is comfortable. Meanwhile, Anita, will you please stop making the food so delicious because I'm putting on weight!' When Somendra goes off for a group, the home team collapses. We wash our hair, sit in our jammies, eat pizza and watch TV.

Alchemy takes care of us. We assistants have to look smart as we travel around the world – we are representatives of Bhagwan. Somendra travels First Class and has the Yves Saint Laurent luggage that he and I chose – I'm his stylist. 'The Boss' and I have outings to Burlington Arcade – he trusts my impeccable taste! We buy cashmere cardigans and soft loafers. He wears hand-made Indian Kurtas and pyjama bottoms. He also has a collection of Cashmere scarves which he gives to us, his team, and people special to him. They are prized gifts. Yogi is very chuffed with his Alchemy scarf.

One evening, Roddy Maude-Roxby comes to Alchemy and announces that he and Jane are going to take Sannyas. Alright! Out with the champagne. So now that's Rashid and Roddy – who both worked with Mickgough at the drug rehabilitation centre in Chelsea. It's an epidemic - James Coburn, Terry Stamp and Diana Ross, who goes to Poona and sings in Buddha Hall. We see her doing concerts later and she is wearing red, getting everyone to hold hands, singing ecstatic songs.

It's December 1980.

'Mum!' It's Yogi, rattling down the stairs. 'John Lennon's been shot!' We are all stunned. We walk up to Hampstead High Street and join the throngs of weeping people. The shops are playing his music and the world and we are grieving over this tragic loss. Our beloved John Lennon. He was a visionary of our time.

♪ ... *Imagine all the people, living life in peace...* ♪

We are allowed to celebrate Christmas (much cooking for me), but on Boxing Day, it's back to work.

We do a group in an old Swiss Chalet. The couple who own the centre are very attractive. Somendra really likes the woman and I fall for the guy. When the group is over I want to stay in Cuckoo Land with him. Somendra gives her my ticket back to Alchemy.

'Enjoy your honeymoon, but there may not be a job for you when you return.'

This beautiful, gentle man and I go to hear Krishnamurti talking in the Swiss mountains. He takes me to the church in his local town where he was confirmed and shows me the confessional box where he had to confess his childhood 'sins' to an abusive old priest. There is no-one around so we sneak inside the box and get it on defiantly.

We go up a very high mountain in a ski-lift and I get hypothermia. I love the farms and Swiss villages, it's a real holiday at last. After a week I return to Alchemy, and I have to clean the toilets as a punishment. I'm playing Bob Dylan on my tape recorder as I work.

♫ *You gotta serve somebody, he may be devil, he may be saint, but you gotta serve somebody...* ♫

It makes Somendra laugh so much that he forgives me, this time.

I'm in charge of running an Irish group. Somendra has asked if we can be met at the airport in a Mercedes as he loves to drive good cars. The Irish group leader has promised that he'll organise one, so I'm horrified to see a clapped out Ford in the airport car park.

'Sorry 'bout the car, me brother was sorting it. Long story ...'
This doesn't bode well. We set off to Killarney. As we drive through the countryside we keep seeing odd people on the road.

'Are ye comin' to the group?'

'Oi can't get the fee together!'

'Well come anyway, we'll sort it out!' Oh God, it's getting worse, and if Somendra is in a strop, it can be misery, and there is only me to look after him. We have about 35 people, and in the end we are out on the deck in the evening light ecstatically waltzing to *The Blue Danube*, the man from the IRA, the housewife, all the odd human beings, coming together in their hearts. Somendra forgives me for the group being so... well... Irish!

Somendra calls me in to his study. It's always nerve-wracking to be summoned.

'Anita, you are a catalyst, which means that whatever is unclear with the people around you, it will come up more intensely. So in this group, you are very useful to me. It makes my life easier.'

'Why can't it be love that comes up?'

'No-one said it was going to be easy,' he replies. 'You are burning off the Karmic residue of many lifetimes. It's a bumpy ride. Tighten your seatbelt, and I want you to illustrate my new book.'

In Amsterdam, we have a group on a houseboat. I'm in charge of this one because I'm half-Dutch. The Dutch have an open and warm way of being, I feel quite at home. The boat can hold a maximum of 100 people, but 150 have turned up. It's an amazing celebration, I just hope the boat isn't going to sink.

The ashram in Poona has instructed us to have a big day for the public and the press, to introduce Bhagwan's work to the west. We hold it at the Café Royal in Piccadilly. Somendra and Veeresh and Teertha will all work with large groups. There will be Sufi Dancing and meditations. We Alchemists are to escort the reporters around. We are dressed in our best suits. I am to accompany a man from The Times. He and I spend the day observing the happenings. It's amazing - hundreds of people, sincere seekers, asking questions, dancing and looking into each other's eyes, and laughing and hugging. Somendra plays powerful music, and has them all collapsing in blissful heaps. At the end of the day the energy is full of love. Groups of people are hugging in the hotel foyer. We Alchemists all come home and talk of what an extraordinarily wonderful event has taken place. Next day, we read in the papers.

SEX ROMP AT THE CAFÉ ROYAL!
FREE LOVE ORGY!

Somendra sends Girisha and I to Belgium to find a European base for his work – he says England isn't ready for him. We find a large, beautiful house in the old part of Brussels, and in September, we all move in. There is a Bhagwan Centre in Brussels, so we have a team of swamis to do the structural work on an attic space that I design. Alchemy is enlarging. Prageet from the bus trip joins us, and now we are a family of fifteen. There are three or four of us doing the cooking and the shopping. I love talking Dutch in the market place. We find a big space in which to hold groups. By now, Somendra is letting me take over in the groups, so I have my mates as assistants. He has bought himself a Mazda sports car – he loves to zip down the autobahns at breakneck speeds – laughing,
'We'll have no fear in this car, Anita!'

One time, we are sitting high in the turret of a schloss, he's having a break and a beedie, looking down below at the group members wandering in the gardens, all in floating clothes, hugging and laughing.

'Look at us,' says Somendra. 'We've become Angels.'

There is a lovely old pub on the corner of our road and in the evening sometimes we pile in there and drink old Trappist beer. There is also a café where Girisha and I love to go with the women. It's very genteel, sells heavenly coffee and sumptuous cakes. The prudish Belgian women, with their tiny lapdogs are very disapproving of our gales of laughter.

Meanwhile, Bhagwan has moved to the US, he is in New York state while Sheila, his secretary is negotiating for a piece of land in Oregon which will be the American commune. Rumours abound.

'In Oregon? Surely it's the most redneck, bible-thumping state?'

'Well, maybe that's perfect.'

We are having an open meeting, all the Sannyasins from the centre, and us Alchemists, when I notice a pair of eyes watching me. A very sensitive face. When everyone is leaving he comes up to me, his name is Vimal. He is very beautiful. Something's happened. I mean, I've had lots of lovers and lovely brothers, but now, this is big. I'm falling, falling, I've had it. I'm now obsessed with this man. My sisters are amused and teasing me, but it's no good, I can't listen, I'm in love.

He is a Scotsman who had been working in the ashram in Poona for two years when he was told to leave. When Bhagwan left for The States, many of the devoted ashram workers were dumped. He had arrived at the Belgian commune a few weeks before, with just the clothes he stood up in, and feeling very let down, so I buy him a coat and boots and kit him out for the winter.

It's October 1981, my 40th birthday, and Alchemy has made a celebration for me. When the feasting is over, I'm in my room waiting for Vimal. Of course, he's been delayed working late in the centre. A pattern is established for our future relationship.

I have to drive Alchemy's VW bus back to London to collect some supplies for Somendra. I stay overnight with Roger and Jehane in Kentish Town. It's lovely to see them and they tell me that Richard (Cracked Cup!) has returned from Poona with his girlfriend, Mary McCarthy, and now they are both Sannyasins and living in a lovely little house in Stiffkey, next to the bridge. I can't resist it – I go up for a quick visit. Their home is beautiful – warm and welcoming. They invite me and Vimal to come and stay with them for the winter. I love this idea, I want to have him all for myself. So when I get back to Brussels I put it to him, I'm very persuasive when I want to be.

'…and anyway, Somendra is becoming too big for his boots, with all these young Germans bowing down to him – it's too much – it's all gone to his head! He's forming a cult.' When I tell him our plans, Somendra says,

'Good. You're of no use to me when you're in your romance bubble, so both of you, go with my blessings.'

Now Yogi has to make a big decision. Mickgough has been on the phone to ask him if he would like to come and live with him and go to school in London. He goes for a meeting with Somendra, who points out that he could go and be a 'boy' with his father, and attend a regular school again, or he could stay here, in this juicy family, Somendra would look after him, and he would have a job as Alchemy's official photographer, travelling with him photographing all the groups. Yogi comes down the stairs with an expanded look in his eye and in tears.

'I'm staying,' he says. Everyone cheers. Our farewells are heartfelt.

'Come back soon, we love you!'

Chapter 14

Vimal

Stiffkey is cosy and familiar. David and Roger are happy to have me close again, although they don't like Vimal. He and Vardan (Richard) build an extraordinary conservatory alongside the river, with windows from an old chapel and I learn the art of stencilling with Asango (Mary), who is a unique and brilliant artist and getting a lot of commissions. I become her assistant. We watch *The Jewel in the Crown* each week, by the roaring fire with Doris the cat. Polly and David often come for supper. David's parents invite us for Christmas. They are a sweet family, attractive but neurotic, so it's a bit of a strain, but they have lovingly embraced Polly as part of their family. David's father is such a gent.

'You could turn the farm organic,' I say, hopefully.

'No, there's no money in it,' they reply.

On Christmas Day we all go to Church. Although it's not my thing, I am supporting Polly. During the service, my spirit becomes sad. Compared to Anubhava's music group, the singing is turgid and repressed. I can't wait to get out and be under the sky again. We are going to a big party in Aylsham, Simon and Sharon will be there. Simon is as mad as ever, and Sharon takes one look at Vimal and says,

'What a drop-dead gorgeous man! I didn't know he was yours!' Vimal reacts as though he has been pierced with a sword.

'I don't belong to anyone! I am a freedom!' He won't have anything to do with me for the rest of the night – another pattern.

For some time, my spirit has been knocking on my psyche, but I keep silencing it – I don't want to hear what it's saying so I've ignored it. But after a few months, I can't stop crying, so I'm going to pack my bag and leave. It seems that Vimal is emotionally unavailable to me and I need to get back into the mainstream again. This one-to-one thing doesn't nourish me any more – I need more people.

I've called Poonam and asked if I can come to Medina, the newly opened commune on the Suffolk border. It's a massive, mock-Tudor house – there are 500 of us living and working here. The dormitories are very full, but I find a bed in the corner of the attic, and get stuck in helping in the kitchens. I'm very lucky to be here because they are already full up, people are clamouring to come. Poonam wants me to help transform this old depressing school, with its dark mock-Tudor panelling and institutional olive-green sofas everywhere. I send for Vardan, Asango and Vimal, and we form an Aesthetic Team.

After many meetings we agree to paint the panelling in the main hall Wedgewood blue, which causes quite a stir – people seem to be attached to the beastly phoney oak panels. We make white linen loose covers for all the sofas. The Sannyasi builders have become a business, 'Sun Services'. They transform the hall and in the dark dining room we paint the panels cream and add mirrors to reflect the garden. Asango and I make large, unique wisteria stencils. It looks stunning. Now we have meditations and meetings, Tai Chi on the lawn, and a bar is built – 'Zorba the Buddha' - a sauna, a healing centre, a kids' house, and a screen-printing studio. In the attics I've designed curtains for all the sleeping spaces but I find it claustrophobic – such a small space. The lovers getting it on at night – I call them the opera singers.

'Ooh, ooh,' They seem to compete as to who can be the most ecstatic.

'Oh shut up! Some of us have early shifts!'

Medina is having an open day. Poonam announces at the pre-press day meeting,

'No hugging – they will only call it sex.' Vimal stands up, and argues determinedly.

'What rubbish! Sannyasins are renowned for lots of hugging!'

'But outsiders don't understand it!'

'We are Bhagwan's disciples – we must be true to ourselves!'

Polly arrives unexpectedly with David one day. She bursts into the kitchen, where I am working.

'I've come to see my mother.'

'She doesn't finish her shift until four o'clock,' says Vera the kitchen boss.

'Righto,' says Polly, putting on an apron. 'What can I do?' she's cracking many eggs into a bowl for our next meal. Good old Polly, getting stuck in. She doesn't like my bedspace,

'God, how can you bear it mummy? There's no room!' I'm putting a brave face on it. As they climb into David's Renault,

'Come and see us in Norfolk!'

'I'd love to but I'm not allowed.'

'It's like a blooming school,' sniffs David. Polly and I are crying when she leaves – we always hate goodbyes.

By now I'm adept at flying in my dreams. Now I dream that I've seen the light, and I'm hovering over the Medina courtyard.

'Come on, look! Look!' I'm calling my friends, but they are busy, with their noses in shifts and meetings.

'But we can fly!'

'Anita! Come down! You've burned the toast!'

Bhagwan has said that a new disease is coming, that will wipe out a third of humanity, and as it is transmitted sexually, we must all wear condoms and rubber gloves, and no kissing. The disease is called AIDS. The shockwaves reverberate through the communes. Selfishly, I think,

'Good – that'll stop Vimal from kissing all the girls.'

When Bhagwan left Poona, the big Mamas had gone around Europe checking out the various centres, and when they got to Brussels, they closed Somendra's outfit down, because he was setting himself up as a Guru, rather than a disciple. He was blacklisted. Yogi was sent to the Cologne commune where he was having fun working on the equipment at the discotheques. Now he has arrived at Medina and is working in the print workshop. I often sneak into his dormitory and pop packets of illicit salami under his pillow.

Vimal and I are not together in Medina. He has his own space and is happily getting it on with whoever he likes. I'm going through my jealousy over this, it's very painful for me. I'm sitting in a tea-break out on the terrace. Below me on the lawn, Vimal is rolling around with a beautiful girl. I'm feeling the knot of nausea.

'Anita, what are you doing?' An arm around my shoulders.

'Experiencing my jealousy.'

'You don't want to do that,' says a friend, pulling me onto my feet.

'Come and help me scrub the potatoes. There is a gorgeous new man in the kitchen.' I can't hold onto Vimal, yet I still have so much love for him.

The ranch in Oregon is holding its first festival and some of us are being sent, and I'm on the list. First, I have to wash my passport, so I get a new one without all the Indian stamps. I'm sad to lose my squashed and bashed up Navy blue and gold passport, with all the wonderful Eastern visa stamps. Royal Thai, Bombay, Penang, Laos – the record of my travels must all be wiped because the US is on alert for Sannyasins arriving illegally. It has shadows of a witch-hunt.

We are packed and taken on coaches to London Airport – it's like a huge school trip. We have chartered flights to Portland, where more coaches pick us up, and in the evening light, we are driven through this extraordinary cowboy country, wild and desolate. Large signs on the road proclaim, 'Rajneeshpuram', and we drive down this vast valley full of sage brush and junipers. They have set up tent cities to accommodate us all. We are decanted into yellow school buses and given numbers. I am allocated a tent with three friends from Medina. There is an enormous hanger for a canteen and in the morning we will see Bhagwan in the Buddha Hall. I know that Yogi has also been sent but now I'm really anxious because this is a very big festival – thousands of people – how will I find him? Outside in the downtown area, there he is. He's working. He's in the audio equipment team in Buddha Hall, so he's very important.

The morning meditation is extraordinary – thousands of us, from all over the world, gathered in this polished-floored tent, sitting in expectant silence as we wait for him to come. And there he is again, beaming and Namaste-ing up on his podium. He sits in his chair and closes his eyes. He's gone into silence, no more words, except when he has meetings with the world's journalists. Sheila and her team are in charge. They have built him a home up in a canyon, while Rajneeshpuram expands. The Sannyasins have built a dam. Rashid is in charge of planting thousands of trees. A farm is being cultivated and a town will be built. It's like the pyramids, thousands of little people, working away, inspired by a dream.

I have to admit, I hate it. I don't like this vast, barren landscape. I don't like the hoards.

'Too many people!' I never liked big festivals, and Bhagwan seems too remote. I mean, I've sat at his feet, and laughed with him, and here he is, a tiny figure, over the heads of thousands of disciples. It's all too much for me but I don't tell anyone, because they are all so fired up and excited.

When we get back to Medina, I'm beginning to feel rebellious. I've rung up my friend Devesh, and he tells me that he's spending the autumn at his vineyard in Bordeaux.

'Would you like some helpers for the harvest?' I ask.

'Yes indeed!' It's always been a fantasy of mine, to pick grapes in the south of France – how romantic! Sun hats on, wine flowing. I've got a few of the Sannyasi friends interested, but it's all cloak and dagger, because we wouldn't be allowed, so surreptitious notes are passed – we are playing truant – and when our plans are complete, we leave notes and scarper, very pleased with ourselves.

We take the boat train to Paris, and another train to Bordeaux. The château is exquisite, set amongst the groves of vines, and Devesh is very welcoming. Behind the chateau is a group of buildings for the workers. He has a new manager in charge, who is officiously proving himself. We have dormitories with iron beds and horse blankets. That night the new manager and his wife serve us with chicken's feet soup and pork, so we have to explain that we don't eat meat. They look at us in disgust. But the wine flows and we get stuck in like thirsty puppies.

Next morning, hungover, we are marched into the vineyards. It's a back-breaking hard slog. As soon as we get to the end of one row, the manager directs us at once to the next,

'Allez! Vite! Vite!' In between we load our heavy baskets into 'panniers'. Devesh and his beautiful model girlfriend come to see how we are all doing, and bring tea. But he's the boss, so there is no time to gossip.

'Alors! Vite! Vite!' And we are back at it.

The next day, it rains. We are crawling in the mud, covered with black plastic sacks and cursing the slave-driving manager. The rain doesn't let up for ten days. Perhaps the hardest physical labour I've ever done, and the fantasy has long since evaporated.

I can't go back to Medina because I'm in the black books. I try to call Vimal, only to be told that he's left.

'Left?! Where's he gone?'

'He's flown to Vancouver.'

Thousands of us Sannyasins are now trying to get into the US. The American immigration authorities are on red alert, so some disciples are moving to Canada, hoping to sneak in quietly, over the borders. I talk to Vimal.

'What's it like?'

'Great – you should come! Lots of people we know. Girisha's here. Get a ticket – let me know when you're arriving!'

I've saved some money from the grape harvesting, I'm staying with my friend Paul, from Norfolk days, who buys my killum, my last possession from Norfolk, and he gives me some Canadian addresses, friends of his, just in case.

I pack my small suitcase and Polly and David take me to the airport. When it is time to say goodbye, Polly has big tears in her beautiful blue eyes.

'I'll miss you mummy, you will come back for our wedding won't you?' And I walk through into the departure lounge and sit straight down, and write her a love letter.

My Darling Daughter,

Whenever and if ever you need me, just let me know, and I'll come straight back, because I love you Polly, for ever.

Your Mum

143

Vimal picks me up at Vancouver airport, and drives me to the house he's sharing with a group of Sannyasins. It has an amazing view over the city, to Whistler Mountain, which is lit up for the skiers. It's my birthday. How often I seem to start adventures on my birthday.

There are a lot of old friends here. Girisha from Alchemy is looking for a house to share and I've got to get some work at once, so I advertise myself as a cleaner – 'Cleaning Transformations'! – I need to make some bucks. The supportive network of the Sannyas world cannot be underestimated. Wherever you go in the world, there's a centre, a hug and a bed. But one rainy day, I'm feeling depressed. I hate this ugly house and this ugly street in this foreign city. So I pull out the list of people that Paul gave me. Here's one that says 'Michael McNamara, Hornby Island' – I decide to give him a call.

'I'm a friend of a friend, and he told me to call you ...' he sounds very nice. I ask if I can come to visit him. He gives me instructions. Up to Horseshoe Bay – ferry to Vancouver Island – up to Buckley Bay, another ferry – across another island – another ferry – it's a whole day's journey.

'Well, one day I'll try and make it,' I say, disappointed.

Vimal's nickname is Veems, and he calls me Neets.

A week or two later, I've decided I want to go to Hornby. I have to persuade Veems to come on this adventure with me. He's resistant as usual. I also haven't managed to speak to Michael, but I figure, it's an island, so he's bound to be there. So on a cold November day, we set off in Veems' VW bus. The huge ferry from Horseshoe Bay over to Nanaimo is amazing. We sail through the Georgia Strait, past many islands, the snow-topped mountains, the blue-grey water, the birds – I feel like I'm on a cruise.

'Are you by any chance going to Hornby Island?' We are surprised to see a good-looking man, about our age, wearing a reefer jacket and boots, twinkling at us. 'You looked like you were. My name is David Cloud. Can I have a lift?' And joining us he begins to tell us tales of the extraordinary place we are about to visit. It has been his home since he left America in the late sixties. There were

144

quite a few US Citizens who had headed north to avoid the Vietnam draft, settling on the remote Canadian islands, hacking back the forests, clearing the ground and building their homes, forming communities, like the original settlers. He had managed to avoid the draft by going for his interview wearing a purple cloak and accompanied by a goat! The difference with Hornby is that they are mostly artists, architects, painters, alternative folk. He regales us with stories and information as we drive up the Vancouver Island highway, which is busy with logging trucks, piled high with massive great trees. We take the ferry across to Denman and finally, the ferry to Hornby. The island is quite small, with a mountainous rock rising above the ferry landing. As we are driving up the hill there is a woman walking along the road.

'Stop!' says David. 'Suzanne, these guys are going to visit Michael.' And she climbs in with us for a lift.

'Brilliant!' she says. 'He's away off-island for the weekend, so I was going to feed his animals. I'll show you what's what and that'll free me up.' We drive to the end of a tree-lined dirt-track road, and at the end is a hand-painted sign saying 'Blue Sky Design'. We park beside a huge glass-fronted workshop.

'Will it be alright to stay, if he's not here?' we ask, as we put our bags in the hall.

'Oh, sure, here's the pony's feed, and here's the cat's food, and help yourselves to anything in the fridge,' and with that she has climbed onto her bike and disappeared down a path into the woods. Well, if this is island living, I like it!

The house is mind-blowing. A huge main room has windows up to the second story and old French doors lead out onto a wooden deck. There is a kitchen on one side, with a large table with a long bench and picture windows behind it, looking out onto the garden, an enormous wood stove has been made from a cast iron cylinder. Wooden stairs lead up to a balcony room, and there is a bathroom with wonderful forest views as you lay in the bath. We are surprised by the first compost toilet that we've seen. There are more stairs leading up to the bedrooms. It's all handmade in wood and glass. Who is this man? From his books, we can tell that he's very interesting. Michael is an architect and it looks like he plays the flute.

We set off to explore the island. There is only one road, which goes all the way around – it's only 8 miles long. The population is apparently 700, which doubles in the summer. There is a small shop which sells everything from building materials to food, and has a post office. We discover the most wonderful wild beaches. The island had originally been settled by ancient Indians and we discover their petroglyphs on the sandstone rocks. We visit David Cloud. The farm he's running is on the south side, a large, open piece of land at the bottom of steep, tree-lined hills. He lives in a log cabin next to the farmhouse, with geese nibbling by his back door, and amazing open views right out across the waters. He takes us to the sauna, it's up a track under the mountain. The entrance fee, apparently, is a few logs of wood to lay beside the furnace. I'm shy about sitting naked in front of all these island folk but luckily, as we step into the main space, the lighting is very dim. I'm clutching a towel around me. We climb up on to a circular shelf and in the dark, hot atmosphere I can make out about fifteen to twenty people, companionably sweating away. Everyone is naked, so I sit on my towel as the wooden seating is piping hot. As my eyes become used to the light I see that the roof spirals up to a tiny round window at the top. It's like being inside a snail's shell. After a while, I'm roasting, I follow someone out of the back door and suddenly we are standing in the star-filled night. There is a sort of sandy edge to a small lake, and we are plunging gratefully into the black, icy waters. This is fantastic. I'm hoping that no Canadian sea-monsters will bite my bare bum.

'Only water snakes,' says someone, and I'm out of there pretty quick. The sauna is a Sunday ritual throughout the winter. I like these island folk. I'm going to come back.

Chapter 15

All Things Bright and Beautiful

It's December 9th 1982, a beautiful sunny day, and I'm cleaning in North Vancouver. For some reason or other, I'm in a very weird space, and I'm beating myself up for it.

'What's wrong with you? The sun is shining, you've got work, how come you're feeling so strange?' When I get back home, my housemates seem somewhat distant with me. I'm down in the basement putting clothes in the dryer, when Veems comes in through the back door.

'I went to your work but I missed you. Something's happened. Mickgough called. There's been an accident. In Norfolk. I'm so sorry Neets, I don't know how to tell you this... Polly is... Polly has died.'

The world stops turning. NO! My heart stops beating. NO! My soul shatters into a million pieces. NO! NO! NO!

I'm sitting on my bed. The women have their arms wrapped tight around me, and we are all wailing and rocking back and forth. Polly, Polly – in my ear – your voice whispers urgently.

'I'm alright mummy, I'm alright.'

The next day they put me in a car going down to the ranch. Tomorrow is Bhagwan's birthday celebration. The office has been told, and Veetasmi has been given time off to be with me, and a bottle of brandy. I fall into her bed and howl. During the celebration, my agony becomes so unbearable that I can no longer contain it. I have to let it go – give it up. And in that void the healing descends and permeates my entire being.

Back in Vancouver, Girisha says,

'I don't know Mickgough, but to call and leave a message like that, with strangers, not to have the heart to speak to you, I'll never forgive him for that.'

Charlie, Emma's husband, picks me up at London Airport. For the first time, I hear what happened. David and Polly, and her best friend Henrietta Cozens-Hardy, and her brother were in a pub and it was getting late. The girls had decided to go home, and the boys stayed for one more pint. Polly had only recently passed her driving test and David had given her a small car. It was loaded up with wood for their stove, because the nights had become icy-cold. Driving home, there was ice on the road, and on a bend, they skidded, and the car flipped over the bank, landing upside-down in a frozen pond beyond. When the boys drove home, passing the spot, they didn't see anything. Getting home, they assumed that the girls had stayed at each other's houses. In the morning the police knocked on David's door with the news that the girls had been found. Two beautiful young girls on the brink of their lives, drowned.

We gather at Emma's flat in Maida Vale. Yogi was in Medina when they told him. We are all hugging and crying. Emma and I both decide that Polly would hate us to wear black. Just as well, as both Yogi and I are in red. Jetlagged, I sleep, and then it's the day of the funeral.

'Simon has organised everything,' says Emma. 'He's been marvellous. David will meet us for lunch in Fakenham. Mick will come straight to the church, the little one opposite David's farm.'

When I see David at the lunch, it's almost unbearable. None of us eat much, but we do drink. We assemble outside the church. Where's Mickgough? I have such an overwhelming need to hug him. Now he's here, but there is some large person in a big, black cloak, shielding him from me – it's Henrietta. We file into the church and David, Yogi, Emma and I are on one side and David's parents, Mick and Henrietta are on the other. The sweet little coffin, covered in flowers, passes us by and is placed in the front. We are sobbing all through your favourite hymn. *All Things Bright and Beautiful*. We all follow the procession into the little graveyard and are given earth to throw. Yogi and I are hanging on to each other. David is in agony. I can't see Mickgough. There is a big black crow between us. We wind across the road to the farmhouse for drinks. It's like a cocktail party. *My daughter's dead. I wish it were me. I want Mickgough! I want a hug! What are we all doing?* Instead, I nod, and drink, and blink back the tears. The hole in my heart is getting bigger.

I stay the night with the Maude-Roxbys, and next day we are driven to St. Margaret's Church in Cley. Henrietta Cozens-Hardy comes from a well-known local family, so the church is full. Once again we stand opposite Mickgough. It's a touching memorial service, and Simon does a reading, and David is utterly destroyed. Once again in the village hall, the drinks, and Mickgough is behaving as though this is a first night. 'She' is hovering protectively around him. I give up on any possibility of contact. Jonathan's mother comes up to me and is talking about something totally else. I can't bear it. I'm in screaming pain.

Days later, they've put your clothes in plastic bags, and they've been delivered to the Maude-Roxbys, and I can't put off this painful task any more. I must go and sort them out. David has asked if he could keep everything else of yours. Of course he can. I don't want your things, I want you. The only thing I keep is a little quilted bag you made. In these neat stitches I see your darling spirit. I go into the end drawing room, light a candle, swig some brandy, and open the bag. Here's the black cashmere sweater I gave you, and your stripey men's jacket. I begin to sort into piles, sobbing all the while. I make a pile for the charity shop. Then I hear your voice in my ear.

'The charity shop?! Are you kidding?! That coat cost me ten bloody quid!' I'm collapsing into laugher and tears.

'So you are with me?'

'Of course! Where else would I be?'

We are all talking about how cruel it was that Mickgough was kept apart from me. Roddy says,

'That's going to take a lifetime to get over, Anita. And what are you going to do now? It's nearly Christmas, and our house will be full, we have the whole family coming …'

149

'Christmas? I never want to do another Christmas.' I want to run away to the edge of oblivion.

'To go beyond, the way is through.'
- Bhagwan

Veems has taken over the farm while David Cloud has gone to Cuba. I'm glad I came here, and can get away from Norfolk, and all the painful memories, and Mickgough and his cruelty, and all the well-meaning people. This is a fresh slate. Yogi remains at Medina, his girlfriends comforting him.

Here, in this little log cabin with a wood stove to cook on, Veems is hugging me. I walk along the shores looking out across the waters to the islands with snow-capped mountains. The eagles sore in the skies, and I can be with my pain. So many tears. How will I ever pick myself up from this? I am annihilated. That I'll never see your darling face again, my lovely Polly. I know I have to keep this wound open. So many tears. I walk, wrapped in oilskins and welly boots, up the mountain, through the Douglas firs and arbutus trees, and high up on the cliff I walk along, the light changing across the Georgia Strait, the fishing boats, the skies filled with birds. Up here, close to the heavens, I can feel you loving and comforting me. So many tears.

After a week or so, Veems is the stark voice of reality.
'You're going to have to get some work together,'
'I'm not ready to see anyone yet.'
'I'm not supporting you financially.'
'But I'm grieving!'
'That's the past. Be here now.' He's a tough Master and I can hate him.

I go to see Michael McNamara. I would like to have left it for longer, but here he is, and he's lovely, and kind, and hugging me. His great wife Kirsten and their daughter Jessica, who flies across the field on her pony, long tresses flying, barefoot in her nightie. Mimi, who's a baby, will really help my heart to mend more than anyone else. It's one of those instant friendships. They give me love

150

and support. We set about spring-cleaning their home. They are being so kind and they get me a job helping John Grunewald sanding his handmade cabinets in their workshop. I'm painting a picture of some wild roses, entitled 'For Polly, Wherever You Are'.

David Cloud is coming back, and we have another cabin to stay in. No electrics. An outside water pump. Veems has to break the ice in the mornings. He's now got some carpentry work with Michael and I have the nearby beach to cry on. Small beginnings.

I realise I've cut myself off from anyone who knew Polly. I have no-one to talk to who actually knew her. People are embarrassed by my grief so I can't share it. It's like another death – all that I was – my family and friends, my home, my identity. I've slotted in an entirely new tape. At 42 years old, I'm starting all over again.

A while later, we are house-sitting a comfortable home up on the north shore. Edward Fox writes me a heartfelt letter here. It's addressed to 'Anneke, Hornby Island.' I keep it as a treasure for a while. The beaches are piled high with logs, bleached white like bones. I'm walking on the sandstone rocks and listening to the sea lions honking. Soon, it is herring season and there are hundreds of thousands of birds around the edges of he island. The fishermen's boats are lit up at night. We chop wood and light stoves, and keep warm. When I am alone, I cry and cry.

I'm sending so much love to Yogi. How has it been for him? I call him from Michael's but it's on the commune phone in the hall in Medina, and I can't really speak to him. I worry about darling David. I hate Mickgough – my anger for him is like a hard lump inside. I'm sure he must feel guilty that he had abandoned her when she needed him. My pain seems to have found a secret place inside where it can hide itself away so that I can keep myself together.

I dream I am sitting in the kitchen of our old home and suddenly you are there Polly. You are standing, luminous, laughing and translucent. Love surrounds us.

But Polly, you can't be here. You died.

You just smile.

Can I hug you? Can I stroke your hair?

I am hugging your spirit in this precious moment. We are interrupted by someone knocking at the front door.

Oh damn. Don't go away. I'll just go and get rid of them.

I go to the door and tell whoever it is that I can't talk to them right now. But when I come back to the kitchen, you've gone. And the old familiar pain returns. I go into the garden, and desperately call.

Polly, Where are you? Where are you?

I'm here mummy.

Where? I can't see you.

I'm everywhere. In the flowers. In the sunshine. In you.

Chapter 16

Hornby

It's a dark and stormy night. I'm worried because Veems hasn't returned from an off-island trip. When he gets to the ferry, the Albert J Savoi, there is no sailing, the sea is too rough. Too rough?! We often go on amazingly rough crossings. The cars are covered in waves as we bucket and heave our way across. It terrifies me. So this night, it must have been really bad. The ferry man looks at Veems dressed in red and wearing his mala.

'There are some more of your lot on Denman. Follow me.' So they drive across the island to a large handmade house standing in a beautiful garden. Veems arrives looking like a drowned rat, banging on the door. He is welcomed by two beaming Sannyasins, Deva Raj and Sudasi.

'Come in, Beloved!' We will become very dear friends.

One day, I'm sitting with Sudasi while she is spinning her wool. She dyes and weaves the most wonderful clothes. All these island houses are made entirely of wood and glass. They all have large wood stoves and walls of stacked wood along the decks and in the sheds. I love the sound of the spinning wheel, it's an ancient sound. We are interrupted by a call.

'Yoohoo!' My heart stops. I look at Sudasi. She looks at me.

'Who's that?'

'You heard it too?'

'Yes.'

'It's Polly. That's her call.' We've both got goose-bumps. We light a candle. It's a magic moment.

Michael and Kirsten have family meetings. I'm impressed. I wish I'd done that! Mimi is playing with her dolls. She's holding a meeting.

'Now look!' she says, 'I need some cooperation…'

I design a herb garden for Kirsten and we go to the beach and heave great flat stones back for the paths. They have an outside bath tub set in the deck, and it's heavenly to sit in the hot water and watch the sun rising behind the trees. Sometimes when I'm once again awash with tears I hear you say,

'Come on. Stop that! Put on your mascara and go dancing!'

I have heard that we repeat the same patterns as our mothers. I look into this within myself. I see the similarity in our emotional make-up. Both wild, impossible spirits, hooked in pain to the men we love. And that we were both nailed to the cross of losing a child. Moe, I know you can feel my pain. I love your bravery and determination to the last, to speak your truth. They also say that intelligence is passed down the female genes, so thank you Moe. I feel I'm echoing ancestral wounds. The pain, the pain.

'It is only through the dark night that the morning comes.'
- Bhagwan

Michael has a dear friend called Dean. His house is in a clearing down a path, thick with huckleberries. He's an artist and a fisherman, and arrives bearing a freshly caught salmon and a bottle of wine. He has built his own home and it's even more eccentric than Michaels, with a wooden ceiling in the living room that swoops, like a Bedouin tent. The compost toilet is out in the field.

155

When I stay there one time, in the winter, I'm very resistant to walking across the frosty field and baring my bum, but actually these bucolic poops are really wonderful. You and nature. And it's made with a little wooden tiled roof to keep the rain off, but there is no door because you are alone in the field anyway. Dean has an upside down rusty car, suspended in a field – his art. His fishing boat is called 'Love and Anarchy' – as he says – what else is there? He's a character.

The islanders have formed a supportive and conscious community here. The co-op shop is part shared by everyone and is central to the community. There is a great community hall, the entrance is made out of a gigantic tree root. All the chairs are handmade from wood and leather. Here, they have theatre, dances, workshops, exhibitions, and movies every Saturday night, with the children in sleeping bags at the front. There is no bus, so we give each other lifts around the island.

Another amazing architect who lives here is so famous that he has disciples. He lives on a houseboat hauled up onto the beach called 'The Spud Queen', and it was he who designed the sauna.

Veems is going tree-planting. We drive the VW up to Campbell river in the far north of Vancouver Island. The tree-planters gather. Veems has his eye on a pretty young woman, one of the cooks. I drive back to Hornby, feeling wretched. But Veems is quite clear.

'It's my freedom, I don't belong to anyone. Only Bhagwan knows about love.' Our life is punctuated by blazing arguments and sweet tender moments. Veems is brilliant, talented, intelligent, funny, sexy and mean. He can cut me up and spit me out with his cruel words, and I love him and hate him equally. He is never happier than when his bag is packed at the door, ready to flee; then he can be the most delightful company.

I'm now living in a little cabin made of driftwood beside the beach. Veems is away tree-planting. I'm so cold I spend my evenings reading with an oil lamp, with my feet in the wood-fired oven. I live alone and after being quite afraid at first, I begin to love it. I slip naturally into a hermit-like existence.

I've got another job. I'm weeding the sod roof of one of Michael's clients. They have a Blue Sky house right on the edge of a promontory, so the roofs are all planted with sedums and bulbs. I'm up on the top looking out at the astounding views. We are surrounded by arbutus trees. Pip is an Englishman who designed the courses for the Olympic Show-jumping. They are very kind to me.

'Anita, come and have a hot tub when you're finished!' Later, I will be sitting in their beautiful spa with a large gin before walking back along the beach to my driftwood cabin. Now they have offered me a big job. I am to fly with them to Calgary where we will hire the biggest U-haul truck, drive it to their ranch, which is up for sale, stuff it full of furniture, and I will drive it back across the Rockies to Hornby. $250, all expenses paid. I'm hoping Veems will come too but he can't get back so it's just me. My heart sinks when I see the size of the truck, and they stuff it full. I drive it in absolute fear and trepidation to the Calgary Hilton, where we'll stay the night before I set off. I can't resist saying to the commissionaire at the entrance,

'Park this will you?' as I hand him the keys. We have a slap-up dinner and I'm talking about my favourite subject – mysticism – to a very interesting woman so I get pissed as a fart. Next day I'm heavily hungover as I set out across the Calgary plains towards the daunting sight of the Rocky Mountains ahead of me in the snow. The truck has power-steering and a comfortable cab. I've got my flask of coffee and Pip's credit card for the expenses. I'm beginning to feel rather powerful. It's going to take about three days. Should I take on a hitchhiker to help pass the time and support me? Well, maybe. But only if he's the most beautiful guy. On the side of the road ahead is a man hitching. As I sail past I see that he is beautifully tanned and wearing a white fur coat and boots. An angel on the highway. But I've passed him by – this is my adventure – I must do it alone.

After the first day, I've really got into the swing of driving this huge, heavy vehicle. I've been through spectacular scenery and the roads have been clear of ice. I stop for the night in a motel which has a pool, so I can swim and relax. Tomorrow are the high passes. My route takes in Banff, Lake Louise, Golden, Revelstoke, Kamloops, and the Fraser Valley. When I stop to fill up with gas, people get chatting to me. They are amused to see this woman in red jeans and red welly boots.

'Where ya going? That's a big rig and a long journey! Well done! Good luck!'

By the time I'm charging down the Fraser Valley I'm in the zone. I'm driving this huge pantechnicon like it's a Mini Cooper. I'm singing Bhagwan songs at the top of my lungs.

♫ *So I let it all go and I'm living…* ♫

Another motel and I can't really sleep. All I see is the road ahead, and tomorrow I've got to drive through the city of Vancouver. I'm more worried about this than the mountains. I haven't driven in city traffic since London in the sixties. I manage without mishap and get to Horseshoe Bay, negotiating my way on to the ferry with the help of the very professional ferrymen. My goal is in sight but will I get to Buckley Bay in time to catch the Albert J? I'm now roaring up the island highway alongside the logging trucks and I just manage to make the last Denman ferry, which will connect with Hornby. The Hornby ferrymen cheer me, it's the most satisfying praise. I drive straight to the Co-op and parking in the road, I tell everyone,

'I drove this across the Rockies!' So they take photos of me. I then drive on to Pip's, let myself in, and get into their hot tub with a huge gin and tonic, as the stars come out above me.

I have to write to my father, to tell him about Polly. It's a very difficult letter to write. All his dreams of coming back to England, seeing his granddaughter married, are dashed. It hurts him terribly, but I don't know that now.

The vehicles that people drive around the island in are incredible. Ancient, bashed up trucks and Volvos. When the police get on the ferry the island drums relay it to the Co-op. There is an announcement over the loudspeaker.

'Cops on the way!' Miraculously all the beaten up unlicensed bangers disappear, driven into the fields and barns. I've bought an island banger with my $250 and one day a pungent old hippy jumps in,

'Another day in paradise,' he says, as he settles into the front seat with his smelly dog. I ask him if the band on Saturday night are any good. 'Does it matter?' he replies. 'They are the only band!' The entire community comes to the dances, the wild witch women, the grandparents dancing with their grandchildren. We dance around, catching each others' eyes in the shared moments of fun and laughter.

An island home

How Jonathan would love the geodesic dome built up high in the trees, and the castle built out of lithographic plates, the house made of straw bales, but the Blue Sky houses are the best. It's Japanese

159

style, meeting the west coast. Post and beam, the flowing lines, the curling roofs following the contours of the land. Tiled floors, polished red cedar windows, each house unique. They inform the Hornby style, which is emerging.

A 'Blue Sky' House

I'm very blessed to be here at this time, and I know it. Actually I begin to have rebellious thoughts. What if I just settle down here, and don't go down to the States? Veems and I have been saving to go to the second festival in Oregon, and then on to California, because we have to get ourselves green cards so we can live on the ranch – I'm not sure I want to live on the ranch – we'll see. In the summer months the water table goes way down. We all have to be very sparing. Short showers. Switch off taps while cleaning our teeth. It's a good reminder. There is a couple who once went to Poona living here. They're wintering in Hawaii so we housesit for a month. It's one of Blue Sky's houses so it's a large and comfy space – with an inside loo! Our friends from Vancouver – PJ and his Norwegian girlfriend come to visit. PJ wants to make a documentary about life on Hornby. We are talking about the ranch. I suddenly interrupt.

'I think it's already heading for its own destruction. Sheila's got the power and it's all going to end in corruption and politics. You'll see ...'

'Oh, Anita, you're so negative! You need tickling!' They tickle me until I am crying with laughter and begging them to stop.

Hornby

Chapter 17

The Road to California

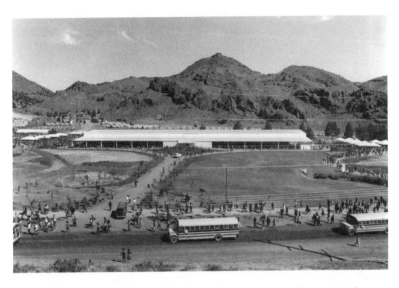

July 1983. We drive down to Oregon for the festival and meet Yogi who is here taking photographs and working on the audio equipment in Buddha Hall. He's a young man now with his own life. It's emotional for me to see him again, after Polly. The mother in me mourns my little white haired boy – got to let go – let go. The ranch is more developed. There is now a town with shops and bars and restaurants. Rashid and his team are turning this desert into an oasis. They have dammed the lake and in the centre is a raft which hundreds of Sannyasins are diving off, while drummers drum. The tent cities spread up into the canyons. Bhagwan is a tiny figure in the distance. Everyday there is a drive-by. He is driving a Rolls Royce along the Sannyasi filled roads, and rose petals are being scattered by an aeroplane – there is now an airport. Bhagwan now has a fleet of 100 Rolls Royces. These cars are notorious. It's pressed everyone's buttons.

'But he's a spiritual leader!'

'He doesn't own them! They've been given to him from some of his wealthy disciples. They're owned by the foundation – He doesn't own anything. He's way beyond all that!'

'But he does love to drive them very fast, around the ranch!'

'But… a hundred Rolls Royces!' This is the way I see it: we are talking about an enlightened Master, and this is his device. What more brilliant way of getting the world's attention than by moving to the most right-wing state of the richest country in the world, and then flaunting a hundred of the most potent symbols of wealth… and, he has the added audacity to have his artist disciples paint them, with clouds and swans and lotus flowers. Well, that's got everyone's attention. He's here to wake up the world, because, as he says, we have to have a revolution of consciousness if we are going to survive what's coming…

Bhagwan is being guarded by Sannyasins carrying machine guns. Machine Guns?! When I see Rashid and Veetasmi I ask them about it but they just accept this state of affairs. Can't they see what's happening here? I sense a kind of elitism going on – us and them – I am never comfortable with that.

All the people are lined up on the road for the 'drive by' and I am alone, wandering off to the lake on the opposite side.

'Anita!' bawls one of the Mas, over a loudspeaker. 'Get in line!'

'No thanks. I'm off to the lake.' All this adulation is too much for me. But on the last day, Veems and I are walking way out on one of the ranch roads, and mounting the hill, comes Bhagwan in his rose-covered Rolls. As he sees us he slows down and the window is lowered. Veems and I are rooted to the spot in Namaste.

'Can you take these roses away?' says Bhagwan. We rush to do his bidding. He smiles and then… brilliant! He does a double-take.

'Hello, Anita!' he beams at me, and away he drives. The glow stays with me all the way to California.

Some of Yogi's extraordinary and unique photos

A little mouse climbs into our VW while we are at the ranch, and now he has travelled with us all the way to Mill Valley, which is steep and wooded, and many of the houses are built on stilts. It's an affluent, alternative Californian society. Van Morrison lives here. The main town square is like Hampstead – full of boutiques, health spas, bookshops, and with a large square in the centre, with benches, and people roller-skating and playing guitars under the orange trees. While we look for somewhere to live we stay with my Uncle Hans and his wife Hennie in their trailer-park home. She had wondered if she should hide the kitchen knives in case we were like the Moonies. Hans tells us stories of the Nazi occupation of Holland – how they managed – eating cats. How my grandmother died of starvation.

'Ja dats true,' calls Hennie from the kitchen. But when Hans talks of the earthquakes here in California, how the roads are like waves, she's in total denial. 'No Hans, dat never happened, it didn't.' It amazes me what we human beings are able to endure.

I find us a lovely home to rent, up a quiet canyon. Four bedrooms, all on one level. A large deck, running the length of the house at the back. It has skylights and big sofas. I'm in disguise, dressed in a green trench coat, with high heels and painted nails, playing the part of a posh lady, bullshitting the owner about how financially secure my partner and I are, about how we need the extra space for visiting family.

'And do you have a favourite furniture polish you would like me to use?' That clinches it. I sign the papers, hand over our last few dollars, for first and last and deposit, always such a stretch, and whistle to the mates – there will be six of us sharing. Funny how, it's at these times, when I've got to find work and a car and pay the rent that my back gives out, and I'm flat on the floor, pillows under my knees, in pain and worrying. There are lots of Sannyasins living and working here, so there is dancing, music and meditations. Veems and I love to walk in the redwoods, on Stinson Beach and up Mount Tamalpais. We will save our money so that we can afford to live on the ranch. Veems's favourite day out is in these massive superstores. He's absorbed with all the power tools he's starting to collect. We have to find ourselves amenable fellow Sannyasins to marry, so that we can get our green cards. There is a side to Veems that drives everyone who knows him mad. It's like a cloud descends, and he becomes black, and 'in his head', and vicious with it. I fight with him then, to survive, because he wants to destroy. Many of my women friends will resort to a Zen stick, in the form of a hefty clout over the head to stop him. But I can't hit anyone, ever, for any reason. So I run away, or I stand and fight, or I jump out of the car as it's going along.

'Stop it! Leave me alone!' I can't live with him, but, I can't live without him. The agony and ecstasy of relationship.

These west coast Americans are great people – I really like them. They are so open and warm and friendly, and 'no-nonsense'. At first, it's alarming, when their opening gambit is,

'Hi. Whadd'ya do? How much'ya make? What kinda car d'ya drive?' We English are so retentive about money. They are always so positive, it's California style.

The TV is on in our living space.
'Oh do turn it off!' I call out from the kitchen.
'No, look,' says Veems. 'It's English. It's *The Avengers*'

167

'I was in it once,'

'You weren't!' I walk back in to see Diana Rigg entering a familiar tie shop.

'I certainly was – and there I am!' In true Sannyas style, I never spoke about my past. Here, now. Even *Doctor Who* was a distant memory, I had no idea that people at the BBC had unsuccessfully been trying to track me down, to invite me to take part in the programme's 20th anniversary celebrations. It is many years later when I find out that I missed the chance to appear in a spectacular story featuring all the surviving Doctors.

I am back to cleaning houses. I get a perverse pleasure from getting paid for what I always used to do for free. It's also a necessary part of a spiritual path, to be humble, and of service. These Californian women are neurotic beyond belief. The carpets have to be vacuumed in stripes and each section of the Venetian blinds cleaned with a special brush. The cookers dismantled and polished, the toilets and bathrooms gleaming. One of my regulars works in real estate. She sets off to work looking fantastic – big hair, big shoulders and impossibly high shoes. But in her home she is a total slob – unmade bed full of pizza crumbs, every surface full of clutter, magazines and dirty knickers – it's such a drag to have to tidy up after her before I can start my work. I try on some of her clothes. Amazing. The cleaner is transformed into an eighties glamour girl! I take the lovely silk shirt and pearls off with a sigh, and get on with mopping the floors and worrying about money, and how much I will make at the end of this day.

Every morning, I wake with a hole in my heart and I remember that you're no longer here, and my spirit flies to Yogi to give him a hug and I begin to accept that this sadness will never ever leave me.

I'm working for two gay professional women. They call me their peach and on their fridge they have a sign which says 'Every Working Woman Needs a Wife'- but they've crossed out the 'wife' and written 'an Anita'! I iron all their shirts and blouses. I never see them. They leave notes and money. Because of the possibility of earthquakes we all carry emergency supplies – stout boots, leather gloves, water, torch and a blanket, in the trunk of our cars – so I ask them where I would switch off the gas supplies should it happen while I'm working for them. They leave me a note – Gas supply Instructions – 'and help yourself to anything in the ice box'.

I see images of Joan Collins – my old rival – starring in *Dynasty* – the ultimate glamour of the eighties, and here I am cleaning houses. It feels like I was another person, in another life.

I'm branching out and have advertised myself as an 'English Gardener'. I'm employed by Launa Huffines. She has a wonderful Dallas accent and is a diminutive, clever and sophisticated fifty-something blonde woman who had got rid of her wealthy hubby some while before. Over the next few years I transform her vast garden. Many of the Californian gardens have been planted by Japanese gardeners to be maintenance-free. The hills are overgrown with periwinkle and St.John's Wort, so I have to weed all this out. Humping huge bins full of weeds up and down the steep hills. I make an English herb garden with herringbone brick paths, a terrace full of strawberries. Veems and I build a deck under a pear tree for her to recline on, and a hexagonal tiled pool with a fountain. She is very good to me, telling everyone that she has an angel working for her. I help her to clear out all her cupboards – these Californians have far too much stuff. A lot of the excess goes to furnish our communal home. I make eight dollars an hour and work eight hours a day. I now become Launa's voice coach and stylist. We go to Neiman Marcus, downtown, and I help her to loosen up the clothes she wears. I love her.

Veems and I live very frugally. No luxuries, no alcohol. But one time, two old Scottish Sannyasi friends – the lads – come and haul me out.

'You need a little treat, Anita!' We start off in a bar in downtown Mill Valley with a delicious tall glass of something called Long Island Tea.

'It's like lemonade!' I say, happily quaffing one or two. 'What's in it?' It's a mixture of brandy, vodka, gin and tequila. I am hauled out of the back of their car in the early hours by my surprised housemates. Veems won't speak to me for days. Ah, but 'twas a grand night. These Celts!

Peggy has answered my English Gardener advert. As I drive up the steep driveway, my heart sinks. More blooming periwinkle, which I bet I have to weed out. It's an exceedingly beautiful home, vast glass windows in the main room, huge cabinets containing their accumulated treasures, an original Shakespeare sonnet, a sheet of Mozart's music, letters from Debussy, Thomas Jefferson, many paintings and sculptures. I get to work weeding the periwinkle, clinging to the steep-sided hills. She likes me. I show her my portfolio and she wants to buy a botanical that I've done, of honeysuckle. I'm relieved, that'll pay the rent. She invites me to accompany them, sailing in San Francisco Bay. Her husband has a beautiful yacht, so we are off for the day, with delicious food on board. I'm wearing a suitable stripy shirt and sunglasses, imagining getting a lovely tan as we sail across the blue waters. As soon as we leave the dock at Sausalito, the wind gets up, the waters turn grey and rough, the yacht keels over until we are braced, feet straining, arms clinging.

'He loves to sail with the jib in the water,' shouts Peggy, cheerfully, above the spray. I'm terrified, and he doesn't let up till we reach the other side, where the boat once again becomes level, and we relax, and eat our lunch, and then we have a repeat performance back to the harbour.

My bank is called Wells Fargo and my cheques have images of stagecoaches. I clean for some cocaine dealers who have guns under their beds. They smoke hash while I iron the frills on their daughters' fussy dresses. I also clean for an art dealer whose whole house is secured with locks, and a bath so vast that I have to climb inside it to get to the walls. There are white marble floors, white leather sofas, huge dark, violent, modern paintings. In their nanny's room where I do the ironing, there is a lovely little Victorian oil painting of English countryside, which comforts me. Meanwhile, Veems is making a lot of money building decks and I'm employed by a very rich woman to cut box hedges in the front of her mansion. She comes to the door at 8:30am, wearing high-heeled slippers, a housecoat, long false eyelashes and lipstick. She has yapping Pekingeses at her feet and with her wrinkled old hands smothered in diamond rings, she walks with me around her extensive shrubberies, pointing with her walking stick to each dead leaf, which I must remove. I also have to tweak miniscule weeds with eyebrow tweezers, and feed her plants with vitamins and stress pills. I cut the box hedges with an electric hedge-cutter, and two days later, they have all gone brown. I'm off.

I read Barry Long, an Australian spiritual teacher. He is very insightful about male-female relationships. He says that women want love, but they advertise sex. I'm sitting in the main square in Mill Valley, so warm and relaxing among the orange trees, I watch the women strutting their sexuality…. hmm. The Californians have bumper stickers. One says, 'B.I.T.C.H. = Beautiful, Intelligent, Talented, Charming and Horny'. Another proclaims 'SAVE WATER – DRINK WINE' and 'THE RAT RACE IS OVER – THE RATS WON!' One enterprising Swami has advertised himself as 'Tantric Lover, to satisfy all your needs'. He is kept remarkably busy.

I'm reading Louise Hay. My new mantra is 'I love myself the way I am'…

I've met a Sannyasi who has agreed to marry me. I pay him the $1000 I've saved up. We spend some time swapping histories, and a Sannyas Minister marries us. A sweet little ceremony, 'helping each other to the light'. Candles lit, much laughter, a meal in a restaurant – a rare occasion. Then I'm off, back to England, to set the immigration wheels in motion. He goes back to Seattle, where he lives. On the flight I watch Mickgough in *The Dresser*, directed by my old friend Peter Yates. I want to say to my fellow passengers,
'I was married to him!'

This time, I stay with Geeta. Roddy Maude-Roxby and she have split up and she is now living with Richard. Norfolk is as I always remembered it. It's early summer, and I'm helping her in the garden. Rashid has built her a greenhouse with a wall of glass bottles, to keep the heat in. I've planted tomatoes and I'm playing them meditation music to see if it enhances their growth.

We go to the Wells Centre, which is now flourishing and successful. There is a large photograph of Michael Gough - 'the founder' … ! Geeta and Richard are still doing the Gurdjieff Group.

171

I'm woken in the mornings by the cacophony of bantams crowing. I ride my old Edwardian bicycle around the lanes. I still can't face our old house, although it's only up the road. It's lovely to see David and Roger again, and I spend a week with them in Stiffkey. Their lamp shop is now a very successful business, but sadly, Roger's brother Mick has died of Aids, and is now in an urn on a shelf in the conservatory. We sit around the kitchen table, drink gin, smoke roll ups, discuss the world, the madness, how Thatcher is ruining England. One day they are off on lamp business. I'm dusting the conservatory when – CRASH – I knock Mick off his shelf, and his ashes are scattered all over the floor. I quickly sweep them up and pop them back into their urn. How he would have enjoyed that!

I have to get some piece of divorce documentation from Mickgough. I'll meet him at his theatre, he's in a play at The Haymarket. I feel disturbed to see his name up there in lights.

'Who shall I say?' asks the stage door man. I can't resist it.

'I used to be his wife.' The doorman looks surprised, and goes to phone Mick in his dressing room. I wait in apprehension, not knowing what I will feel when I see him again.

'You're looking well,' he says, as he comes down the stairs. 'Shall we have a spot of lunch?' I can't speak, I'm afraid I'm going to cry. We are sitting in a busy eaterie, crammed in awkwardly with others, so conversation is tense.

'So what's he like?' he asks, with a mixture of sadness and bitterness.

'Oh I don't know, it's just to get a green card.' Polly is holding our hands. We don't say much more, it's too much for us both. He turns and waves to me as he steps inside the stage door. This is the last time I will see him.

Back in Norfolk, one morning before dawn, I get on my bike, pack a flask of coffee in a backpack, and go to the little churchyard where Polly is buried. There it is, close to the wall, a headstone of dark, grey marble. 'In small proportions, life may perfect be.' – I don't remember the full inscription on the headstone. It has no meaning for me. Simon and Mick chose it without consulting me. After a while I hear the lambs in the field beyond. I watch the sun rise behind the hills of David's farm. I feel softly peaceful.

I've found the telephone number of Lady Dorothea, the cousin, and she lives not far from Melton Constable Hall, the house where *The Go-Between* was filmed. She's invited me to tea. Geeta drops me off at the gates and I walk along the drive in the warm sunshine, and soon I see a perfect, small Tudor manor, surrounded by a moat, nestling in a landscaped garden. By the time I've crossed the bridge and reached the front door I'm in an altered state. What is it about Elizabethan houses? I pull the bell in the oak door and follow 'Stevens' across the creaking wooden floor to the drawing room. It's quite dark, the walls are panelled. 70 year old Dorothea is on a mat on the floor, in fishnet tights doing yoga.

'Have a seat – shan't be a mo! I've put some photo albums out for you to look through.' She puts on an antique kimono. 'Stevens, we can have tea, and would you call Johnny and tell her to come? Yes, you see, there's your father, with Julian at Harrow...' I'm staring at these images of my father, posing, smiling behind sunglasses, with his foot on the running board of his Lagonda. 'Alaric was very handsome,' she sighs. 'So popular with all the *gels*. Ah, here's tea!' The sliver teapot, the cucumber sandwiches, I'm in an Oscar Wilde play. Here comes Johnny. She's in a wheelchair, long, lank hair dyed jet-black, scarlet lipstick, her wrinkled old hands wafting her long cigarette holder.

'He was the only one of the family with the guts to get out.' Her voice is a gin-sodden drawl. 'Buggered *orf*. Quite right too.'

'Anneke's been living in an ashram in India,'

'Poona eh? One of your ancestors, Richard Temple, was British Resident in Hyderabad in the eighteenth century. He spoke Hindi and wrote a book on the psychology of Hinduism – had a native wife – well many of 'em did in those days – that was long before the Raj. I say, Dorothea, you're not going to ask that frightful couple from Blickling to your party are you?'

'I'm having my seventieth in a fortnight Anneke, I would love you to come. Now I must get on with writing the invitations. Do see the gardens on your way out. The tree peonies are particularly good right now...'

Eventually I am called for my interview. I've been to Oxfam and bought white clothes! I'm sitting in the waiting lounge at immigration in the American Embassy, nervously trying to remember my lines. I open a magazine on the coffee table, the centrefold is a huge photo of people doing Tai Chi on the lawns of Medina, and a big article about Bhagwan. I snap it shut, abruptly and act like I'm bored because 'I'm not interested in things like *that…*'

I breeze through the interview, my acting skills so useful. They believe me totally and they give me a card which claims me to be a resident alien. Yes! Now, when I land in San Francisco, they say,
'Welcome to the United States'. Amazing – we have always had hassles when we've crossed the borders, and my nightmares are always about being in the wrong country with the wrong bit of paper.

I've joined a cleaning agency. They've sent me on a job – some bloke who's got into a pickle and needs his house blitzed. I'm given a key and when I turn up with my little personal vacuum cleaner and rubber gloves I let myself in and the stench hits me. Dog shit, cat wee and stale beer. The place is absolutely disgusting. How can people live like this? I open all the windows, get garbage sacks and start scraping the shit off the carpets and clearing the empty beer cans. I go into the bathroom. There are turds in the shower tray. Oh God. I wake up in this moment. Wait a minute. I don't have to do this anymore. To hell with the money. Thank you, Gods, for giving me this extreme situation. I go back to the agency and hand in my resignation.

Bhagwan has announced that we no longer need to wear orange. How I've missed wearing blue jeans! I buy turquoise t-shirts in the thrift shops. A few days later he has said how sad he is that we were all relieved not to have to wear orange any more. I think he's lost the plot, but I daren't tell anyone.

Chapter 18

Cloud Hidden, Whereabouts Unknown

Bhagwan's secretary Sheila has become all-powerful at the ranch. They have bullied their way into the local town, Antelope, among other things. They want the vote so they can take over the local politics. The ranch has invited all the street people in the Midwest to come and live and work on the ranch. They are bussed in, in their droves. The experiment is extraordinary. American street life is the toughest existence in the world, and here they are, surrounded by loving, kind people, with clean clothes, food and fun work. They become transformed. Many of them are deeply healed. Sheila gets them to vote, to swing the local election so that she can have even more power but their votes are illegal as they aren't residents. They bus the street people away again, but there are many who stay on and become disciples. The power has brought corruption. It's all a microcosm of the world. It's become a hotbed of intrigue, and then, it all erupts. Sheila and her gang have taken all the funds and flown off to hide in Switzerland. Bhagwan's closest disciples, who take care of him, put him in one of their comfortable private jets and get him out of there. The rumours abound.

PANIC! STOP PRESS! Bhagwan has been arrested in Charlottesville, for, of all things, a trumped up charge of immigration fraud. He was fleeing in a Lear jet, when it landed to refuel. There are heartbreaking images of him in chains and handcuffs. Bhagwan! He is a religious leader! Why is he in chains? This is the peak of American paranoia. We can't get any news. There is a pop radio station which keeps us up-to-date with information. All other news of him is buried by the government. We are all very upset and disturbed, and I want to go to the ranch now, to be part of this happening.

Veems says he's not ready yet so I hitch a lift up the coast to Oregon. When I get to the registration they are officiously pissing me about with forms.

'Don't fart about!' I say. 'I'm here! Here's my money! I've come to support!' They give me an A-frame high up in a canyon, sharing with a German bloke. Well, I've finally done it, and Bhagwan's not here. I'm picked up by a school bus. The driver wears rabbit ears and is playing Wagner. I'm back in Bhagwan's world.

Bhagwan returns, he must go to court in Portland, so we are all on the runway, waving him goodbye. The sentence is deportation so they fly him to Cuba, where he can't stay because the US pressures the Cuban government. Marlon Brando offers him an island, a wealthy Greek lends him a Greek island, but the police hassle him off, and it seems there is nowhere on the planet that is safe anymore, for this man of truth. The highest mountains in the world will shield him, our Beloved Master goes to the Himalayas.

It's the coldest I've ever experienced on the ranch – 25 below. I'm grateful for my silk thermals and the down-filled coat and fur boots. Late at night, I'm standing outside my A-frame, looking out across the canyon in my nightie, shivering and smoking a beedie. I've got a wonderful job. I'm transcribing the interviews that Bhagwan has been giving to the world's press. It's inspiring and brilliant and sometimes very funny, but no wonder they were trying to get rid of him. Once again he'd been exposing the hypocrisy in politics and religion. I'm working with another woman up in the press office.

'It's too noisy in here,' I say, 'Let's find somewhere else to do it.' So we take ourselves off to a corner in the downtown bar, so we can watch what's happening. We are told by the main office that we should go to the lounge of the hotel and keep our ears open. We've become spies, because the CIA has infiltrated the ranch and are in disguise everywhere. The energy in the ranch is so high, I haven't eaten for ten days and I'm getting divinely thin. But today, I manage some sprouts in Magdalena, the main canteen, joined by Rashid and Veetasmi. The rumours are exploding by the second.

'What's happening? Is it all finished?' Rashid's going to follow Bhagwan to the Himalayas. Veetasmi is going to Australia. People are taking the school buses and filling them with equipment and supplies looted from the offices. There are rumours that the army is coming, to break it all up. But still, the Sannyasins are laughing and hugging and making music! I'm afraid of the army marching down the canyon – we are like sitting ducks. What am I going to do? Miraculously, there's Veems in his down coat and fur boots, looking anxiously for me. He's come to the rescue – good old Veems.

We jump in his VW and drive away through the snow, afraid of being stopped by the cops or shot at by the local redneck Christians.

When the dust settles I get Veems and me a lovely little studio in Fairfax, looking out over the rural hills, and I get a job at Smith & Hawken, a famously wonderful garden shop. They employ me because I am an English gardener, but I don't know any of the Latin names. I like working here, we are a friendly team, and gardeners all over the world are good people, in tune with the earth. The shop is run by two brilliant men who are into 'alternative business'. There is quite a lot of snobbery about English gardens, Vita Sackville West's garden, Sissinghurst, the white garden, becomes a pilgrimage for the wealthier clients.

Today I wake up for the first time, in years, and I'm not immediately reminded of the huge hole in my heart. It's 1986 and Veems has got another girlfriend, and so I'm going to leave him to it. Now that Bhagwan's back in India, there seems less point in being here in California, so I'm going to follow my heart and go back to Hornby.

My team at Smith & Hawken give me a farewell party. I say goodbye to my Sannyas mates and I pack my bags and my paints. Veems is sweetly helping me to pack my car. This is when he can be so loving and sweet – when I'm leaving. I set off along the coast up to Canada. I pass Mount Shasta over Grants Pass, driving nine hours a day, staying in motels, it's a scary adventure, all alone. I head up into Washington, cross the Olympic Mountains, catching the ferries to Vancouver and Horseshoe Bay. Back on the now familiar Vancouver Island highway, I arrive on Hornby Island after three days. Michael is delighted to see me. There have been many changes. Kirsten has left him for Dale, the children have grown, he has a new girlfriend, she has a hubby, life on Hornby continues. I stay with him at first, we work well together – drawing, architecting, a shared focus, supporting each other. But now I hear of a house to rent, up the road, and I want to live alone this winter, and really devote myself to my painting. I would really like to focus on it, to see where I can take it.

This house is upside-down. Its living room is at the top, a lovely kitchen with windows looking out across the lawns to the forest on the second floor, and the bedrooms are on the ground floor. I get to work. I'm very disciplined. Up early, meditating, painting till lunch, rest, walk, more work, another meditation, supper, a drop of Canadian TV (not very interesting, mostly ice hockey). I don't see anyone for weeks. The friends get fed up. There is a banging on the door.

'Anita!' It's Kirsten and her new man.

'Go away! I'm a hermit! I don't know how to talk to people anymore!'

'We've got a pizza and a bottle of champagne, so let us in!'

I have been reading therapeutic books about relationships, I'm always trying to get the root of my endless struggle to understand it all. Nowadays they are talking a lot about dysfunction, victims and boundaries. Lord, I think, these books are written about me! But how does one change the pattern? I see that I am attracted to the beautiful and brilliant, but their dark sides also appeal to me – the danger and unpredictability. Too bad Mr Normal doesn't do it for me.

After a few months, Veems comes for a visit. We have a lot of love for each other. The workshop in this house has a great table saw, so Veems is busy doing some work for Michael while I'm upstairs painting. I come down to bring him some tea. I'm feeling happy and content.

'You're dreaming of 'domestic bliss' again, Neets,' says Veems suspiciously, like they are the dirtiest words in his vocabulary.

We go over to Sudasi and Deva Raj's for supper and to try their sauna, which they have built into their house. We sleep up on a balcony under the eaves. They have built a wind organ against the window, which lulls us to sleep with heavenly notes. But one day the woodstove in the sauna spits out a log while they are out, and the whole house is burned to the ground. This is a regular occurrence on these islands. Their stack of *Rajneesh Times* become floating cinders which land on the flowerbeds of the garden, so tucked under the shrubs there are wonderful messages,

'Let go, celebrate everything … just an overnight stay'

Veems and I are admiring their total acceptance of this experience. They stay nearby and immediately set about building another beautiful home, but this time, in cement and plaster, Adobe style.

I call Yogi on his twenty-first birthday.
'I'm starting a painting, with love, for you.' Later, I ask him,
'Did Mickgough give you something nice? A party? A present?'
'Uh, no.'
'What?'
'Well, I asked him if I could have some driving lessons but Henrietta said "Too expensive. If you want to get a book or something, give me the receipt"' I am incensed with rage. All this stuff about Mickgough the generous Patriarch. What bullshit. He's in a play in New York so I write to him, care of the theatre. I tell him what I feel about him not honouring his son's twenty-first. The letter returns some months later, unopened, in Henrietta's hand, it says 'Return to Sender'.

I've been living very frugally on my savings, drinking a south American root tea and eating cucumbers. I'm much too thin but I love feeling so light. I reach amazing spaces in my meditations. This morning, I experienced myself when I was a fish.

I get a terrible bout of strep-throat. I've been in bed for a week and I'm not taking the pills because they are huge and I can't swallow them, so my temperature is roaring higher and higher. In my delirium I see myself walking up a long path towards a very bright light in the distance. There are tall beings on either side, all dressed in flowing white robes, and it seems as if they are beaming exquisite love into me, as I am drawn higher along the path. I'm floating now. There is someone very familiar in the distance, with their arms open to me, but I'm not sure who it is, just that I love them. I'm floating upward, dissolving into the light …

'Neets! Neets! Sit up and swallow this!' I wake up to Veems's anxious face and swallow the dratted pill and I feel utterly, utterly, bereft. That had been such a beautiful and love-filled experience, I felt I was going home, I don't want to be back here.

March 28th, 1987, and I'm having supper with Michael and friends when out of the blue, I tell them how I used to be in a programme on TV in the sixties, called *Doctor Who*. I tell them how wonderful Pat Troughton was. I rarely talk about my past. A few days later, an English friend calls.

'Do you know that Patrick Troughton died a few days ago?' He must have been waving me goodbye as he went. I wonder where Michael Craze is now, and what he's up to? I'm so far away from that world now, it's like it was another life that happened to another person. I'm thinking about dear Pat. How much I loved him, what fun we had on our lovely show. I chuckle to myself, as I remember Cybermen, Daleks and ridiculous giant crabs, and the laughs with Mike and Frazer, how we teased Pat and got drunk with him, the draughty locations that we found ourselves filming in. We were so lucky to have him take over from Bill Hartnell. The nation accepted him so easily. One of the finest actors of our generation is gone. I expect the programme is long since finished and forgotten.

Veems and I are driving over to see some friends near the ferry, when I see a 'for sale' sign.

'Let's go and have a look,' It's a boring box of a house but it's only $45,000. 'I think we should buy it.'

'You must be crazy,' says Veems.

'Yes, but I still think we should buy it.' Veems has saved enough over the years of work in Mill Valley to put down a deposit, and it means that the monthly payments wouldn't be more than I could earn on Hornby, and Veems could come and go. Michael and all our friends encourage us and we sign the papers and finally have a permanent home on Hornby. We have to rent it out at once, paying the deposit has stretched the finances so we must return to Mill Valley to make a stash, enough so that we can do the structural renovations.

This time in Mill Valley we share a house with an English woman who used to live on Ibiza, until she took Sannyas. Veems goes on with his building work and I become an assistant to a dynamic woman called Jean. She drives a BMW, has long glamourous nails and she is an energetic decorator. I'm making good money.

Jean gets me a job with an interior designer who only employs the best painters. We are doing a penthouse in downtown San Francisco. It's a beautiful apartment and weeks of professionally paid work. At the end of the job I've gone in to do the touch-ups, as the carpets and furniture are now in, the owner is there and he is placing an exquisite little oil painting of sailboats on his mantle shelf.

'That's lovely!'

'Yes, but my interior designer, won't allow me to put it up, because the colours are wrong,'

'It's your home!' I say, 'and you're only employing her!' He likes me. With horror, I notice little pale stains all over the ceiling in the master bedroom. I can't believe it. I'm going to have to repaint the ceiling and the bed and carpets are all in. Gloomily I go off to the paint cupboard to see if we still have the bedroom paint, when the owner says,

'Have you seen in the bedroom?' Oh, God. He's going to be mad.

'Yes, I know … but … um …' I begin to apologise.

'It's the night sky,' he says.

'It's what?'

'It's the sky, on the night I was born.' He closes the blinds and the ceiling is full of stars. Wow!

'Yeah, they charged me two thousand bucks – do you reckon that was a good deal?' Thank God I didn't paint it out!

We've all been reading *The Holy Blood and the Holy Grail*. It's riveting. This book turns so many old ideas upside down - there is so much intrigue and I feel quite shaken up by it. I think of Robin when I read how the Cathars were massacred on Friday the 13th. That was his birthday.

I get a postcard from the man I married.

'Thank you. Nicest marriage I ever had. The divorce has been paid for, love Anu.' Great, but now I want to live in Canada! I'll still be in the wrong country with the wrong bits of paper!

We've been very focused and worked for six months. Veems has bought a second-hand Airstream travel trailer. It's like a silver bullet with riveted aluminium walls and a futuristic fuselage body which we pull with his big Ford truck. I scrub the wood panels and leather seats and we fill it full of all the lamps, carpets and stuff for our new house, which I've been collecting from the thrift shops. A TV is stuffed into the toilet for when we cross the border. Veems is worried about being searched by the Canadian border patrols.

'I'll flash my painted nails and say "I never travel without my TV!"' We don't stop in trailer parks on the journey up, but in wild cougar country, where we cook our tofu and brown rice, and sleep safely in the Airstream. We both get six month visas.

The house is half way up the mountain so the driveway is very steep and the Airstream full of furniture struggles, but eventually we manage to park it in the garden, and we live in it while we work on the renovations. I paint the dated pine panelling; Veems makes a massive wraparound deck; the basement has a wood stove, workshop and washing machine, so upstairs is always warm. We make French doors in the living space and bedroom so we can walk straight out onto the deck. There is a forest behind us, some apple trees and a woodshed. Veems makes a lovely square table that fits the kitchen area exactly, and that's it, it's done – simple. It's great to have a home again but it's not like Church Farm House - that was my passion. But as we lean over the deck railing looking out across the Georgia Straits towards the snowy mountains of Vancouver Island, I feel ready to settle.

Our two neighbours are old disciples of Bhagwan. Will is a specialist in rolfing massage and Lyn has two young children. It was their house that Veems and I stayed in a few years ago. As soon as the renovations are complete, Veems is off back to California and I am left to get on with it. I have inherited a microwave, but I don't trust it. When it's on, I can feel the ends of my hair vibrating. The owner of the farm that David Cloud manages wants his large old farmhouse redecorating, so I ask Michael's friend Deb if she would like to help me. We become a team. A big new wave of 'Faux Finishing' has started in England. I learned the art of marbling and scumbling with Mary McCarthy. I'm ahead of my time here on Hornby – they haven't yet heard of Jocaste Innes – but it's coming. We jokily refer to our outfit as 'Faux to Go'. We are both very focussed. I stencil some tiles in the kitchen. We use lovely colours everywhere. We scrape and sand and repaint the exterior. It's weeks and weeks of wonderful work. We form a business – 'Debanita' – painting and decorating. I handle the business side. Me! Who could never do 'sums' at school. I work out percentages, the fees and all the bills. I feel quite empowered – I can do it! Over the years to come we will paint most of the houses on the island. We also become part of the Blue Sky design team, fine-finishing the handmade kitchens designed by John Grunewald, climbing scaffolds, painting atriums, hanging off roofs, painting soffits turquoise, and I stencil wherever I can.

I take my supper down to the beach below my home. Deb and her children have a barbecue, we swim. Life is good.

The island has an innovative recycling depot. It's years ahead of its time and environmentalists come from all over the world to study it. We all meet there on Sunday mornings. Everything is compartmentalised – everything is recycled - there is no rubbish collection on Hornby. The Blue Sky houses have recycling bins built in to the kitchens. There is a bottle pit where you can hurl your empties in with a roar. I furnish my house from the 'free shop' and I am delighted to find a pair of Calvin Klein jeans which fit me. The children's clothes go round and round.

We work with Dean on his old sailboat. We strip the mahogany down and oil the wooden decks. It's weeks of summer work, sanding and varnishing, and now at last, it's in the water and we sail it up north, to Desolation Sound. We pick oysters off the rocks and cook them there and then on a fire. We visit Michael's friend Hugh, who has a Blue Sky houseboat. It's wild country, no roads. He is smoking a lot of dope, playing fantastic music, fighting with his woman. He has a power-boat to go to the stores.

Rog has written to tell me that Tony Quayle has died of cancer. He was a man of such integrity and I loved him. When we finished working on the series *Strange Report* in 1968, he sailed his boat, the Jenny Rose, to Greece with his family. I always loved what he said about acting, that he wanted to be as transparent as possible, so that the workings of the heart could be seen and communicated. He was one of those very rare beings – a loyal man.

The excellent dentist who we call the Tooth Fairy, operates out of a converted school bus. Half the week he's on Hornby and half on Denman. It's very efficiently run.

Kirsten is now running the Co-op in a very large new building which has a café and a post office, and now there are unique shops around a green. In the summer, visitors arrive on the island from all over the world – the market place begins to look like 'Goa meets the West Coast'. When we go shopping, it can take up a lot of time

184

because you know everyone you meet. Kirsten and the Co-op team have hung Groucho Marx masks at the checkout, so if you are wearing one of these, it is a sign to your fellow shoppers that you wish to be left in peace.

I sleep out on the deck all summer long. Sleeping under the stars, waking up at dawn, the bats streaking home to their eves, a bath and a march up the mountain road, and out onto the cliffs. I can walk all along the edge till I'm looking down on the cove where the boats are moored. Then home, to load up my equipment and I meet Deb at the job by 9:00. At lunch-break, if it's fine, we have a swim and work on till she has to fetch Zeke, her son, from school.

We're working with the Blue Sky boys. During a tea-break they mention that it's whaling season.

'But how do you know when they are out there?'

'Because you hear the blowing, shushing sound.' I come back home and the doors and windows are open. I'm putting the supper on for Veems, when I hear it.

'Whales!' I shriek as I gallop down the steps. Veems is coming up the drive in his truck. 'Whales!' I cry as I tear down the road to the beach. And there they are, a big pod, moving down the strait. These majestic creatures. Veems joins me on the beach, we are jumping and shrieking. When there is a sighting like this the ferry switches off, so all the passengers can watch this pod of Orcas on their way south. You are not the same person after you've encountered a whale. That summer, there is a beach party on the flat sandstone beach, where the petroglyphs are on the north of the island. Some remarkable musicians are playing, a large crowd has gathered, wrapped in blankets as the sun sets and the stars come out, and then I see the Northern Lights for the first time. The skies are alive with a floating, undulating rainbow light-show, descending curtains of shimmering golds and greens, pulsating shots of red. Very powerful, and a bit spooky.

'You should display your paintings at the Hornby Fair,' says Michael. He is a great supporter of my work, which honours me, as there are some exceptional artists working on this island. The Hornby Fair is an annual event. It includes a fancy-dress parade –

everyone goes wild with their costumes, sitting on their cars and wagons as a colourful cavalcade of battered Volvos goes around the island. In the school field the tables are laid out and on a pretty cloth, I've got my watercolours, botanicals of irises and sweet-peas, which have been framed by an islander. They look lovely. There is music, dancing and feasting. I sell my Iris to Jim and Judy Saks – they are like the King and Queen of Hornby – so I am over the moon. At the end of the day I've sold out and that night in the hall, I'm dancing away with all the friends to the local rock band – 'The Noisy Neighbours'

'I'll have whatever she's on!' says one of the Denman lads.

Jim and Judy become very dear friends. They have homes in Cleveland and Florida but this is their favourite. It's up the road from us, an exquisite Blue Sky house. The Saks's play a supportive role in our community, and Judy gives splendid parties. She has a lovely light studio where she does her painting, and Jimmy has a garden where he grows his dahlias. Their house is filled with books and art and antiques, and up at the top is a little place to hide away and read. The living space is a large round room with windows over the wide deck – the views are stunning. A John Grunewald spiral staircase leads to the bedrooms where there is an outside hot tub. I grow to really love these two wonderful people.

I'm learning the art of Zen wood chopping. It's a meditation. When you are really centred the logs split open like apples but when you're not – then the axe wedges itself deep on the edge and it's a nightmare getting it out.

Chapter 19

Rashomon

'Would you like to direct a play for the Hornby Island Theatre Trust?' John Grunewald and his friends are passionately committed amateur theatre members. They love to tread the boards and usually they have a retired professional directing them, but this season he can't do it.

'But I've never directed before!' Then I'm reminded. *Whenever you say no, a door closes. Whenever you say yes, the doors open wide.* 'Yes! I will!' Holy shit. What have I let myself in for? I have the weekend to find a play from the library, meet the cast on Tuesday, hold auditions, and be ready to start rehearsing by Friday. Michael says that they mostly do old and tried favourites – drawing room comedies, Canadian style. I'm pouring through the plays. What shall I choose? I am struck by a Japanese tale – *Rashomon* – it's all about aspects of truth. I like it and I don't think the staging would be too demanding. Only four main characters so it shouldn't present too many problems ... little do I know!

I meet Richard and Serena. He's a Professor of Social Anthropology and she is a retired teacher and potter. They run the 'Pizza Galore' business in the Cardboard House Bakery, and they live in a house that Richard built himself in the woods. They are the heart and soul, along with John and his partner Bonita of this theatre group. I cast Richard as the wigmaker, John as the samurai, Bonita as the wife and Glen, who is a West Coast painter, as the husband. Dean's ex-wife will be the soothsayer, and Helen from the post office, the mother. We meet in each other's houses twice a week to rehearse. We have three months before the hall is booked. I love community theatre. It's like in the ashram. There is no commercial pressure, we are all here because we love it. John and Michael are working on the sets. They make a revolving platform.

Stevie, who is one of the island's most talented artists, is going to make the ninth century Japanese costumes, and Keith's wife will do the make up. We have inspiring meetings, researching Japanese paintings and costumes. The kung-fu teacher works with John and Glen and they choreograph a thrilling fight. One of the island's musicians composes and records the music and the thunderclaps. Dale does the lighting. Everyone puts in 100%. It's coming together amazingly, but Veems is back, and is concerned that I'm too involved with the play and not working as much as I should, so we are fighting, which I don't need.

Yogi and me on Mount Jeffrey

Our opening night draws near, and Yogi comes to visit. He flies in a little four-seater plane from Vancouver, he steps out, grinning - he loves a good adventure. He is working now as a photographer for the London auction house, Sothebys. He is looking wonderful and I'm a happy mummy. We have a special 'Welcome Yogi' dinner at Michaels. Dean's bought a salmon, we have lit the fire-pit and are having deep discussions. Everybody on the island is into computers, which is very boring for me because all they talk about is floppy disks, but Yogi is very up with this new technology. After dinner, Michael turns to me.

'Look what happens to an intelligence, if you don't constrict it.' He means my Darling Son. He is brilliant and beautiful. He loves

188

the house, thinks Hornby is 'far out', and naturally fits in. he films the *Rashomon* rehearsals for me because I want the actors to watch themselves. I'm very choked up when he leaves – I hate saying goodbye. I sob like a baby on the ferries back to the island, but the show must go on.

The actors find watching themselves very useful – like rushes – you can iron out the little habits and mannerisms that as actors we can adopt. We are rehearsing in costume, to get the movements right. Our opening night is imminent. And yet, and yet, it's not there, and I don't know what else I can do. There's just some kind of holding back. My heart sinks when I see the banner across the road. 'Hornby Island Theatre Presents – *Rashomon* – Next week – 7:30.' Next week?! Oh God! I hold an emergency meeting with the actors, I'm going to wake them up. I'm taking a risk because they might exit stage right.

'Well, I don't know if we've got a play.'

'What?!' There are indignant cries.

'Only Diane is really good. All the rest of you, are 'acting'. Richard is too New York Jewish, Bonita – a ninth century Japanese woman doesn't stride about like *Annie get Your Gun*, and Glen and John, it's not a dance! We want to see you kill each other! So, shall we get to work?' This trick works wonders. I learned it from a director I worked with in the sixties. On the day of the recording he told me how rotten I was, and it made me drop my 'niceness' and be the bitch he wanted, but he took a big risk and so have I, but my friends pick up the gauntlet and we get down to work. Michael and Dean have brought in half the Hornby Forest. Stevie has painted a bamboo backdrop. The make-up lady has glued Velcro behind the actors' temples, and attached elastic around the back of their heads, so they all have great slanted eyes – and on the night, nobody recognises them! The costumes are superb. We do the make-up in the round bar. I love painting Richard's wonderful face as the wigmaker but I have to tell him to keep still because he talks so much. On the first night the hall is packed, the word has gone around that this may be something different. The play begins, it's magic. It all works – the revolve, the lighting. Kirsten is cueing the sound box, the actors have all become alive and I'm thrilled with their performances. In one memorable scene, the Mad Medium

Soothsayer is dancing wildly in the forest, the drumming comes to a crescendo, there is a deafening thunderclap and she screams and falls prostrate on the ground. Blackout. A terrible moaning sound as she raises her white, mask-like face into the spotlight, and out of the blood-red gaping mouth echoes the voice of the dead samurai,

'I'm in the dark, now.' It's a dramatic spell-binding moment. Glen and John leap off the stage and their fight explodes into the hall, and is terrifying. We have a standing, roaring, stamping ovation. Next day, I call them all in to give notes. We have five more days and should go on improving all the time. This is the art of theatre and we all love it. We do voice warm-ups before make-up each evening. But one night, many of the cast are off, someone's cabin has burned and they are the fire-fighters. We will have an extra night - a benefit performance, to fund the building of their new home, with help from volunteer neighbours. This is a supportive community. John says,

'The community wants to know who this Anita woman is, who has directed this play. So I'm going to call you up on the stage on the last night.' I'm terrified of this. I'm in fear all through the performance. I'm glad I borrowed this lovely kimono. When the moment comes I walk through the standing, clapping, cheering audience, and climb on to the stage and take a bow – it's my moment and I love it. When it's all over they have a tradition of taking down the set before the party, so we all muck in, hauling fir branches out of the side doors, packing costumes and props, the tables are spread with the food that Shirley has prepared for us, and we are dancing and celebrating our success. But. Oh spite. Oh hell. Veems is dancing and flirting with a local woman. I pretend to ignore it. They continue and are getting more into it. Now my night is ruined. I can't bear to watch them.

'I want to go home now, I'm tired,' I say to him.

'Go on then. See you later.' She flashes me a knowing smile and they go on dancing, so angrily I drive home alone, cursing and trashing him. When I wake up it's 2:30 and he's not back. How could he do this to me, on this of all nights? Once again I'm in the madness of jealousy. I get in my car, drive to the entrance of her driveway, and sure enough, there is his truck. I want to trash it, and him. Sobbing and growling I try to let the air out of the tyres but I can't do it. Finally, in desperation, I chuck mud all over the

windscreen. I drive home, I won't be here when he gets back. I turn off the heat and open all the windows to let the cold night in.

'It won't be cosy for you. I deny you that!' I pack a bag and go to Deb's. She finds me in the morning curled up on her couch, under a fur rug. She knows how I feel.

'He's jealous of your success! What a shit! What are you going to do?'

'I want him to suffer!' My mind is going nuts, with rage-full thoughts, which turn later to pain and tears. I put on boots and a coat, and walk down the path to the beach, to a magic place at the end of a long spit. I wedge myself into the white bleached logs and watch the sun set behind Vancouver Island. I see the columns of smoke, emerging from the pine woods on Denman – the islanders' stoves are lit. I cry my heart out until at last I feel empty. And in these quiet moments I hear the voices of ancient beings, healing me. I feel like I'm in the presence of... grandfathers.

'Thank you, thank you! But I'm not of your tribe – I'm English!' They are laughing and loving me. When I get back to Deb's, she and her man, Russell, are making supper. I tell them of feeling healed down on the spit.

'Didn't you know the spit is an ancient Indian Healing Place? Where the elders – the grandfathers – could be consulted?'

Russ hands me a small, crumpled note.

'Veems came, and left you this.'

'I've got work, back in Mill Valley. I'll catch the next ferry. I'm sorry you're reacting. There is only love, Veems.'

Russ opens the first of many bottles.

Chapter 20

Rappi

The play receives huge accolades. One American visitor says she's never seen anything better on the New York stage. They want us to perform it again in the summer festival. We hear of a few American directors who would like to come and work with this community theatre. Things are taking off, it's great. Meanwhile Debs and I get back to work. We are doing a makeover on a large B&B on the north shore. After the months of involvement with the theatre group, life begins to settle down again.

How quickly the summer passes. We fish for salmon, putting them in our freezers for the lean times in the winter. The island is worryingly expanding and there are many more summer visitors. Some of them are freaked out kids from the streets of Toronto. The islanders try to help them integrate, giving them food and work.

Now it's autumn, and I need a load of winter wood. My usual woodman, from Denman, has gone off to do a sweat lodge meditation, so someone called Rappi, who is a friend of Michael's, is going to deliver some later today. I hear a truck's wheels skidding as it mounts the steep drive. It's a veteran Chevy, faded red and chrome, piled high with wood. I've come out in my jammies to greet the woodman. The door swings open and this smallish blond-haired man, with soft green eyes steps out. Our eyes lock. We are embarrassed because we have really met, in this moment.

'You'd better come up,' I say. 'Some tea?' We sit opposite each other at the kitchen table, we talk of life and death and pain and the music of Tom Waits. The light has faded and it's beginning to snow. Together, we stack the winter wood. He's got to catch the ferry back to Denman. I'm shivering as I go back into the house, but not from the cold, but because I know, with a mixture of excitement and dread, that I have met the next man in my life. Later that night he phones.

'Are you single?' He says he's a musician and a deep-sea diver, a marine biologist and a passionate birder. He's thirteen years younger than me. He smokes roll-ups, drinks like anything, lives in a cabin on the beach on Denman Island, which is filled with diving gear and bird books.

On one of our first dates, I watch while the flames consume this old fishing boat that he used to live on, hauled up on the beach. He's having a ritual burning, moving on from his painful past. He gives me two baby ducks. We listen to Roy Orbison. He plays the mandolin. All the friends are fed up with us because we spend our time in bed for weeks. We can't get enough of this yummy mating!!! He's got some very good friends on Denman. They are musicians, singers and songwriters and they have a band. I go to the Denman Hall to hear him play. It's different from Hornby. This is a bigger island and there is a darker element to it. It's a huge crowd of strangers and they are drinking, so it feels rather dangerous. Rappi is a star, and he's very popular, and everyone wants to know who this older woman is that he's now seeing. My ego likes that he's being chased, unsuccessfully, by lots of local women. But do they know his vulnerability? His pain? We were both abused as children, so we share that place. He really loves me, so we are healing each other. How happy I am to see him appear at the top of the outside steps carrying a chicken and a bottle of wine. Often, he has no money and I've begun to write cheques, down at the pub, for beers and smokes, supplying him with ferry tickets. Well, we all have to help each other.

Veems rings from California to say that he's off to spend some time in Poona. Bhagwan is back there now and has changed his name to Osho. I don't tell him about Rappi, not yet.

In the spring the waters around the island are full of sea-lions. Rap takes me out in a small dinghy with an outboard. He and his friend have a six-pack. We motor out to where the action is. These massive creatures, bigger than our boat, are splashing and honking.

'Could they tip us over?'

'Yeah, if they decide to be playful.' Rap sees my fear. 'Would you feel safer if we tied up to the buoy?' But the outboard motor has died, the fellas are tucking into beers and enjoying themselves, and we are floating amongst them. One huge sea-lion emerges from the water, a face full of whiskers and stinking fish breath, but she looks me in the eye and we make contact. Now she slips back into the water, under the boat, and I am not afraid any more. We are all God's creatures.

I'm going to get some eggs from a powerful black woman who lives in a half-finished house off the main road. By her back door, next to the logs is a large fridge with a message written boldly across it. *Keep the faith baby!*

At the end of the summer when the last ferry load of visitors leave, the ferry goes round in a circle, hooting its horn. There are great cheers from the islanders, who are gathered at the pub for a celebration. Now, the island is ours once more!

Rappi introduces me to *Star Trek: The Next Generation*. I am immediately hooked. Nothing gets in the way of our weekly fix. I hadn't bothered with the original series, but now, the focus appeared to have moved from the science, to the characters and the relationships, which make it so captivating. I tell him about my own adventures in space and time, as he had never seen *Doctor Who*. Someone has lent us the most wonderful video – they think we will like it because it's English. We sit down, and are blown away by this story of two actors, struggling at the end of the sixties. From now on, Rappi and I will quote from it regularly. Richard E Grant is wonderful as Withnail, but I am particularly struck by the young actor who plays 'I'. His name is Paul McGann.

The Halloween Dance at the hall is one of the highlights of the year. Everyone goes to extraordinary lengths to make unique costumes. The hall is decorated from floor to ceiling, in branches from the woods, and there are lights and spiders' webs. The band members are in costume. I've dressed as a New Age Witch in a silver-blue wig, with blackened teeth. I'm unrecognisable, which gives me great freedom to cackle at one and all. I love the islander who has come as an outhouse, so he's sitting on the loo. Kirsten is marvellous as a lecherous bloke with a moustache, and the inside of her jacket is hung with watches. There is a group of real witches on the island, so they don't have to dress up much! I really love this community!

Rappi wants to check out our star-signs.
'Never mind if we're soul-mates, just buy your own ferry tickets!'

Veetasmi calls me from Australia in the middle of Friday night.
'Osho has left his body.' The telephone lines across the world are buzzing. The news reverberates around the planet. Thousands of Sannyasins are connected in these moments, to his spirit, dancing amongst us all. What happened? He had become paralysed down one side of his body, the side on which he always slept. He had been saying that the Americans poisoned the mattress in that Charlottesville jail with lithium, so slowly, slowly, our beloved Master had been disintegrating. I close the curtains, unplug the phone, light the candles, put up all the photos of Bhagwan and my friends. I play the music of Chaitanya and Anubhava. I dance and cry and shout and celebrate as he showed us how. *Celebrate Everything.* I talk to you, beloved Bhagwan. I don't know what went on at the end of the ranch. There had been so many rumours and so much speculation. I had stayed clear of it all, just stayed simple, with my connection to you. I'm in deep gratitude and feel so blessed to love you. You are in my heart forever.

On Monday morning, I blow out the candles, put away the photos, and set off for my work. Here, now.

'Once you've got the message, hang up the phone.' – Alan Watts

Now Veems is coming to Hornby on his way back from Poona. He is coming to tell me how it was when Bhagwan left his body, about the shock, and celebrations, how his lawyers are now busy trying to prove how he died. It's what we do with men of truth. We crucify them or poison them. This is how Bhagwan went. But his vibration goes on in us, like seeds, scattered around the planet; stardust; pockets of laughing, dancing, hugging Sannyasins, waking up.

I tell Veems about Rappi. He looks hurt and surprised, but he has to accept it, because he's got girls in every port. He goes back to Mill Valley, and I am torn because I love them both.

My visa is nearly up. We go down to the immigration office in Nanaimo. It's always nerve-wracking; these people are very good at interrogation. I'm nervous, even though I've worked hard on my story. We are waiting to be called up. One officer looks like a Nazi from hell. Oh dear God, please don't let me get him. No, I'm beckoned to another. What will he give me? Six weeks? Three months? Rappi notices that the officer is wearing a *Star Trek* badge.

'Ah! Best thing on TV!' says Rappi. The officer gives me a warm smile,

'And Patrick Stewart comes from your country!' I get a six month red stamp. Once again, science-fiction comes to my rescue!

I rent the house out for the summer to fund a trip to Poona. Bhagwan's birthday celebrations will be a massive gathering this year. Rappi is scrabbling around to get the dollars together as he wants to join me. On the way, I will stop off in England to see Yogi, and Rappi wants to see Norfolk, as I'm always going on about it. When we arrive, Geeta doesn't like him, but Jehane does. She, Rap and I go to see an astounding Monet exhibition before we go to the airport.

When we join the long queues of chattering Indians at Heathrow, my body says,

'No, no, not this again … I won't be responsible!' I don't listen.

Arriving in Bombay, Rap is devastated by the beggars who crawl up the sides of the bus, which is transferring us to the local airport. It's his first time out of Canada, so it's a big shock. He's also nervous of the Indian airline that takes us to Poona, as the cabin fills with thick, white vapour. On the outskirts of Poona, it's more like a Rabelaisian nightmare than the lush, tropical paradise he's been expecting. Everything is covered in monsoon mud. It's squalid and Biblical once again. But when we walk outside our hotel, that first morning, he is down on his knees with delight, absorbed by a skink (a wormy thing in the dust!).

Passing the German bakery, it's all very familiar. I haven't been here for eleven years, and it's much busier. The road to the ashram is literally a flea market, with stalls and vendors, beggars and hundreds of disciples, dressed in maroon. We have to sign in and have Aids tests, photos, security checks and much more. There is a day or two of official business before we are allowed to enter. Rappi is mesmerised by the whole scene, the parrots flying everywhere, the size of the fruit-bats in the trees. We have to buy robes, as Western clothes are no longer allowed. There are now lots of Germans in charge. We wander down the road looking at the stalls full of robes. Rappi doesn't think that the maroon colour suits him so he chooses one in black, with a white belt. He's fascinated by the beautiful women hugging and dancing.

On the third day we are allowed in, so we go to Buddha Hall to hear a lecture, but are looked at most suspiciously. A Swami accosts Rappi with questions about his black robe. We didn't know that only Commune Therapists are allowed to wear these. Rappi is fed up and thinks it's all a silly trip, but we find him some plum-coloured trousers and matching shirt, and once again we are allowed in.

We have rented a room in the back of the ashram, in the workers' quarters of a large Indian mansion. We go to the early morning meditation in Chuang Tzu. As soon as we walk through the gates of his home, his presence is with me. The garden is more deeply lush than ever. It's as though the plants are radiating the love. We are all wearing clean, white socks on our feet. In silence we pass by his immense library and into the hall, now enclosed by vast windows, with the beautiful garden all around. We file past his white marble memorial stone and I read,

'Osho. Never Born. Never Died. Just visited this planet. 1931-90'

High up in the ceiling of this astounding space is a huge chandelier which dims as we sit cross-legged on the marble floor. The musicians play their sitars and flutes, and we close our eyes.

♫ *Disappear into the Blessed One...* ♫

When we open our eyes again, the garden is bathed in sunlight. The birds of paradise are calling to each other. The bamboos are dancing in the breeze. We walk very slowly past his pond, which is filled with carp, and back out into the hustle and bustle of the ashram morning. Veems is here with his new girlfriend. I'm still disturbed by him. We sign up for 'The Mystic Rose'.

It is Osho's last gift to us all. It's described as a corkscrew into one's innermost being. A three-week long process. The first week we will laugh for four hours every day, the second week we cry, and the last week we are in silence. The large room can hold 60 people. There are 60 cotton-covered foamies with pillows, blankets and tissues for each participant. The lights dim, we are all on our beds, there is loud music and drumming. We are blindfold, and we start to laugh. At first it's forced. Ha, Ha. Ha. But after a while I'm totally into it, rolling around on my back, holding my knees, giggling and gurgling like a child. When we come back out into the world of the ashram, we must stay inside ourselves. No talking. So although we can listen to the lectures, dance and eat, we stay in silence. We wear badges – 'Mystic Rose' – so we are left alone, but we don't feel isolated.

It's tricky being in our room without speaking. I'm miming a lot but it's also good, because there are things emerging within myself, which I can connect with better when I'm quiet. By the end of that first week, I am ready to howl. We all explode into the crying. The whole room is filled with sounds of sobbing and howling. The man next to me is roaring in Spanish and beating his mattress. I wait to see what wants to happen in me. I find myself taking my pillow and I'm cradling it in my arms. It's you, my unknown Beloved. I'm rocking back and forth and moaning. My heart is broken. It feels like the aftermath of war, all the beauty we had created has been destroyed, and here you are, lifeless in my arms. Every day I wait to see what wants to happen, everyday it's the same.

It's the last week and we will sit in the glass walkway that was specially built for Bhagwan. It allowed him to wander through his garden without being affected by his allergies. It's all quite Zen-like. The white marble, the black meditation cushions, the bell sounds, we close our eyes. I am disturbed by a whooshing sound outside. A German Sannyasin is busy power-washing the windows. I've lost it and I want to kill him! My mind is off on a tirade. Why now?! Couldn't he wait? Once again, the duality.

The unendurable is the beginning of the curve to joy.

Rappi is at the other end and has his first taste of… he's tapping his watch…

'What happened to the time?' We are both in an amazing space when it's over. Rappi's dropped years of pain and rage. He wants to explore further, so he signs up for a group called 'Cutting the Roots of Fear', and I get Dengue Fever. For a week, I am delirious and in acute pain. Rappi is very worried that I'm dying.

When I recover, we head off to spend our last ten days relaxing in Goa. The ashram has changed. It's hard to let go of the memories of that magic time in the seventies. I think they're turning it into a religion. Isn't that exactly what Bhagwan said he didn't want?

We take pillows and valium on the night bus from Poona. In the heat of the Indian night we are woken by bumping and rattling, to see our driver is busy racing another bus around a totally blind corner. We take more valium, and pray.

At first light, we all pile off the bus.

'Panjim! Panjim!' We are stiff, and tired and angry. This isn't Panjim! We are in the fields, under some coconut palms.

'Yes Baba, here you take taxi!' It's a set up. The bus rattles away and the taxi driver now demands far too many rupees, to take us to the town. How Goa has changed over the years. Large signs at the beach proclaim, 'No Drugs' and 'Police Patrol'. We find a room behind a huge sand dune and spend our days roasting on the beach. Rappi finds a dead sea snake. He says it's the most deadly, so I'm rather put off swimming. We have found our own shack café, run by an enterprising boy who we love.

'Come Baba, I make you crab salad!'

'No, no, we don't have many rupees, just rice will do.'

'But Baba, next year you coming?'

'Well maybe…'

'Then next year, you paying.' His trust humbles us. As do the saffron sellers. They walk along the white hot beach in their black cotton suits and attaché cases.

'This is saffron, Baba,' Each strand of the crocus stamen is carefully harvested in the hills of Kashmir. They sit down to bargain. There are piles of it, and they have scales.

'How much?' Now I know how much saffron costs in the west, and this is astoundingly cheap. But Rap is doing his bargaining spiel.

'No, no, it's too much,' and he offers less than half. With a shrug and a sigh they close their case and trudge off up the beach. We are left feeling our ugly, greedy, western-ness.

I am still in love with Veems and I found it very disturbing to keep bumping into him and his girlfriend around the ashram, so it's a relief to be away from all that. Just here, with Rappi, for the last few days before we return to London. As we shelter in the shade of a fishing boat, all the beach wallahs come by. The boys with chopped pineapple on ice, in tin boxes on their heads.

'Hello, froot!'

One woman, we call Hats. Rappi buys one of her embroidered Tibetan hats and now she won't leave us alone.

I'm resting in our room with the fan on when looking out of the window, across the sandy path, I see a block of apartments and on one of the balconies is Veems and his girlfriend. Oh horrors. Do I have to endure more jealousy and pain? Gods, can't you give me a break? Veems is quite wealthy now, so they have rented a motorbike and they roar past us on their way to Anjuna market, while Rappi and I wait for a bus.

What comfort, to sink into our seats on the flight home, with a large glass of decent wine. I decide to let go of my Sannyas name. Rappi says 'Neets' sounds like a depilatory, so I've gone back to being Anneke, and it feels right.

Chapter 21

Third Marriage, On the Rocks

We spend Christmas in Norfolk. Rappi busks outside Larners. He looks so adorable in his Tibetan hat, his green eyes sparkling with humour in his tanned face. He plays rock tunes on his mandolin, the stuffy old town folk look away, embarrassed. After a whole day in the cold, with his fingers freezing up, he has managed to make fifteen pounds, which he spends on a Christmas Hamper for us.

Britain is now at war in the Gulf. The jet bombers are based nearby, they fly overhead in the morning, cause major havoc and devastation, and are home again by teatime. We need to get back to Canada, in case the airports are closed, but we only have enough money to fly to Toronto. My heart is heavy as I hug Yogi goodbye, in Roger and Jehane's living room in London. He says to Rappi,

'Take care of her,'

'I will.' He promises. Promises, promises.

We stay with one of Rappi's sisters outside Toronto. She lives in an original 18th century log home in the deep snow. We go ice-fishing on the nearby lake and Rappi skates about like a bird. We redecorate her home for her, drink all her homemade wine, and make enough money to fly back to Hornby.

It's heavenly to be back in my lovely, light, clean, simple home. The French windows in my bedroom look out into the woods and it's always warm and cosy. I pick up the threads of work again. Kirsten wants me to transform the co-op and I'm designing stencilled panels to go over the fruit and veg displays.

I get a letter from Veems.

'Neets, I'm coming to my house next month, so I'd be grateful if you would now move out. I'll pay for a month's rent for you somewhere else, while you make other arrangements. Love, Veems'

'What?!!!!' I have emergency meetings with the friends. He wants to kick me out.

'What do you want to do?'

'Live in my little home! I've made it so beautiful.'

I go to see Jim and Judy Saks. They help me with sound advice.

'You've made the payments for four years – that's $12,000. You could take over his share and buy him out.' So I let Veems know that I would like to take over the mortgage, giving him double his original deposit. As Jimmy says, to double your investment in four years is sound business. But Veems is furious. He thought he could just get rid of me, so he's objecting and forcing the price even higher. This, from the man who was always talking about being 'more loving'. Ha! Judy is painting a portrait of me. I sit in her studio looking north across the islands, worrying about the finances, feeling totally insecure. Neither of us like the painting when it's finished. The anxiety is written all over my face.

After what an eternity of agonising back and forth, until I'm quite at the end of my tether, the nightmare is finally over, we've settled, but the price is very high, and he knows that this is going to be really hard on me, trying to earn this much money. Work on Hornby is naturally limited. He buys a house on Denman Island and returns to California in his Toyota Landcruiser with his girlfriend.

Rappi suggests that he moves in with me, to help with the rent and bills. I'm not sure this is a good idea as he is an enormous liability – his work is erratic to say the least. More often than not, I'm supporting him. But he moves in anyway and I immediately feel the little house isn't large enough for the two of us, so we design a studio for me above the garage. I have found a wonderful twelve by nine foot window at the recycling depot. Together we plaster the walls and I do a terracotta finish, which becomes my trademark. And another dream is fulfilled – I always wanted a studio.

Studio Hornby '92

The next thing is that I have to become legal, so Rap and I must get married. Once again, I feel reluctant to move our friendship in this direction, but hey, it's only really a piece of paper. Or is it? Anyway, we do it totally. Helen, who runs the post office, is a minister, so we choose some wonderful sayings from *The Prophet* by Kahlil Gibran, and Sitting Bull. Deb lends me an Afghan wedding dress and Rappi borrows Will's jacket which is too big for him. We have the ceremony down on the flat, sandstone rocks in the sunset. As the tide comes in, we are drinking Greek wine with our friends. Next day, hungover, we swim and relax before going back to work.

Rappi is now part of the building team, creating amazing fireplaces. Now that I have my studio I can have quite a few projects on the go. On my table I work on botanicals, and I design some closet doors for Richard and Serena. I paint them to look like stone-mullioned windows, looking out onto a mountainous landscape.

I find an old iron bath tub. I re-enamel it and paint the outside like marble and the feet gold. Out on the deck I have heavenly baths watching the deer grazing through my garden and the eagles high in the sky.

John Grunewald is directing a play and would like me to co-direct. It's a very well-written piece about sex and religion in the Blue Mountains in the 1930s. On the night of the auditions in the hall, Rappi is picking up a script and announcing,

'I'll read this!' When he has finished we are all silent. He has moved us all so much. John gives him the part and we start rehearsing three times a week after work. Quite often I just feel exhausted after a long day of hanging off scaffolding and climbing ladders, but once we start rehearsing I am totally energised.

I see Sarah Miles on the telly. She is lounging on the lawns of her mill-house wearing Edwardian lace and a huge, expensive straw hat, playing croquet with her Labradors at her side. I don't sleep that night – seeing my old school friend is very disturbing. We had been such buddies at the Arts, but later she became very ambitious and cruelly cut me out of her life.

It's my 50th birthday! Fifty?! How can that have happened? I still haven't decided what I want to do when I grow up! I growl and snarl.

'No party. Leave me alone!' I want to hide in a bush. I walk up the mountain and sit in Jim and Judy's lovely garden, surrounded by dahlias. They are back in Cleveland so I'm alone. When I get back to the little house there is a bottle of champagne, some sugared almonds and a card from the friends, saying '50? Holy Shit!'

The play opens and once again we have a standing ovation and Rappi particularly receives a lot of praise for his deeply moving portrayal of an abused Hillbilly. He's been bitten by the bug. He wants to be an actor.

I'm suffering with terrible sweating, mainly at night, and emotionally, I'm all over the place. Serena suggests it might be the menopause, but I was told by Dame Josephine Barnes that I wouldn't go through any symptoms because of my hysterectomy, but it seems she was wrong. I get the book *The Change*, by Germaine Greer. What gifts she has given to us women. First, *The Female Eunuch*, and now this, all the information and insights, massively researched. We start a menopause support group, I go to a few meetings. I feel so much better about myself, these other women are really suffering the extremes of changing hormones, the drenched beds and murderous rages, the depression, exhaustion and pain.

It's all too easy to work, work, work, and to never have a day off. So today, I'll just get the lawn mowed and then I'm going to take it easy. Funny how all my men seem to have an aversion to cutting grass! I'm chilling out, feet up, exhausted. The phone goes.

'This is Steve Walker. We *Doctor Who* fans have been trying to track you down for years! You're very elusive! Would you be willing to give us an interview?'

'You're kidding me! People are still interested in *Doctor Who*? I can't remember. Remind me.' We have a long chat, which transforms itself into an article in a magazine called 'The Frame'. I'm blown away. I tell all the friends. 'Do you remember me telling you about *Doctor Who*? Well, they have invited me back to the UK, to go a convention.' Wonders never cease.

Rappi is going to do an audition for a drama school in Vancouver, and I am flying back to England.

Chapter 22

This Too Shall Pass

I meet Gary Russell, the editor of *Doctor Who Magazine*, at my friend Devesh's flat in Chelsea. Devesh lets on that he had himself played The Doctor. I had never known that he had doubled for Jon Pertwee, and flown his own Microlight in an early seventies story.

I have to take the train to Manchester and I meet Mike Craze, at Liverpool Street Station.

''Allo Duchess! 'Ow ya doin'?' We pick up as though it were only yesterday. I'm feeling pretty nervous, not knowing what to expect.

'You'll be alright, they will be thrilled to see you.'

'But what do we have to do Mike?'

'Just be yourself Duchess.'

'Well who else could I be?' Mike tells me how Pat Troughton grew to love doing conventions.

'In fact,' says Mike, 'He was at one when he had his heart attack. The day before, he was on stage and he talked about us.'

At the Piccadilly Hotel there is a large crowd of people, and a real buzz about the place. The guest list includes Jon Pertwee, Sophie Aldred, Deborah Watling, Sylvester McCoy and others. When it's my turn to be interviewed on stage, I am waiting at the back of the room. 500 people are seated expectantly. Gary gives me a glowing introduction.

'As you all know, we have searched the world over to find her, and at last here she is, loved, as the first sexy *Doctor Who* girl Polly, it's... Anneke Wills!' The audience is on its feet, roaring approval, as I walk down the centre aisle. I'm blinded by flashbulbs. It's an amazing moment and I am quite overwhelmed. I stand on the stage, bowing and waving as the accolade continues. I feel like a star. I kick off my shoes, curl up on the sofa, and start answering the questions. They know all about my time in the show and I manage to make them laugh. Afterwards I sit at a table, signing autographs. I meet all these lovely people, who show me pictures in books of me and Mike in the stories. I'm holding the queue up because I'm so fascinated with it all. They know so much about the show. Everyone wants to have a photo taken with me. I'm so blinded by the flashbulbs that I can't see to sign my name. Later, I listen to other actors' interviews with great interest. In the evening, at the dinner, I talk with Sylvester McCoy, who makes me laugh, and I meet Debbie Watling who I remember from my early acting days. She was my replacement on *Doctor Who*. We talk about Frazer Hines, our old mate. He's just written a book and Mike's going to give me a copy. This is all so incredible for me, after all these years. I had no idea *Doctor Who* was such a phenomenon. I meet the latest in a long line of *Doctor Who* girls – Sophie Aldred – who is 'real' – I love her at once. The dinner table is long and hilarious. Sylvester McCoy is such a character, and Jon Pertwee is presiding. My first *Doctor Who* convention is over and I've had the most wonderfully rewarding time, and they've booked me for another, in Hammersmith, in a few weeks.

I go to Norfolk and stay with Mary McCarthy and her family, now living in a gorgeous farmhouse, where Keith Barnfather makes a video about me for his *MythMakers* series. I'm number 26! Mark Ayres, who has provided music for *Doctor Who*, does the sound, and Nick Briggs does the interview. He is an aspiring actor, and he is careful to make sure that every detail looks right – his jacket, his nose, his entrance! It pays off, because he will go on to be involved in many *Doctor Who* productions. We film on the beach at Holkham as the tide comes in, and as an additional location, they suggest my old home, Church Farm. This fills me with dread. It is fourteen years since I last saw it. Nick and Keith are very persuasive and supportive, and they literally hold my hand and wipe away my tears as I confront the past, at this home that I had loved so dearly. I sit on the bench in the yard, as with joy and sadness, memories of family life with Mickgough, Jasper and Polly come flooding back. The video becomes one of the most popular in the series.

Geeta and Roddy were having a drink in the Jolly Farmer before it closed and got talking to the owners of our old home. Roddy told them how I always said I haunted it.

'She does!' they said. 'When we were hanging our chandelier in the kitchen, we felt it!' - no wonder – 'And someone opens the attic door,' – Polly's room. I find this an interesting phenomena – you can haunt somewhere while you're still in your body!

There is nowhere in the world as beautiful as north Norfolk in the summer. The fields pale gold with wheat, the hedgerows ebullient with wild flowers and butterflies. I missed this landscape so much while I was away. The old friends are trying to persuade me to stay.

'Come home, we miss you! Find a little cottage!' They've given me a nickname – 'Anneke the Brave'. We get some prospectuses from the estate agents. Geeta and I like the look of a cottage near Brancaster. It's opposite a church, with a small garden in front. Oh God, the state I get into when I'm thinking of buying a property. If I put the Hornby house on the market I could put a deposit on this cottage. I don't think Rappi would transplant very well. Maybe I would like to live on my own.

We go to see an exhibition of paintings on our way back, and extraordinarily, bump into my old friend Douglas Gray, of The Alberts. Still wearing a kilt and smoking jacket, but now with glazed eyes and reeking of booze. Back at Geeta's, we talk. I'll have to move quickly. The cottage won't be on the market long at that price. I feel rushed and pressured and I can't hear my inner voice, so I drive to the cottage on my own. There is no doubt about it, it's a darling little house. I can see myself being here, but what work could I do? I'd have to start all over again. All this moving around plays havoc with gaining a reputation, and actually, I do miss Rappi – his laughter, his spirit and his music. I think of coming home to this cottage on my own, after a Who convention, and there would be no-one to share it with, except Douglas Gray, who would become a nuisance, and I would be a sitting duck, for all the old bores of the county to prey on. I'm not ready for this move. Not yet.

I'm looking forward to attending the big *Doctor Who* convention in Hammersmith but I feel pressure to look my best. On Hornby, I enjoyed the freedom of sitting in my painter's clothes and welly boots in the pub. No make-up, hair scraped into a ponytail. Now, I'm making a big effort – I've got a reputation to uphold, and I want everyone to love me. I go to the hairdresser and tell her to start cutting. She does, until it is really short. That's good – I look younger, and Rappi will like that!

There are lots of guests who I am looking forward to meeting. The wild and wonderful Katy Manning, who is so unbelievably feminine that she is irresistible to one and all, and makes me feel like a chap! Andrew Beech, the organiser, is flying around like a whirlwind. By now, I've got a rough idea of the history of *Doctor Who* since I left in 1966 so I'm looking forward to meeting Tom Baker – he's an eccentric and an original – right up my street. I have heard that while he was playing The Doctor, he lived under the arches with tramps, and turned up to rehearsals with his toothbrush in his pocket. I have to ask him about this, and there is an urgency because later I will be on the flight back to Vancouver, and I'll never get the opportunity again. So during his talk, I am down at the front, sitting cross-legged on the floor and at an appropriate moment I grab a roving microphone and ask him if it's true, but in his inimitable way, he avoids answering me directly, going on with his story about dogs and bus stops.

At the end of the convention the actors are assembled on stage. The various companions are coupled with their respective Doctors and are hugging each other warmly as the audience applaud. I feel isolated – my Doctors aren't here. In the line up, the nearest Doctor to me is Peter Davison, who I have never met. The moment is slightly embarrassing for both of us, as I stand, alone and Doctorless, with a shy Number Five behind me, not quite knowing what to do.

I go back to Roger and Jehane's with the bouquets given to me by the convention organisers. I absolutely love being given flowers. Plonking them in a vase on the kitchen table, I put on an apron and get on with their endless washing up. It brings me down to earth after all the attention I've been receiving. *Don't give it to the ego.* While I've been away, Roger's career has gone stellar, and he is now a household name. I've been loving his portrayal of Trigger in *Only Fools and Horses*, which we get in Canada, and Jehane has raised three boys and become a significant poet. Yogi only lives up the road and comes for supper, a roast chickie in the rayburn. It feels poignantly like shadows of our old family life. I try to be brave – holding back the tears when we part – it will always trigger the same pain. Goodbye, goodbye.

Rappi meets me at the little airport in Qualicum. He is tanned and his green eyes are soft with love, as we rattle back to Hornby. He is very fired up. He's just got his acceptance for the drama school in Vancouver. He starts this autumn. But how can he manage? He will apply for a scholarship but that won't come into effect till later. I'm very touched by his enthusiasm and I want it to work for him, as it had done for me when I was a child. So maybe, I am his Fairy Godmother, as Lady Jane Vane Tempest-Stewart was mine. (I just love that name!)

'Let's put the house on the market and move to the city. I'll invest in you!' I refuse to consider the consequences of this, it just feels right. Anyway, I simply can't go on working as hard as I have been just to keep the bills paid. I've painted the pub, the medical centre, the Co-op and most of the houses. Maybe I could find more consultancy-type work in Vancuckoo, as Rappi calls it. The friends are very dubious that this is a good move. But I've always followed my spirit voice. Now is not the time to falter – when I get an idea in my head, I'm unstoppable.

We have emotional goodbyes. This wonderful island, full of loving friends has been a haven and has comforted me during those agonising times as I put the pieces of my shattered heart back together. Later, they were so supportive of my creative endeavours. I shall always be grateful and there will be a special place in my heart for Hornby. I love you all, I won't forget you, thank you.

We load up Rappi's truck and are off to the big city. I've taken out a double mortgage and put the house on the market – it won't take long to sell – properties are at a premium on these islands. We have rented a house in the east end of the city. I don't like it here but it's near Rappi's drama school so we'll manage. He's had his hair done and some professional photos taken. As the weeks go by I fall into a deep, dark, bleak space. I'm missing my friends and my lovely island home. I feel like my spirit says 'let's go' and Anneke follows, with all the luggage - the fears, the bad backs and the lack of funds. As I step out of the ugly little house, in the street full of other ugly little houses, the neighbours are mostly Chinese, and don't speak. I mourn the support of our lovely community. This is the mean real world. A voice in my head says,

'What are you doing here Anneke? You should be out on the downs!' A voice from the future says,

'Not yet, not yet…'

There is a big street – Commercial Drive – at the top. It's full of Chinese food shops and hip food halls. It's quite a cool scene but I don't know anyone, and Rap is becoming more and more emotionally unavailable, as he gets more into his course. I cry and cry. I feel lost and hopeless in this huge unknown part of the city. It's industrial and noisy. I have to get another car and find some work, and I'm feeling a lack of support and lament the love of my friends. I've painted a sign on my door to remind me, *This Too Shall Pass*.

I manage to heave myself up by my boot-strings once again. I have connected with an old actor who refurbishes Datsuns, so I get a good car, I find a store that sells the environmentally-friendly paint that I like and I start to make my life happen here. An old client from Hornby asks me to redecorate her apartment in Kerrisdale and gives me my most favourite instructions.

'Here's the key, transform it in your inimitable style and call me when you're done.'

I like it much better over this side of the city. There are wide avenues of amazing, large turn of the century houses. Streets full of blossoming trees, Italian coffee shops, 'art movie' cinemas and alternative book shops. Much more my scene!

I've gone with Rappi to pick up some supplies. He's dancing lightly back to the car with a light in his eyes, and I know in that moment that he is in love, and not with me. I push the thought away. The house has sold to some friends of Richard and Serena, who are delighted to have their own island home, so we have to go and collect the remaining furniture and the cast iron tub that I enjoyed so many baths in out on the deck.

We put the bath tub out in the back garden of the ugly thirties house and within a week it has been stolen, ripped off from under our noses. I want to go and see *Remains of the Day*,

'I've seen it already,' says Rappi.

'Who with?!'

'Oh, one of the students,' I know at once that this is a betrayal. We are falling apart at the seams.

I make friends with some Sannyasi women living in Kitsilano, in the west of the city.

'Why don't you get your own place over this side? We'll support you to be free.' So I tell Rappi I'm off and he goes into full abandonment mode. He's so thunderous to be near and I can't reach him anymore.

I take a room in a house full of Sannyasins and I am back amongst the laughing, hugging Osho-lovers. It's a large community.

There is a big meeting in our house one evening and I really like the honesty with which they communicate. As I'm settling into community living, I am beginning to get work as a designer. Serena has a plan to rent a house in Mexico for three months this winter. We scour her Lonely Planet guide, and choose Patzcuaro, an authentic old town, near a lake in the state of Morelia. Girisha is coming from Seattle, so is PJ, who made a film about Hornby, way back, and Mu, an artist, and Yogi will come for two weeks over Christmas. It's another adventure, and I want to put some more space between Rappi and my bruised heart.

I have a big commission from a Taiwanese coffee shop to do an eight foot painting of roses that they want to use for their logo. I tell them that I'll bring it to them in the spring.

Chapter 23

All Passion Spent?

We think it will be great to live in the town, go to the market every day and get to know the locals. My mother's spirit is rejoicing. She loved Mexico because, she said, it reflects the flavour of old Spain. We pick up the key from an office and take a taxi high up on a hill above the town where a large house stands alone. It has lots of rooms, extraordinary tiled sunken baths, a first floor living room with a fireplace and views looking out across to the lake, and there's a big flat roof where we can sunbathe and hang our washing. It's all quite dirty, so we find buckets and cloths and start cleaning.

I'm having a pee in the upstairs bathroom when all of a sudden there is a huge rumbling sound and the whole house is rattling. My instant thought is,

'The others are really getting into the scrubbing!' Seconds later, the others are shrieking.

'Earthquake! Quick, get out!' I'm scrambling down the tiled stair case pulling up my trousers. Everything is shaking and rattling. We stumble down the garden path and stand together in the road. Almost as suddenly, it stops. I am very shaken. We have no phone, no radio – oh God – what's Spanish for 'earthquake'? I feel very far away from everything I know and love, and I don't want to die here, so I make myself a temporary bed by the door, with my shoes and a torch for the next few days, until eventually the fear goes.

We go into town for food and wine and to explore. Ancient squares with porticos, bars and lush gardens, a big market, music everywhere and the Purepeche Indians who live here. It's so colourful. We have a meal in a café, drink local beer and fall in love with the Mexican scene. Out on the nearby lake the fisherman have butterfly shaped fishing nets. There's a magical island in the middle.

We take a boat, serenaded by the Mariachis. Every day we have to pass the abattoir on our way to the market. I meditate on life and death.

It gets cold at night so we have a load of wood delivered. We lay on the roof, practice Spanish and brown our bodies. We cook a parvo (that's a turkey), drink jugs full of tequila and all agree it's the best Christmas ever. Viva Zappatta! Quelle hombres! Muchacho!

One of the artists who lives here takes us out to an incredibly rural stone village, where the wooden mask-makers work. She knows the family. We all gather around the table in the kitchen, which has one bare electric bulb and we are served chicken foot soup – and I get the foot.

'You have to eat it!' whispers our friend with a fixed smile. 'It's a big insult if you don't.' I couldn't. But we know it's a privilege to be at home with these people, the old granny who is 102 is pumping water from the well in the yard. The youngest son is beautiful. In

this lovely face you can see his whole tribe, all his ancestors, and
with his nimble hands he carves wooden angel and devil masks.

This evening over supper I'm telling stories of Peter Cook, The
Establishment, and how Pete and Dud had entered the halls of
comedy fame, never to be forgotten. The next day we walk into the
town. There is a printers which also has a fax machine, and I have
received one from Gary Russell, to tell me that Peter died last night.
How very sad. I think of Wendy and her daughters. I know how
distraught they'll be. When I last saw him, I had a feeling he wasn't
long for this world. He was too bright, too clever. Nothing of this
mortal coil could hold his interest for long. Alcohol and his
intelligence had consumed him. Good luck my darling old friend, in
your journey to other realms. I'm lucky to have known you when
your star was in ascendance.

Girisha and PJ have fallen in love. They leave with Mu and Yogi
and now it's work time for me and Serena. We live and work for
another month, eat a lot of tortilla soup, and then we head off to
Malaque on the coast for our last relax before heading back to
Canada. I've been keeping a journal, like I used to years ago.

[畫作名稱]：ANNEKE的玫瑰
[原作收藏]：ROSE HOUSE 古典玫瑰園本店
經營者於1995年4月收藏於溫哥華
[作 者]一位漂亮、率性的加拿大女畫家：是我在追莎華一家小畫廊邂逅的。她的玫瑰充滿陽光和嫵媚、色彩濃柔細膩，一個人獨來獨往、喜歡喝咖啡和聊天，字寫得好漂亮。她叫做ANNEKE

玫瑰般的午后夜晚　知心的人　相繫在ROSE HOUSE

The rose painting is finished and I roll the six-foot canvas up in a plastic drainpipe and lug it around on taxis, buses and planes back to Vancouver. The Taiwanese clients are delighted with their painting and it will advertise the Rose House Coffee Shops for years to come.

Rappi has got himself a studio apartment in the basement of a home a few blocks away, owned by a Greek family. I go to see him. Damn, damn, damn. I had hoped that by putting space and time between us it would hurt less. On the table in his bedroom is a photo of a very young and beautiful girl from his drama school, who he is now in love with. How many more tears can I cry? It's all very well telling myself to 'let go' but it seems to me that you simply have to be ready and present for when it happens – you can't actually do it. As Devesh would say, 'Hindu footwork – saying yes to your no'.

Mu suggests that I go to see the renowned psychologist Mahmud Nessman. He's a Sufi, and a lovely being. I go to see him in his offices near the river and sinking into a leather armchair under a skylight I pour my heart out. I tell him everything, from the beginning. After the years of pillow punching and catharsis I'm ready to just sit and talk and be heard. Really heard. As the weeks of seeing him go by I am healed by the very quality of his listening heart. He wants to know who taught me to be so hard on myself. He encourages me to love and respect myself – about blooming time. Now at last, I am mature enough to process it all, take responsibility, forgive myself, move on. Like a ripe fruit, falling off a tree. I see how the child went in search of her father, trying to mend the wound. This is essential work. Now at last, I begin to feel free. When I look in the mirror I see that – I'm beautiful! For the first time, I'm not judging myself. After many months, one day, I'm walking along the beach to listen to the folk festival, when I suddenly feel as though I have just shed a huge backpack. I feel light and free and strong.

♫ *So I let it all go and I'm living…* ♫

Now, my life in Vancouver can really begin. I get a lovely first floor studio apartment near the university. Every morning I walk in the nearby woods. I've made a very good friend, Hazel. She is a very successful designer and she has a shop on 10th Avenue, my new neighbourhood. She gets me a lot of work and together we do a massive colour scheme for the Richmond Hospital. I'm painting a mural for a young Chinese man who has an apartment down town. It's for his child's nursery. During a break we get talking.
'So what do you do?' I ask him.
'I'm in real estate,'
'What sort of properties do you sell?' he opens the glass doors

and waves to the skyscrapers around us.

'These.' He says, and I had been worrying about my fee!

I've been reading *Anatomy of the Spirit* by Carolyn Myss. She is talking about keeping promises to yourself. I decide to give up smoking, for real. Three days of hell and madness, as I suck plum stones, drink water and watch the large nicotine snake inside me change into a small worm. I feel so empowered that I am no longer a slave to it. A test. I go to see *Angels Over America* at the theatre. Standing outside on the terrace in the interval, with a glass of wine, this is the very moment that I would love to have a smoke, but I've made a promise to myself.

The Ladner Arts Council wants me to have an exhibition of my work and some of my botanicals are in downtown galleries. I'm kept very busy at the framers, my reputation is blossoming and I'm selling a lot of work. A designer employs me to do some stencils for a bathroom of a mansion owned by one of the busiest lawyers in Vancouver. I measure the space and cut the designs out of oiled manila card. Swags of acathunthus leaves, with birds and butterflies. It's going to be really striking. Mary would be proud of me. I go to a meeting where the rich and spoilt wife is holding court. The glass designer and other professionals are in discussion. I'm waiting patiently while they talk about whether brushed brass should be used for the handles of the shower doors or not. I'm wearing a four million year-old ammonite on a chain around my neck. I'm bored now and playing with it, and suddenly, I'm struggling to my feet, shovelling my designs into my portfolio, I've seen the light.

'I can't!' I protest. They look up, surprised. 'I can't do this. There are people in this world with no food, no homes. This is nonsense, it's only a sodding toilet!' This is the kind of work I so wanted to get, and now it doesn't feel right, indulging wealthy people in their madness.

The evenings on Jericho beach are so special. Greek and Italian families in the sand and in the distance, big liners on their way to Alaska. The snowy slopes of Whistler Mountain and the tall, bronze shining buildings of downtown, sparkling with prosperity and hope for the future in the sun's last rays. What a place!

Vancouver really works. I've got a great female doctor who supports my determination not to have HRT, so I'm mainlining evening primrose oil. I also have a Sannyasi dentist, Mahmud is giving me strength and my hairdresser saves my ruined hair (so many times I risked my colour in cheap salons; so many disasters). The bookshops are stuffed to the rafters with ancient and modern esoteric wisdom. In previous centuries this knowledge was secret. Only if you had attained a certain level of consciousness could you find a teacher... But we are running out of time, so the Gods are making it universally available.

My friends are encouraging me to get it on with a Russian journalist who's keen on me, but I'm very resistant.

'Go on, put some sexy clothes on!'

'Like what?!' Later, dutifully in the throes, I ask him to stop. 'Let's have a cup of tea, and just talk.' I can't do this anymore. It seems... irrelevant. But the Gods don't don't give up. An attractive fifty-something film producer, a Toronto businessman with silver hair and a yacht, who woos me with Mozart, but I'm so enjoying being able to focus my energy on my work, and having fun with my mates, the need for 'the other' is evaporating. Besides, each one of these guys needs too much work!

♪ *I'm not looking for another as I wander in my time...* ♪
- Leonard Cohen

I've been caring for people since I was eleven. Now I want to give all that love, energy and nourishment... to myself.

Down under the Granville Bridge is the market. It's huge and busy and has such a great atmosphere. I am in the courtyard having a cappuccino and people-watching. There are jugglers and children and seagulls and a band playing. I'm suddenly missing Robin. Oh my darling brother, you would be in your sixties now. You would have become something very big, such talent, such ambition you had. How we would enjoy sharing life. Over the years when I think of Robin, it's always painful, not knowing what happened to him at the end. The explanations were never satisfactory; we had felt powerless to do' anything about it at the time. In that moment of sweet reminiscing the band strikes up a tune. It's the theme from *Orpheo Negro*. Our favourite film, our song.

I have taken a stall at the Van Dusen Show. It's like the Chelsea Flower Show. I shall be in the craft tent and I am taking all my little oil paintings. I've made a sign, 'English Gardens, Anneke Wills'. As I am driving along the wide, tree-filled road to the show, Carolyn Garnham, my childhood friend, pops into my mind. We all lived in Burnham Beeches during the war – Jasper her brother, Robin and me. Carolyn Garnham?! Where in the world are you now? No time to think more of her, because I am queuing up with all the other stallholders. I've brought a large tablecloth to cover my stall, and the paintings glow. It's very busy with people because it's raining outside and a Thai woman is selling her handmade rain-hats like hot cakes. I'm sitting down now with my nose in my lunch basket when above me I hear a surprised, English voice.

'Is it Anneke Willys?'

'Yes, but… how do you …?'

'It's Carolyn Garnham.'

'I'd just been thinking about you… how extraordinary.' She had heard about Robin's death, and she was so sorry.

'And sadly, I have no photos of him.' I wail.

'Well, I have, so come and see me.'

How amazing, and I can't wait to see a photo of you. It's been 30 years, and I can't remember what you look like.

I go to her beautiful home on Vancouver Island. We sit on her sofa looking at photo albums and there you are! I am staring at an image of you, aged seventeen. So endearingly young and lithe.

'I never told him I loved him,' says Carolyn, her eyes filled with tears.

'He's letting you know that he knows, right now.' Robin is with us as we are both locked in this timeless magic moment, when in the background I hear the voice of her husband.

'Oh, You believe in reincarnation do you?' Never mind belief, when you know, you know.

It's the summer holidays and Yogi's coming for a visit. Hooray! We spend a week on Hornby, having barbecues on the beach and catching up with friends. It's beautifully hot. Then we take a ferry to the mainland where we meet two friends who spend every summer canoeing amongst the lakes in the wilderness. We rent canoes and set off up Haslam Lake. We have enough supplies to last a week. We make camp on an island, so we won't be bothered by bears. It's one of the best adventures we've had. We swim and cook on the beach, and sleep under the stars. When we leave we make sure we leave no trace.

It's hard to enter the city again having lived in the wilderness. Before Yogi leaves we go to the Imax cinema, the newest technology. When I come back from the airport having seen him off I feel so bereft. It gets harder and harder to say goodbye to him. I'm back at the apartment and I am curled up and crying my eyes out. One of my friends tells me,

'Just let your heart break.' We spend so much of our lives trying to prevent the pain but it is exactly this that makes us truly human.

I go into partnership with a friend and we take over a large empty space on West 4th. We transform it into a gallery called 'Anneke, Calen and Co., Decorative Art'. We fill it with painted furniture, screens, floor-mats, shelves full of the work of Hornby Island potters and candle-makers. My paintings are on the walls. We play good music, have a grand opening, and everyone comes to celebrate with us.

Let the beauty you love be what you do. – Rumi

Chapter 24

It's Back, and it's About Time!

One day, a couple of actors come into the gallery. I overhear their conversation.

'So are you working?' says one.

'Yeah, I'm in the new *Doctor Who* film,' she replies. I just about jump on her with a barrage of questions. It turns out that Sylvester McCoy is in Vancouver, making a *Doctor Who* film, and that Geoffrey Sax is the director, so I get the unit's phone number, quite a cheek, but hey – it's *Doctor Who* – in my city!

'Unit Office?'

'Is Geoffrey there?' I'm blagging it.

'Yes, who is it?'

'Anneke Wills'

'Just a minute, I'll put you through.' My heart is pounding. How presumptuous of me.

'Hello Anneke, how nice to hear from you!'

'Geoffrey,' I start babbling nervously, 'I hope you don't mind but I had to tell you, I'm here in Vancouver, anything I can do… sweep the set floor… I'd love to be a part of…'

'Anneke,' he replies, 'I can't give you work but we would love you to come to the wrap party as our guest.'

Now, someone called Bill Baggs is on the phone.

'We'd love to film Sylv and you, in your shop. We're making a film about his farewell.' I am delighted. They are making the first new *Doctor Who* in eight years and me and my gallery are going to be part of it. Well, sort of. They film Sylvester coming to the door of the gallery and I pop out in a mini-skirt and boots, and we have a hug. Sylvester talks to me about my time on the show, and about my life in Vancouver. When we have finished, we are joined by the

227

brand new, as yet unseen Eighth Doctor, Paul McGann, that actor from Withnail & I. I fancied him. He's beautiful, and shy, and real. If only I was twenty years younger…

The wrap party is in a posh restaurant down town. Everyone is there, the director, the producer Phil Segal. I feel so at home with all the actors. Afterwards we go to a large, wild, Irish pub. Daphne Ashbrook is dancing and Sylvester is showing off, lit up and mad. He is playing the spoons, and he is a master at this particular art. He perfected it with *The Ken Campbell Roadshow*, where he stuffed ferrets down his trousers and hammered six-inch nails up his nose. A massive bald-headed, tattooed bouncer stands arms akimbo above him.

'What's going on in this corner?' Sylv is blissfully unaware, playing the spoons up the man's knees and thighs. There is no stopping him, and we are all holding our breath. Is he about to be annihilated? No. He merrily plays his spoons on the guy's chest, which is above his head, and suddenly, magic happens. The bouncer melts, and laughs. Sylvester is delightfully, innocently drunk. My last sight of him on this grand night is at his hotel, at three o'clock in the morning, chattering away to the X-Files actors returning from their own night out.

Paul McGann and his wife come to the gallery. Like all of us, he is hoping that the new *Doctor Who* will be a smash hit and that he will be in Vancouver for the next few years.

'You must come to the conventions!' The colour drains from his face and he changes the subject and starts asking me about the city, and places to live. I like his wife, a spirited event organiser. She tells me that while he was working on *Doctor Who*, she had asked the concierge at their hotel,

'Which areas in the city would you advise me to stay away from?' Jumping in her cab, she's off to check them out. Gutsy woman! A *Doctor Who* fan in Vancouver invites me to join him and his friends to watch the premiere of the new film. After all the hype and expectations, the film is received with mixed feelings. We have long debates on the balcony, overlooking the city, and I am not sure about any of it. This was not the programme I remembered.

Something was missing. It's a pity, because Paul is such a good actor and sexy with it… despite the wig.

Life back at the shop continues. I've found a wonderful remnant store and I'm having tapestry cushions made and they are selling well. But it can be very slow, and my partner's wife has just had a baby, he rarely has time to do a day, so I'm minding the store, beginning to feel trapped and worrying about the finances, because we're not making any money.

I've been invited to a big science fiction event – 'Visions' - in Chicago. 1500 people. Brian Blessed is here, it's the first time I've seen him since he told me in the BBC canteen that all the *Z-Cars* actors fancied me. I'm wearing a lovely flowing blue dress and as soon as he sees me he says,

'Aah! I can see you're alive!' and he tucks me under his arm. The fans love him, and so do I. He's huge and he never stops telling extraordinary stories. He is so energetic but is he mad? This event is very different from the two that I've been to in England. We don't stop signing for hours, they keep us very busy. Way back in the fifties, when Sarah Miles and I were practicing our autographs, little did I know that I would sign my name thousands of times in one day. I am glad I didn't change my name to Anneke Delicatessen. There is an enormous Monet exhibition at the Chicago Art Institute and they kindly give me time to go. I stand in the bitterly cold queue for hours but finally, there they are, the paintings I know so well. During my next panel on the stage, I am asked if I enjoyed the exhibition.

'Yes, but by the time I got to the shop all the cards had sold out.' As is the generous wont of the fans, they bring Monet postcards to my table. Bless their hearts. I love these people. How come our little programme can reach across the world and join so many people together?

When I get back to Vancouver I buy Brian's book, The Turquoise Mountain, about how he climbed Everest at the age of 64, with a broken toe.

Since I lived in Burnham Beeches as a child, I've always loved walking in the woods, and I do yoga regularly. But now my friend

229

Donaleen wants me to come with her to gym. I'm very resistant. The main room is like a nightmare, pumping bodies, sweat, loud music. I walk straight through, and out the other side.

'Let's go and have a latte and a cake down by the beach instead.'

I've got to close the gallery. If we were prepared to hang on in for a few years, by then the surrounding area would be more affluent and we would do well. Even though we haven't made any money, the gallery has been a success. Everyone loved it, some artists displayed their work for the first time, I sold a lot of my paintings, but it's time to get out before I lose my shirt, so I'm now working in my apartment. Rappi has joined the out of work actors' profession, split up with his girlfriend and wants to meet up with me. After all that we've been through I'm very apprehensive. We walk through a park by the side of the beach. He's bought some seeds with him and shows me how to hold my hand out and keep still – and amazingly a red-winged blackbird is soon perched on my open palm. I can feel its weight, and its trust, and I'm looking into its eye. With opened hearts, we walk on hand in hand. I have so much love for him, but now, very firmly, just as a friend.

I have another exhibition at the Delta Arts Council, and one of my pastels is hanging in a group show at the Bau Xi – the most prestigious gallery in Vancouver! I'm very excited about this, and all my friends go to visit it. I'm glad in the end that it doesn't sell, because I've promised it to Yogi.

I have decided to paint a portrait of Pat as The Doctor. I shall do it in oils. I have various images of him to work from. This is fantastic. I feel him so close, especially when I paint that 'far horizons' look in his blue-green eyes. Darling Pat. When it is complete I'm pleased. Well, perhaps someone would like to buy it. How much could I ask? $50? I hear him explode,

'Fifty Dollars?! At least a hundred! Make some copies and you can sell those as well!' Thanks Pat!

Yogi phones to tell me that he's going to Capetown.

'You must go and introduce yourself to your grandfather. They've moved from Johannesburg… let me call them.' I dial the number hoping I have the time right. By my reckoning it should be early afternoon. I get his wife.

'What do you want? It's the middle of the night!'

'I'm so sorry, I wanted to talk to my father. Shall I call back in the morning?'

'There's no need. He died a few weeks ago.'

'He died? What did he die of?'

'Oh Anneke, it's the middle of the night, I can't go into it!'

'Well I'm sorry it's the middle of the night but I need to know!'

'He was 88 and he had a heart attack. And you really hurt him you know.'

'I'm so sorry.' What a ghastly conversation, but here it is. The death of the parent. It's very big. Even though he was never there for me, his absence has been a vital factor in my psychological make-up. I need to talk to his spirit. Once again, I unplug the phone, close the curtains and light the candles. I place the pillow in the front of me on the floor, and cry and rage and beat the pillow and wail. I become that damaged child. When at last my hurt is expressed, in the silence that ensues I hear his voice.

'Don't you think it hurt me too?' I am stunned. It hadn't ever occurred to me that it had been hard for him to leave Robin and me, to live with that guilt all his life. I forgive you my daddy. Would you be my angel? You could help me with my painting…

I write to Elsie, expressing my sorrow and to ask if I could have one of his little drawings. I never hear another word and the next time I am struggling away on a canvas I hear a voice.

'Not a purple shadow! You can't put a purple shadow!' Angel or not, I said help, not criticism!

231

It's August 1997 and I've been invited to the Isle of Man for a *Doctor Who* weekend and Tim Craxton's daughter Shauna has suggested I have an exhibition sponsored by her charity at a gallery in Hampstead, so it all fits in rather well. It's a lot of work, packing all the paintings and having to get them re-framed when I arrive in the UK.

'This is gettin' to be an 'abit Duchess!' says Mike Craze as we meet on the train to Liverpool. The weather is bad and the ferry has to be washed out after the last crossing because so many of the passengers were very sick. Oh my God, I'm going to be throwing up in front of the fans. Our Captain hugs the coast for as long as he can and then announces,

'Ladies and Gentlemen. Hang on to your hats, it's going to be rough for a while!' And it was. The Isle of Man *Doctor Who* group are old friends of Mike's and he has spent holidays here with his son.

'You look much older than in your photos!' says Ben when he meets me. Ah, the honesty of youth. He looks so like his dad when he was young. Mike's a big fan of *Eastenders*. Whenever we meet he's always telling me I should watch it. We have a great time. On the Sunday morning I'm talking to some of the fans in the hotel lobby, when I notice pictures of Princess Diana on the televison.

'What's that they are saying? Hang on … listen to this,' We are all gathered around the TV as we hear the shocking news. We can't believe it. When I get to Liverpool I go the cathedral. There are queues of people already lining up to write in the condolence books. It's all happened so suddenly, we all just feel the need to connect. The taxi driver in London says,

'You should see the flowers at Kensington Palace.'

I get back to Roger and Jehane's and we are glued to the news. We take a bus down to Hyde Park. The perfume at Kensington Palace from the flowers, in the warm August weather, is overwhelming. What an extraordinary scene. Thousands of very stunned, quiet people, grieving for their fairytale princess, and acres of flowers and offerings, candles and cards. It's a crowd filled with tenderness and tears. A week later we watch the funeral on the television. The note on the coffin, with the small bunch of white roses, that says simply 'Mummy', moves us all. We listen to her brother's extraordinary speech, and watch the corsage start on its journey through North London to Allthrop. We jump in the car and park near the Finchley Road. People are coming out of their front doors. We are all heading in the same direction. I've plucked a rose from a front garden. We hear helicopters overhead, and pushing forward through the crowds we see the hearse. I throw my rose and magically it lands on the bonnet. We sit in the garden and drink a toast to the beautiful and tragic Diana. A little while later in my bedroom at Roger's, I'm doing a watercolour of her brother rowing a boat filled with flowers across the lake to the island where she's buried. This image moves me very much. Suddenly the air is filled with a very expensive scent. What's that? I step out onto the boy's landing, sniffing, it's filled with footballs and posters of Mohammed Ali - nothing feminine here. Back in my room there is the fragrance again.

Shauna Craxton is a musician – of course – and asks if I would like her to play the flute at the opening. This turns into a full-blown concert in the main room and me and my work have become a sort of sideshow! I was her father's favourite girl and she's getting her revenge at last. I have to have my photo taken with one of the sponsors – the fattest, oldest, Russian Princess, dressed impossibly in baby-pink, but we have a great party and Yogi is wonderfully organising the drinks and nibbles. I feel loved and honoured by my friends – there are people from Norfolk, from Poona, from the fifties and from the sixties. The work looks good and Jim Broadbent buys a painting of Patzcuaro, because he went there once. He has to go on to some posh ceremony; he's a big star now, so he's out in the road changing into his dinner jacket. Gary Russell also buys one of my paintings. Roddy Maude-Roxby and Rashid are happy to see each other again. I sell a lot of work and it's a grand night, although I'd invited John Craxton but he refused to come and I'm incredibly hurt by this, and don't understand why.

Edward Fox is playing Macmillan in the West End and has got me a ticket. I've been hassling round London all day and I haven't eaten anything and I'm wedged happily in my circle seat. The play is slow, with not much movement… I fall fast asleep, and wake myself up with a loud snore. Everyone is looking at me. How long was I snorting away? Heavenly to see Ed again, my darling friend.

With Roddy and Rashid

I'm back in Vancouver in my little flat, but somehow, I can't settle. I'm telling Donaleen how much I miss Yogi, and love the English countryside.

'Anneke, if I could wave a magic wand – bing! – what would you say to a little cottage in England?' This time, I don't hesitate.

'I'd ... say... YES!' We are both stunned by the force with which I have instantly replied. Then her eyes fill with tears.

'Oh my God, you're going to go, and I shall miss you, dear friend.' But when the spirit says it's time to move, I have no choice.

Now there is much to do. I call Edward Fox, because he had offered me his second home in Dorset if ever I needed it for a visit. I go to Hornby and take a few paintings. We have a farewell party at Michael's and the friends buy some of my work. I sell all my books – again. I shall have to travel very light because I don't know what's ahead. I buy essentials. Vitamins, hiking boots, paints. I have to laugh because the *Doctor Who* fans always ask me if I have any of the clothes I wore in the show in 1966. I've hardly got anything from last week! I have a garage sale and sell the contents of my flat, and yet another farewell party in Vancouver. I'm always very blessed with such good, talented friends, and I seem to spend my life saying goodbye to them. By the time I get on the plane I feel quite liberated. No keys. A small suitcase and a large portfolio, and I'm going back to England.

Chapter 25

The New Millennium

I walk round the corner on the Kentish Town Road and buy a car for £500, which leaks and breaks down for the next year or so. Ed and Jo's empty house is remote and haunted but I love Dorset. Although it's June, it's bloody cold, so I sit, huddled up against the Aga, listening to The Archers. I have the house for six weeks so that I can become acclimatised and work out where I want to live. I don't want to go back to Norfolk – too many sad memories. Although I have been such a vagabond over the years, now that I am approaching 60, I want to be settled somewhere. As I explore my surroundings, I realise that this is it. This is perfect. I go to the offices on the large estates to put myself on their lists for a little rented cottage. The lists are 700 people long, so when I run out of time at Ed's I go to stay in a friend's yurt in Glastonbury. It has a red front door, it's a fantastic structure, and very cosy when there is a storm. But it's only temporary, so I move to another friend's cottage in Wiltshire, where I'm watering her garden and worrying, when the man from Saville's calls me.

'Got a cottage. Might suit. Can you come down tomorrow?'

It's near Corfe Castle in Purbeck. As soon as I see the lattice windows and the expanse of the overgrown garden, which looks out over the castle, I say,

'Oh yes please, this will definitely suit me!'

It has one tiny bedroom, a wood stove, it's very dilapidated and it's very cheap and I love it to bits. The previous tenant, a nice young woman, is bailing out of a relationship. She wants to be rid of all her furniture. Brilliant. For £50 I get a Harrods sofa, an Arts and Craft pine table, all her pots and pans, a mattress and an old TV. The first morning I walk up the lane past the church, exploring. As I reach the peak of the hill I can see I'm high up on a down, and the road leads down through the fields to the sea – my own beach – it's a long steep path and the beach is sandy and wild. I can't believe it. This is where I now live. Apart from the wood stove there is only one night storage heater. The carpet is very thin over a concrete floor. The bathroom is off the kitchen, there's one cupboard upstairs that reeks of damp and I'm worried about being cold this coming winter. In Canada electricity was cheap and ubiquitous. I shall have to lay more carpets and knit myself a stripy hat to sleep in! I buy long johns but in the deep winter I still sit on the sofa wrapped in a blanket with a cold nose.

The cottage is in the centre of the village so I am surrounded by neighbours. Dave plods down his garden every evening to feed his chickens and to dig his huge, business-like veg plot. I ask his advice, but he has such a broad Dorset accent I can't understand him. Mind you, neither can Margaret, his wife. On the other side is 70 year old Charlie. He was born in the village and worked here as the plumber on the estate all his life. These are real country people. This whole village was built for the workers of the Lord of the Manor. Perfect eighteenth century cottages. Mine used to be the room where the brass band practiced for the high days and holidays. We are under the shadow of a grand church, with a big tower, and the bell-ringers play on Sundays.

'Bloomin' ole' bells. Bugger 'em!' Grumbles Dave. This I can understand.

There is a young couple up the street who are having twins. We all meet up in the evenings at the pub. The Gods send me an angel friend. Richard and his dog Snorbitz. He does all the renovation around the village and over the next few years he will help me to install a gas stove, builds terraces and a greenhouse, which Yogi gives me - fulfilling another dream - I always wanted a greenhouse. Our landlord holds 'local nights' and cooks us all great food.

I have a commission. To paint a barge on the Kennet Canal belonging to the owner of a large plant nursery. I'm going to trade with him – a painting – for some plants for my garden. I've taken some photos and done some sketches and I'm climbing over a bridge in the warm, late summer sunshine, when along the canal comes a barge, painted Navy Blue. Somehow, it reminds me of something but I can't quite make the connection in this moment. I stop and lean over the bridge, and as it comes nearer, I see its name. The Tardis.

'Hello Tardis!' I call. The head of a young boy pops out of the hatch and seeing me, replies,

'It's Polly! Dad! Come and look! It's Polly!' They invite me on board for tea and a chat. We inhabit the same magic world.

I'm going to plant all the flowers that the snobs despise, to give them a chance. Yellow gladioli, peach coloured roses and dahlias. I dig my garden to the sound of the church bells. This is the land of my ancestors. Over the years I had seen such countries. Mountains, jungles and wild forests. But I love with a heartfelt passion the cows in the fields, the mighty English oaks, the villages, the pubs, and the farms.

By the time Yogi comes to see me for his birthday I've painted and restored much of it, dug the garden, and I've cleaned out the old pig sty and turned it into a seating area.

Pat Garwood, an old school-friend, lives in nearby Swanage. When I tell her I've moved to Kingston, she says that the pub here had some framed photographs of the *Doctor Who* cast. I decide to go and see for myself, so Yogi and I head off to The Scott Arms, and then, it all comes back to me. This was the pub we stayed in when we filmed in the local caves. I pester the landlord to turn out his attics but sadly we never find the photographs.

'Someone must've nicked them.' He says.

I go visiting all the local Elizabethan houses. I wore a Tudor costume in an early telly when I was 11, and I had an overpowering sense that I knew how to live in those clothes, and ever since then I have had a strong connection to those days. I had an ancestor who was an Elizabethan hero and one day when I have the time, I shall research him. I've wandered around the garden at Athelhampton. In the tea rooms there is a large picture of Tom Baker as The Doctor. This is where they filmed *The Seeds of Doom* in 1975. I have gone for 30 years and barely thought about *Doctor Who*, and it is uncanny that it is suddenly and unsubtly spreading its rubbery, green tentacles into every aspect of my life!

In the local paper I see an article about Carlotta Barrow. She was a girlfriend of Robin's, and was also a student at the Arts Educational while I was there. I give her a call and go to see her. When I step into her charming living room, looking out across Swanage Bay she says,

'Robin loved this room. And it's hardly changed since then.' Robin, Robin, you are always with me. Carlotta and her husband used to work as designers in TV and movies, but now they are a 'dynamic duo' painting and sculpting, so we plan a joint exhibition.

With Julia 'Toots' Lockwood at her 60th birthday party. She drinks gin and smokes like a chimney, but she still looks great!

Garth Bardsley is writing a biography of Tony Newley. We have lots of meetings and talk endlessly on the phone. He has read the letters that I had sent to Tony following Polly's birth. When he hears the full details of the abortion and everything, he weeps. Although it is deeply painful for me we both agree that the time is right for the story to be told. This will have great repercussions in my family life so it feels like a big responsibility to speak out. Leslie Bricusse is on the phone. After all these years. He says,

'You were the best thing that ever happened to Tony.' What a beautiful thing to say. I don't go to the launch, it doesn't seem appropriate. Joan Collins has a front seat. Garth's book – 'Stop the World' – is riveting. It's startling for me to read my drama all over again.

Yogi now spends every Christmas with me, for which, I am a deeply happy mummy. We go on a special long walk to Durdle Door. We make a fire on the vast beach. He sees his Dad as much as he is able, but Henrietta makes it as difficult as she can, and it makes them both sad because they have so much love for each other. Her fear is so destructive. Mickgough will call him up,

'She's going away, any chance you can come?'

On Christmas Eve, after the pub, we go to midnight mass, but it's no good – I disrupt the service with my giggling. Yogi takes me home to the cottage.

'Badly done, mum.' I'm chastened. At breakfast time, he's grinning. 'Ha! I got that from Alan Rickman in *Emma*. I've been waiting to use it!' In front of the wood stove, watching telly, eating roast pheasants, I make brandy snaps, and we light a candle for Polly.

The *Doctor Who* friends seem very happy to have me home again. We have a reunion with Mike Craze and Frazer Hines at the BAFTA building, off Piccadilly. I don't know, as I hug Mike goodbye, that this is the last time I shall see him. They call me with the news of his demise and we are all very shocked. His funeral is heartrending. As his coffin slides forward and the curtains close, the *Doctor Who* theme music plays. Off to another dimension, Ben. We have all become such a family. I'm honoured to write a piece about him for The Stage. My dear friend, I'm really going to miss you. I start watching *Eastenders*.

Rob Craine had been a close friend of Mike's, and used to take care of all his bookings and fanmail. He now will do the same for me, which is brilliant because he's in touch with all the Who events and I'm getting a lot of fanmail, which amazes me.

Carlotta is having one of her soirees at the front of the row of houses. We sit looking out over the bay to the white cliffs of Harry Rocks. Carlotta's mother bought this house just after the war, so she's part of the fabric of the place, and all the painters and writers, the local literati, gather for lovely food, wine and laughter. We plan to go to Devesh's barn in the Dordogne to paint and help him with his walnut harvest. The sand is scattered over the road as we walk along the front to see a movie. I love this place. Thank you, angels.

A shop called 'Tenth Planet' has opened in Barking and I am invited to do a signing at the opening ceremony. It's absolutely stuffed from floor to ceiling with *Doctor Who* merchandise. There is no sign of the show coming back to our TV screens, and these shops are a vital cornerstone in the fan community. I'm chatting away, and signing photos when the owner, Derek Hambly, hands me the phone.

'Anneke, there is someone from Finland on the phone for you.'

'Eeva-Liisa Kannikoski!' I say. 'Hello Eeva-Liisa!'

'Anneke how did you know it was me, after a lifetime?' She asks me to come and visit, and tells me that she has letters and poems from Robin. She was his first love. In the winter, I fly to Helsinki to see her. She lives in a cabin in the woods, in deep snow. We drink Kipis (warm, deadly alcohol with raisins in it) and read Robin's love letters to her, and howl. He was such a poet, such a visionary. She tells me how, they were planning to go to Australia to start a new life, and that he had finished writing his book. We talk of the strange circumstances of his end, so long ago, disappearing into the mists of time. She has one lovely photo, I can really see you again, after so many years. There is a separate sauna house and up the snowy slope, an outside dunny. The sheds are full of barking dogs, which she breeds. I have to pass a Pyrenean Mountain dog called Clinton on my way for a poop.

'Don't touch him, he'll have your hand off!' warns Eeva-Liisa. I talk to him from a distance, and bow. By the time I leave, he's licking my hand.

Eeva-Liisa drives like a maniac along the snowy roads and takes me to the main Marimekko shop in Helsinki, the designer I wore in *Doctor Who* and for most of the sixties. She likes to lie on her divan beside her wood stove, chain smoking and drinking kipis. I go for long walks across the countryside. Robin was always going to come here but never made it so he's using my eyes. I know Eeva-Liisa was very special to you and that you loved Carlotta, but now, that's it - I'm not chasing up any more of your girlfriends!

I've been invited to make a guest appearance on the Clive James Show. Whenever these events turn up my first thought is always,

'Agh! What shall I wear?' It is the old childhood trauma, which came out of the austerity of the fifties, of not having good enough clothes, still absolutely in place. I don't think we ever get rid of our neuroses, they just overwhelm us less. I set off confidently in a £1.99 shirt, courtesy of The British Heart Foundation. I'm joined by Jacqueline Pearce and Nicola Bryant, a fellow *Doctor Who* girl. There is a live audience and I am quite nervous. Suddenly, he's mocking us. He says,

'After all, you were only there to look pretty and scream. How about doing a scream for us now?' How degrading! And then, drooling over Jacqueline,

'You were my goddess in *Blakes 7*!' Afterwards we are all in the green room, Nicola and I want to set him straight about the role of the *Doctor Who* girl, and Jacqueline wants to thank him for his extraordinary accolade, but his mind is elsewhere, and we are ignored. This is the first time I am confronted with this view of *Doctor Who*, and of us companions. It won't be the last, and I never accept it.

I meet up again with David Hughes, that 'quiet, sensual moralist of the lettered left'. He has become one of the most elegant prose writers of his time, film critic for The Sunday Times, book and theatre critic. I collect and read his eleven novels. We have wonderful lunches. He is a loyal and generous friend and we share deep love, which we'd been unable to express in the sixties because of Mick and Mai. Now we're old we can hug and giggle. It is David who tells me that Mickgough's wife Henrietta has been warning all the old friends not to have anything to do with me - that's why John Craxton didn't want to see me. This woman's hatred is so cruel. *What we do in life, echoes in eternity…*

I am reading all of Hardy's novels. One night I'm in the pub with Charlie.

'Have you been to London, Charlie?'

'Nope. But oi bin to Dorchester!' My neighbours are the Hardy characters come to life.

I am eating fish and chips, having lots of cream tea therapy and visiting luscious gardens. I watch the boat race, the Chelsea Flower Show and Wimbledon. I'm weeping at the beauty of Galileo running his heart out to win the Derby. I am revelling in Englishness.

The new millennium is upon us. The media is full of nothing else. Millions of pounds will be spent on fireworks and celebrations. Everyone is planning parties. I don't see anything to celebrate. Since most of my family is in heaven, I light candles and send love. But after 2000 years, what have we achieved? We are more violent, more greedy and more dishonest. We are busy polluting the very planet we live on, and everyone is getting drunk. On 1st January 2000, I think I'm the only one without a hangover.

I have written to our MP to ask exactly why so many of the experimental GM crops are located in Dorset. I'm deeply suspicious of them altering our food. I've written to the local council to complain about various building works, in progress in the village – I've got a voice and I'm using it! The garden has been abundant this year. Enough sweet peas to put on all the tables at Carlotta's sixtieth, and so many beans and courgettes, I had to fill bags and hang them over the front door knobs of the neighbours. This summer I have been invited to 'open' my garden on a village open day. I am flattered, and in a panic. I must finish the weeding and cut the edges around the borders, but it does look lovely and the veggies are a picture. I sit in my greenhouse drawing, as total strangers come and poke around, scribbling in notebooks.

'Is this an eremurus bungei?'

'I don't know, I got it from the Spar shop!' When the final visitor has left, Mick and Shani cook a feast. We have a party in the garden. We light the lanterns, and drink more wine as the stars come out.

There is a yearly fete in the grounds of the big house. The queues

243

Painting with flowers

of cars start filing through the village very early in the day. This is a grand occasion. As tenants, we have special passes.

People picnic around the lake, there is a band playing on the lawn in front of the house. George III used to visit this house. The stalls are of the best quality, everyone is dressed in summer finery. Carlotta and I pay to see around the house, sniggering at the dreadful decoration. Not what we would have chosen! When Carlotta was a set decorator, she worked on many episodes of *Poirot*. We both have trained eyes.

John Nathan-Turner was the producer of *Doctor Who* from 1981 to 1989 and it appears that it was largely under his influence that the programme declined somewhat. Many of our episodes have been lost, Mike and I have been a bit overlooked in recent years. But not any more – I'm back! I'm now high on the list of favourite companions. When I meet JNT at this big summer event at Longleat, I like him at once. He's so wicked and funny. I always wanted to visit Longleat. Going down the drive I get this feeling. I should live here, The proportions seem to fit me...

There is only one Doctor I haven't met, and he is the star of this wonderful day. He sits in the Orangery, in his costume, holding court, signing autographs. I jump the queue and introduce myself to this larger than life character. I am immediately struck by his warmth and intelligence. I know I could learn a lot from him. Too bad about *that* coat! I have now completed the set – I have met the magnificent Colin Baker.

A *Who* friend of mine is doctor of botanical sciences in California. She has created a flower and called it 'Polly'.

It's time to make a pilgrimage to my mother's grave in Devon. When I arrive at the large cemetery, I think I will remember the lay of the land but in twenty years the trees have grown and I am lost, so I go to the office. We look her up in the ledgers. Here is her name. Johanna Catherina Willys.

'But,' says the attendant, 'Because the plot was never bought there will be no headstone, just a metal number, and unfortunately the teenage boys climb over the fence at night and steal them, but the number is...' I set off, feeling determined. I thought it was being taken care of by Tilly and her husband Bob. They must have been strapped for cash. We've lost contact over the years. When I get close there are three or four unmarked mounds. I don't know which is your grave. How sad. I sit down on the grass, amongst the mounds, and weep. When I open my eyes, there is an orange flower beside one of the graves. I hadn't noticed it before. Moe, is it you? I haven't the money to buy your plot. I'll get a friend to carve 'Anna' and your dates on a beach stone, and I'll put it here anyway. I drive home, heartbroken, that your brave and passionate life had no memorial, I must do something.

'No need,' comes the answer. 'I'm always with you. Just plant more orange flowers.' Marigolds, nasturtiums and California poppies all feature in my gardens from now on.

I'm going to be 60 this year. How is it possible? It seems as if this life has flown by. I'm getting grey hair and arthritis, I can't see and I can't hear so well either! Lord, maybe it's time for me to don my slippers and cosy up with those books that I've always meant to read. Sounds good… but actually, the Australian fans have invited Colin and me to visit them in Sydney. So I'm off on another adventure! After the interminable long and cramped flight, during which I kept doing lots of leg stretches, we arrive in the warm Australian morning. My hotel room is bigger than my cottage. I love Sydney and the gathering of people. Katy Manning is mesmerising.

'Do you like my boobs? Thanks to Liza Minelli!' she says with a big wide smile. All the men melt around her. Andrew Beech takes us to dinner and to a performance at the Opera House, and Gary Russell has come especially to join us. He's been working on *The Lord of the Rings* in New Zealand. Our Australian hosts are lovely guys who take us on a boat trip around the harbour and to a wildlife park and arrange for Colin and I to climb the Sydney Harbour bridge. We are both apprehensive about this - neither of us are very good at heights - but we are determined to do it. We are put in special gear and go through training with harnesses, and then we start the ascent. By the time we get to the top, Colin and I have fallen in love with our instructor and we're hugging him. What an astounding view. When we come back down we sit in a restaurant and quote *Withnail & I*.

'We want the finest wine available to humanity. We want it here, and we want it now!'

Hungover, we go to the local radio station to be interviewed. I am in awe of Colin as he articulates the worlds of *Doctor Who* for the listeners. He explains how *Doctor Who* is, on the surface, a battle between good and bad; a traditional fairytale; but how in fact there is so much more. Over the last few years I have realised that *Doctor Who* has become enshrined in the public's collective consciousness; it has become a British institution and a worldwide phenomenon. And now, captivated by Colin Baker, this most colourful and intelligent of Doctors, I begin to understand why it has affected and inspired and supported so many people. Nearly 35 years since I was in the show, it's keeping me busy and has become a significant part of my life. The programme is being kept alive by the thousands of fans, many of whom have become accomplished film-makers and writers. Gary Russell, with his company Big Finish, acquires a license from the BBC to produce new stories as audio plays. Rather than being forgotten, *Doctor Who*'s finding its feet again. During one of the interviews with Gary, I am astounded when he uses the phrase 'sixties icon' to describe me.

'Go on, I wasn't!'

'Yes you were!' I hadn't considered this at the time. For me, it was a great job but I went home after work to get on with my family life. I run the idea I've had about writing my story past Gary.

'I wouldn't bother. A lot of work, and I doubt if it will sell.' Colin says,

'If you want to, write it anyway!'

It's September, 2001. I am weather-proofing a slatted screen which is leaning against the wall in the entrance way to my cottage, but the wind is so wild, I can't keep it steady. Everything is being blown around, it's like *The Wizard of Oz*, so I give up and go inside. But I feel awful. Depressed and freaked out. Instead of trying to block the feeling I decide to sit down and write it. I write,

'It feels like witches time. Dangerous time. Dark energies are without and within.'

At 6:00 I put on the news but I have the sound turned down because I'm on the phone. My eyes are absorbed by these strange images, of a plane, flying into a skyscraper. I thought this was the news, but it seems to be a movie. What's going on? On September 12th, we all wake up to a different world, a dangerous world in which no-one is safe. A few days later, I am glad to be at a *Doctor Who* Convention among my new friends. It's a comfort to talk to Barry Letts, because he's a Buddhist.

I have to decide what to do about my 60th birthday. It's difficult because I would love all my friends to come, but they live all over the world, so I think I'll just have a small celebration in the pub with those who can make it. The flowers start arriving early in the morning. By the end of the day the cottage looks like a florist's, filled with cards and messages from all over the world, so much love. At the pub, we have some great local musicians and we dance. Wendy Cook makes me a special cake and it's a sweet evening. I feel the importance of the love of good friends. Ever since the attacks in New York I have felt the need to be quiet, at home, cosy. I love walking out on the downs above the sea and coming home to soup, made from my own veggies.

Celebrating my sixtieth with Jehane, Wendy and Yogi (above) and with Roddy and Andrew Beech (below).

There is a massive upheaval on the estate. The big house is up for sale for over a million pounds. Potential buyers have been arriving in their helicopters. The buzz in the pub is that Kylie Minogue is interested. Ha! They wish! I've saved up £400 and a local computer guy is selling me a second-hand laptop. He's cleaned it up, wiped it. I go to Wareham to attend some classes. We sit in the old station. I have headphones and a screen and would you believe it, it's Tom Baker's voice in my ear, inviting me to click on 'Tardis' so we can go off on an adventure together!

As soon as I have cracked this computer lark (I'm so resistant), I mean to start writing my autobiography. People have been nagging me to tell my tale. Well I will! And my mother and Robin are already in my head, reminding me of family stories. But this screen and keyboard scares me, and I am worried about getting lost, and then I'll be in a rage, because I don't know how to do it, so I just keep practicing Solitaire – I can do that!

After the ranch, Veetasmi, who has gone back to her old name of Persephone, had won the pools, and gone to the Australian outback to run a healing centre. Now she's back, and I have found her a thatched cottage in the very next village. We all rally round to get her comfortable and she loves her new home. One winter Sunday, I'm driving back home from a visit with her, looking forward to some soup and putting my feet up and watching *Eastenders*.

Opening my gate I immediately notice my windows seem very black. I open the front door and I am instantly enveloped in a suffocating cloud of black smoke.

'Shit!' I slam the door shut. I bang on Dave's door.

'Dave! I've had a fire! I'd better open all the doors and windows!'

'Don't you do that, that'll go up in flames! I'll call the fire brigade.' The sound of the fire engines coming up the hill is a great relief. The fire chief checks with me as I sit in a neighbour's front room,

'No animals? No people? Give her a cup of tea. We'll come and tell you about the damage.' Persephone's come and is hanging on to me – I am shaking with shock. After an interminable time the fireman comes back. How kind and professional they are. When I step back in, my little home is ruined. It's mostly smoke damage. Totally black and filled with noxious fumes. There had been an electrical fault. The TV had blown, next to the wood-basket and the firelighters. It would have been a lot worse but for the fact that there was no air. If I had have opened the windows, the whole place would have exploded.

Over the next week we salvage what we can. We have to wear rubber gloves, wellies and masks. My books, paintings, fabrics, carpets, all my music tapes and videos, laptop have melted. Personal photos, all ruined. I have no home insurance. I've lost the lot. The estate's insurance will pay to have the cottage cleaned and repainted. I stay with Persephone, which is an added strain because we'd had a set-to – it's when she becomes the 'head-girl' that I start snarling. I cope with the situation as bravely as I can – but I am exhausted, saddened and freaked out. We offload much of the furniture into various sheds around the village so that the painters can make a start.

Then, I'm in Los Angeles at a *Doctor Who* convention. People are so kind and understanding, sharing similar memories. A fire is a real cut into one's physical reality. It shakes one to the very core. Three months later when the cottage is finally dry, I work with the painters sent by the landlord's insurance company, because they're hopeless. Mobile phones under their chins, paint brush in one hand, sandpaper in the other,

'No, no, no. Get out of here! I'll do it!' After many months, it's all looking fresh and beautiful, I've even had a laminate wood floor laid, and I'm planning to get another laptop and start all over again, but first, I'm going to have a tiny break, with Wendy in Devon. When I get home there is a letter from the estate office

'… since the sale of the house we have had to vacate various cottages and we now give you your notice to quit…'

I read it again because I can't believe it. 'Notice to quit?' They need my cottage for their gamekeeper. After all I've been through, my darling little home… I walk out among my ebullient flower beds

and the whole village hears my cries. The friends and neighbours are outraged for me.

'We'll have a protest! We'll march on the office!' But I don't seem to have any fight left in me. I feel utterly deflated. It is impossible to describe the extreme trauma of a house fire. Losing everything, and now this. Dear God! I'm getting too old for this!

Half-heartedly I start to look at new places. But since I've been here the rents have risen. I've been living high on a hill, beside the sea, overlooking the castle. In my life, I have been lucky enough to live in such idyllic places – places where other people go to have holidays, and now, all I can find is a basement flat in Swanage. Persephone and I get on the internet.

'Perhaps if I go further west?' We see a tiny cottage in a Devon field, with hills behind. As we continue our search we lose that cottage as we scan through so many. One estate agent says,

'We've got a rural cottage and are showing it tomorrow. Can you be there?' We drive to Devon after breakfast. As we walk up the hill to the rear of the property, I begin to get goosebumps.

'But this is it! The one I said I liked the look of!' The estate agent politely tells me,

'There are fifteen other people interested in this one.'

'But I want it! I deserve it! And I'm a great tenant!' I bombard them for a week and finally they give in.

Me at 60!

Chapter 26

The Land of My Ancestors

How many farewell parties can I have?! This move seems like the ultimate wrench. I have grown to love this place so much, my dearest friends, the beaches, the hills, my sweet little home and my garden. Our farewell party is very touching. Lots of tears and I feel so sad. When I arrived in England four years ago I had just a portfolio and a case. Now I have to hire two removal lorries – ah well – it's mostly garden furniture, plants and my collection of Purbeck marbles and fossils I shall take with me.

In October 2002, I drive to the hills of Devon, and my new life. It's on a farm and has been freshly painted which is good because I'm running out of enthusiasm for decorating. There's an old wood stove, one night storage heater, a carpet on a concrete floor, one mouldy cupboard… There is a big shed filled with rubbish – of course – and various levels of totally overgrown land. Wendy Cook is half an hour's drive away, other than that, I don't know anybody here. I close my curtains at four o'clock and feel alone. As the winds howl down my 400 year-old chimney, I read all about old Devon life, the farms, the villages and the stone circles. There have been people living on this piece of land since Saxon times. I love listening to the cows in the barn next to me, the farm life all around. The smell of manure is like nectar to me – I always wanted to live on a farm.

I write to Simon Gough who I had entrusted with my trunk of family photographs all those years ago. A distraught Sharon tells me he ditched them all, but she has been through her own albums, and sends me the few little pictures of Polly, and those days, that she has. I can't believe he could do that. This means Yogi has virtually no pictures of his childhood. What a horrible thing for Simon to do – I despair of him.

While we all watch the horrors of the war in Iraq, I work off my frustration with our leaders by clearing and digging the land. Cutting brambles, digging out nettle roots, humping piles of stones is great therapy. By the spring I've mended the steps and walls, dug beds and planted sweet-peas, the farmer has cleared all the rubbish from the shed for me, and I've put in skylights so I can use it as a studio. In the village, the shop, the post office and the pub have long since closed. Many of the cottages are second homes, closed up for most of the year. The farmers and the fisheries are struggling, how very sad this is for our ancient English way of life. If only they realised this planet is a living organism we wouldn't be in the devastating mess we're in. There's no-one intelligent in charge any more!

Rashid has come back from Mallorca where he has spent a few years building sacred spaces. He has moved into a house in North Devon and has become a beekeeper and has fifteen grandchildren. And of course, the hills of Devon are alive with the sound of Sannyasins making their music.

I've been digging out the hill in front of the cottage and have discovered an old cobbled yard. I find a Charles II coin, a clay pipe and an old pitch fork. I love the feeling of generations of country people having lived here. Old cottages have so much soul. This is the line that the farmer likes to feed back to me when I'm grumbling about the damp! A friend has bought me some flower seeds from Monet's garden in Giverny. The prettiest little blue flowers that he loved.

Gary Russell is directing a three-part story for Big Finish, especially for *Doctor Who's* 40th anniversary year. *Zagreus* will be released on CD in November. I'm playing the mother of the current companion and I'll be appearing with four Doctors! It's 80 degrees and there is no air-conditioning in the studios, but we actors set it aside. Gary is a consummate director - many ex-actors are. India Fisher and I work well together and when we finish the scene where

I talk to her from beyond the grave, everyone's in tears. What a gift for me to be in this esteemed company. Back at work! Headphones on, script in hand – I was trained to do this and I love it! In another story, I get to play a female dinosaur! In the green room at the studios there is a familiar face. It's Ian Hogg, a respected Shakespearian actor. At the end of the day, we are nearly finished, and Gary says,

'I need a little adlib roaring.' So Ian and I are looking at each other from our booths, enthusiastically roaring, snarling and growling across the studio.

'Best therapy I've had for ages, darling!' Says Ian as he steps out of his booth.

The anniversary is Andrew Beech's big moment and he has bitten off more than he can chew and organised a massive convention in the London Hilton. It's chaos, thousands of queuing fans, snaking around a huge staircase. Some of the fans seem disappointed; it appears that the event is not living up to the hype. The BBC has produced a huge book called 'The Legend' which we are all busy signing. This is Paul McGann's first convention. He's interviewed by Jason Haigh-Ellery. At first he's shy and on edge but Jason asks insightful questions and it's great to see Paul relax, open up and enjoy himself. The *Who* audience is very special, because they love you. They know all about your work and they're on your side. In the evening there is a disco. Michael Sheard is the life and soul and Jon Culshaw is there doing his Tom Baker impressions. In a small reception room in the bowels of the hotel we actors are plied with champagne and no food. After two hours we're all pissed and ready to party, but the stewards have all disappeared. Finally in frustration Wendy Padbury and I and our gang stagger down the corridors listening at lift shafts for sounds of the celebrations. Poor Gary Downie never makes it to the stage to receive an award on behalf of his late partner, John Nathan Turner. The look of betrayal on his face haunts us all. This is the last of the big *Doctor Who* conventions. A while later I am talking to Cary Woodward at a small event in Birmingham. He is a delightful, warm Welshman and he is wondering whether a convention in Swansea would be a success and whether he would be able to organise it. My recent experience at Panopticon has left me with strong views on how a convention should be run. Cary and I chat at length. No more than a couple of hundred people. Treat the actors and fans with respect. He is fired up and away he goes to start planning.

Frazer is in an Agatha Christie play in Torquay so he's coming to visit me. I'm out early, cutting the brambles in the lane. I don't want his Merc to get scratched. After lunch we go up on the moors and he has a snooze in the warm sunshine. He's excellent in the play – what a good actor he's become.

They have bought out *Strange Report* on DVD. They include an interview with Roger Lloyd Pack and me, filmed on a bitterly cold day in the old locations. The Embankment, Little Venice. I've borrowed a leather jacket from one of the crew. The mikes are kept running as Rog complains,

'Bugger me, I wish I'd worn long johns!' I'm reminiscing about working with his father, Charles. In a way, the person I speak of is familiar and yet she's someone else. Our cells totally change every seven years… so who was Anneke Wills back then?

I'm having lunch in Brixham, and when I see the replica of the Elizabethan ship, The Golden Hind, I experience a haunting and disturbing sense of déjà vu. It's time to see what I can find out about my ancestor. Robin had always told me about Sir Richard Grenville. I'd always thought it would involve many hours in records offices. We Google him. Boom! Immediately, all this information. And even, an image. I'm looking into the eyes of my old relative, 500 years later. Apparently he had a home a few miles away. Filled with excitement I drive down to Buckland Abbey, which he had rebuilt when he acquired it in the 1500s (so renovating old houses is in my blood!). I stand in a large panelled hall. On a table is a model of his ship – The Revenge. I feel the ancestral arms stretching out across the centuries and enveloping me. I feel the glow of Robin's smile as I realise that I have found our ancestor. His home, his story. On the way home, I'm driving on the very same road he would have used. Among my fan mail is a letter from a Commander in the US Navy, just back from a stint in the East, saying how much his family have enjoyed watching old episodes of *Doctor Who*, and asking if any of my family were in the navy… I tell him about Richard Grenville fighting the Spanish in the 1500s.

Of the many events I do, my least favourite are the large collectors' fairs - thousands and thousands of people swarming around the massive halls of the NEC. However, one time, I meet up with Angela Douglas again. Last time I saw her was in the sixties. She's tentative about renewing our friendship – she's heard I'd become a hippy and a religious nut. We plan to have lunch together in London. At one of these fairs, I meet Tim Hirst, his wife Su and Sophie her daughter, a teenage girl in a wheelchair. She is beautiful and I spend some time chatting to her, she wants to be an actress. Su's necklace catches my eye. It contains her dog's ashes, so we are talking about the spirits of animals.

When I'm reflecting on my relationships with the men in my life, I forget all the pain. I only remember the quality of my love for them. They were the perfect mirrors for me – true soul-mates. We have this mushy idea that a soul-mate is someone who is going to make it all safe and perfect for you. Actually, they come to show you what you need to learn, and often it's very painful. I get fed up when people call them 'failed relationships'. If I had needed to live in a safe bungalow with sunflowers, that's what I would have been given. I came here to learn about love and loss and betrayal – to 'burn off the karma of many lives'. And yet, with Mickgough, I feel blocked. It wasn't the physical abuse that had occurred in the sixties, that was a crime of passion. It wasn't even the infidelity and the controlling. It was his inability to give me a hug or look me in the eye at Polly's funeral. I've been returning to this place for years and each time comes a firm 'No'. I can't forgive him. I know I have to let it go, otherwise, I'm not free. Now is the time to deal with this, and just when I need, here is a gentle soul called Tom, who facilitates hypnotherapy sessions called 'The Journey'. He starts by guiding me back to the scene. Instead of a grave dividing us, there is a fire. I have to leave my body and enter into Mickgough, and look out from his eyes. It will take a while for me to accept this instruction. But as Tom says,

'If you want to let it go…' I am quite practiced at coming out of my body and as I see Mickgough before me my spirit flies across the fire and slips inside him. Oh my God. He's in such agony. I can't bear it. I realise – poor Mickgough – he couldn't have hugged me –

it would have destroyed him. Now I understand. He was frozen in pain. I cry for him. Now my guide says,

'Some loving soul is now taking both your hands, and reconnecting you with love.' I look across the fire, and there you are Polly, shining and golden, with hands outstretched to us both. Such tears, such melting, such dissolving. Tom tells me to speak it out loud.

'I forgive you.' Now at last, I am able to talk openly to Yogi and Emma about their father with love and compassion in my heart.

Mark Ayres comes down to record a narration, which we do in my kitchen with a duvet against the window to block out the bellowing of the bull in the field. In the evening we go to a local pub for supper. I've stopped smoking for years now, but when I'm in a pub, I can't resist it. I go over to a group of people and ask,

'Can I scrounge a roll-up?' As I am making my rollie, one of them says,

'Excuse me for asking, but is that by any chance Mark Ayres that you're with?' I am greatly surprised by this.

'How would you know that?'

'Because he's a bigwig in the *Doctor Who* world and we're fans!'

'Really?' I say, with all innocence. 'Would you like me to introduce you?' They chat to Mark, who loves the joke that his fans don't have a clue who I am.

We have a party to celebrate Yogi's 40th at Roger and Jehane's. It's a warm and sparkly evening of his friends past and present. He's greatly loved and he's become the 'best in his field'. The girlfriends bake him a chocolate cake in the shape of a bike, because he cycles to work every day. I can't believe he's 40. How our lives fly by.

The BBC has seen the light! They are bringing our programme back. We all have great expectations. Over the fifteen years it's been off the air, the technology has developed out of recognition, and so has the acting, so it should be good. During the week I potter around my garden, wondering what this latest incarnation of the programme, and The Doctor, will be like. Someone called Russell T Davies is in charge and apparently he's a fan, so it should be in good hands. On the Saturday, my parsnip soup is simmering on the wood stove as I settle down on my sofa, expecting a warm nostalgia trip. Wow! Forty five minutes later I am still pinned in my seat after the whirlwind that has just exploded from the television. State of the art effects, with luminous acting from Billie and Chris, the first episode is quite simply, stunning. Rose is a companion in the Polly mould - contemporary, brave and sexy, and Christopher Eccleston is a Doctor for the 21st century, dark and unpredictable, but with the required eccentricity and charm. This is going to be a very successful series and overnight, we fans have all become cool. A few days later we hear the news that Christopher Eccleston is leaving the role. I feel abandoned all over again. I'd only just got The Doctor back! The future seemed so certain, but now, who knows? And then I remember that we felt the same uncertainty back in 1966, when William Hartnell left. Will there be a new Doctor? As usual, the media is full of rumours and fantasy castings but we are all delighted when a couple of weeks later, a young actor called David Tennant is confirmed in the role. This is great news – I had seen him in *Casanova* and thought he was fantastic. I think he'll be better than Christopher Eccleston, actually!

One of the episodes is so blooming frightening that I find myself wishing my sofa wasn't right up against the wall. 'Are you my mummy?' haunts me for days, I remember those gas masks – so scary. Prior to the series returning I had been approached for interviews in two national newspapers. This is always very difficult for me because I have never sought publicity. I am well-known in the *Doctor Who* community but I am also protected by it. I am reluctant, but the bottom line is that I have bills to pay, so needs must. Both the Mail and the Mirror send intelligent, modern women to interview me in my kitchen. The Mirror wants to talk about the new series and the journalist asks me for advice for Billie, which is then misquoted. Barbara Davies from the Daily Mail focuses on my past, and particularly Tony Newley – she has read Garth Bardsley's biography of him. On one hand it's all very uncomfortable for me but on the other, she is an understanding woman. I feed her home-baked bread, lend her my wellies and take her up to the moors to climb a tor, have a primal moment for herself. These journalists lead such intense lives.

Before the article comes out, I have the painful task of telling Yogi, after all these years, that Mickgough wasn't Polly's dad. I am so afraid that he will judge me and I am grateful for his great big heart, when he says,

'She was still our Polly.' And Emma agrees. This secret that I have carried for so long is finally laid to rest. Such a relief.

Cary has organised his first 'Regenerations' convention. I am very impressed because he has sent me a ticket to Swansea - this is the first time I have ever travelled first class. My dreams of being spoilt at last are soon dashed – the buffet service is finished till Birmingham where I change trains to Cardiff. It has broken seats and also no food left! The convention is beautifully organised, all the details taken care of so that everyone can relax and have fun. It's a star-studded event – lots of guests and on the Saturday evening we are very moved by a Welsh Male Choir. The Marriot Hotel is a perfect location on the edge of the bay, and everyone agrees that this is the best convention ever.

Dear Anneke,

I read with interest the interview with you in the Daily Mail. For many years now it has been on my mind to try and make contact but I had no idea how to find you. You won't know me but in the sixties, I rented a flat in Camden Town to your brother.

The morning he died I had visited him and he seemed very nervous, his hands were shaking as he put papers into his briefcase. He told me that since childhood, he had been searching for the Holy Grail, and that he now knew where it was and was going to find it. He couldn't tell me where he was going, only that it was a chapel near Edinburgh. He said that if certain people knew where he was going they would stop him. He took his bags and said goodbye. The next thing I heard was that he had been found dead at Euston Station. When I returned to the flat to pack up his belongings it was empty and I assumed that you had been in, although I knew you didn't have a key.

Life went on and I forgot about Robin until 1985 when I read a book called 'Holy Blood, Holy Grail'. In it there was a passage about a young journalist on the trail of the Holy Grail and the Templars, who had been found dead on the railway tracks. That night I dreamt of Robin and could not get him out of my mind. I realised where he had been going – the famous Rosslyn Chapel.

I wonder whether you are entirely satisfied with the explanations you had previously received about the circumstances, and I felt that I owed it to Robin to share my recollections with you.

Out of the blue, I have received the most shocking and disturbing letter from the actress Coral Atkins, which has shaken me and reawakened the mystery surrounding Robin's death. I have been at home with his spirit for so long now and suddenly I am thrust back to that devastating time. When it happened my mother was babbling on about him being murdered but for me, that was too much to think about. Mickgough had encouraged me to focus on the raw experience of the loss and not to get caught up with revenge and justice – it wasn't going to bring him back. My mother was in Spain at the time, drowning in wine and tears. I had my small children, a career, and a life to get on with. Even though it was clear that Robin had died following an assault, there didn't seem to be any serious police enquiry – certainly – I was never interviewed. The witnesses said he was sitting alone at the bar when a stranger came over and punched him to the floor. He died in the ambulance. These are all the facts that we knew, except that shortly before, Robin had told us that he was using the pseudonym, Richard Grenville. Now the mystery obviously deepens. You were on the trail of the 'Holy Bloodline', years before the publication of *Holy Blood, Holy Grail*. Why didn't the police pursue the case? What happened to your manuscript and all your possessions? Who was behind it? I wish I'd known this when I was younger. I'd have been banging on Scotland Yard's door next day. Coral and I talk of becoming sleuths, but after all these years, the trail has surely gone cold, and we may never know the truth of what happened to you, my beloved brother.

Wendy Cook is writing a book about her life with Peter. It seems the world is interested once again in the people who defined the sixties. We spend some evenings sharing our memories of those days, Our children playing together, the laughter and humour, the talented people. We remember The Establishment, discovering The Beatles, Dudley's piano, the scene in New York, the innocence and enthusiasm. It must have been so difficult living with Peter, who was such a big presence, and the splitting up was torturous. She thinks I should write my story as well.

'Nah – I burnt my laptop!' She is very concerned that her editors might insist on the usual sex and drugs exposure. This has always been one of my doubts, that if I were to write my story, it wouldn't be my own authentic creation. When *So Farewell Then* comes out it's a brilliantly well-written book, and she rightly feels proud of it, and she seems more at peace now.

Chapter 27

Self Portrait

In September 2006 I am at the second of Cary's 'best ever' conventions in Swansea. The usual crowd is here and by now I am well and truly part of the *Doctor Who* family. I don't call them 'fans' – they are my friends. I have a strange sense of satisfaction that this time, I have one of my old friends with me. Cary and I are delighted to invite Roger Lloyd Pack to 'Regenerations' following his appearance in the show earlier in the year. He and Jehane always wondered why I enjoy these occasions so much, and what I do at them, well now, I can share it with him. People say it must be nice for us actors to get together to reminisce at these events. Actually, we're more likely to talk about where to buy comfy shoes and how to keep the squirrels off our bird feeders.

On the Friday night I'm outside the hotel chatting with Tim Hirst. He's been listening to a radio programme about Tony Newley and he's asking me about my life. As people have done before, he suggests that I should write my autobiography, and as usual I come up with the same set of answers.

'I can't get my head around computers...' Tim doesn't take 'no' for an answer.

'You just need someone to type, while you pace up and down and *create*!'

'But the editors… the publicity…'

'Well, I'll take care of all that for you,'

'But… publishers!' I remember Wendy's recent experiences.

'We'll try one of the *Doctor Who* publishers – Telos or Big Finish – or we can self publish!'

'But it wouldn't have much about *Doctor Who* in it!'

'No-one will mind, the fans are interested in you… ' He seems very confident. Maybe this is my next challenge. I find myself saying,

'Alright then, yes, I will.'

Tim wakes up with a massive hangover, wondering what he's let himself in for, and I've been up late in the bar, excitedly telling anyone who'd listen,

'I'm going to write my story!' Later that day I'm on the stage being interviewed, with Louise Jameson. Someone in the audience asks if we would ever write our autobiographies. Louise is definitely not keen on the idea.

'Oh God. My kids would find out all sorts about me!' I tell everyone that I have at last decided to do it, so David Bickerstaff, who is the host, asks the audience who would buy it. Every single hand goes up. Alright! Now that I've really decided to write my story, my mind is going bananas, and it's all coming flooding back. It seems to me, that what with one thing and another, I've had a hell of a fucking life! I know that there is no point in doing this unless I tell the whole story. I can't start dividing it up into what's nice and what's not. I begin to think about all the people who might be upset by it, but you can't have lived your life authentically if you haven't pissed a few people off. I will start on the first of January. There are other projects to clear out of the way before I can sit down and get focussed. We formulate a business plan. We decide to self-publish. I like the idea of having total control – no editor to cut out my special memories, no publisher to insist on the content. After all the times I've been misquoted in the press, I like the idea of being in charge. I'll do the writing and Tim will do everything else. We'll raise the money by offering people the chance to pre-order. We set up a website, and the pre-orders start coming in, which is exciting but also nerve-wracking, because as yet, the book is little more than a mad chaos inside my head. As a meditator, this is the total opposite of my usual practice because my mind is now full of anecdotes and anxieties.

Tim has been on to BBC Wales and they invite me to visit the set to watch David Tennant filming. I can't believe it – I'm chuffed to bits! The date they have suggested coincides with the special *Children in Need* concert at the Millennium Centre which Cary has already invited me to. So I'm off to Wales for this once in a lifetime experience. The Centre is buzzing with excited crowds. Many of our old friends are here and there isn't a spare seat in the house. Before the show begins the monsters from the latest series are wandering around the audience, frightening the children, which they love. David Tennant runs out on to the stage wearing a gold suit, to a standing, ecstatic, roaring audience. We are treated to a spectacular evening - a total multi-sensory experience and it is hosted with wit and charm by David. The next morning, me and my keen team of buddies arrive at the BBC studios half an hour early. We start our tour in the art department where we watch artists designing landscapes for spaceships and aliens on their computers. What strikes me at once is their level of enthusiasm for the show. This is not just a job for them, it's a passion. They take us everywhere and show us everything. We are like kids in a toy shop as we wander around a vast warehouse filled with everything from the Face of Boe to the Torchwood Range Rovers. It's a far cry from the prop cupboard at White City in the sixties. We are all slightly spooked by the Torchwood set. The attention to detail is astounding, and the interrogation room is really creepy. But now is the moment I've been waiting for – to step back into the Tardis after all these years – fantastic!

It got bigger and it's nothing like the Tardis I remember, which was made of plywood and assembled for each recording. The attention to detail is impressive - the binoculars, the spanners, the weird alien artefacts on the console. This is a special moment – how could I have known, 40 years ago, that I would be standing once again in the Tardis. Is that Pat and Mike, dancing around the console chuckling?

We are taken to the location. It's an old house which is doubling as the basement of a Manhattan theatre. How strange - despite the advances in technology and the bigger budgets, it's all quite familiar – cables everywhere, it's draughty and the tea table is a mess. We go down some stone steps into the cellar where the atmosphere is one of quiet focus. I am greeted warmly by the director James Strong and I am humbled that everyone seems to know who I am. David is rehearsing a scene with Hugh Quarshie. We watch for a while, trying to be invisible, before there is a natural pause and… at last… David comes over.

'Doctor, how lovely to see you again!' And with that, his face breaks into a massive grin and we fall into each other's arms. I am so taken up with this moment that I forget to introduce my gang,

but he is charming and introduces himself to the others with a modest,

'Hi, I'm David.' We get chatting, and I tell him how, for me, Pat Troughton was the ultimate Doctor, and how I feel that he has the very same quality, which seems to delight him. He wants to know about my autobiography.

'Are you going to spill the beans?'

'Oh yeah! All of them!'

On the train home, I am beaming from ear to ear. I feel honoured and satisfied and exhausted.

I'm sitting in my local launderette - I tread as lightly as I can - reading about Joan Collins's many wardrobes, all over the world, and her collection of 500 pairs of shoes… My mother once told me how when she was a glamorous young woman in Rotterdam in the early thirties, fussing about which pair of shoes to wear, her mother commenting,

'If you only had one pair you wouldn't be so anxious!' I never met my grandmother, yet recently I've become aware of her presence in my life. She who died of starvation has been looking out for me all the time. As for Joan's collection of shoes… I'd rather have a shed full of wood.

Yogi comes for Christmas as usual. I have told him about the book and he is as encouraging and supportive as ever. We hike way up on the high moors to a hut circle, it's exhilarating and bitterly cold. He loves some of the early stories of my life, which of course, he has never heard. Children are never interested! I'm putting off telling him how candid I need to be about his father, so in our fireside conversations, I am staying focussed on sunken houseboats and stolen Christmas decorations.

On 1st January, I light a candle and I start. Angela Douglas has bought me a set of pencils, and Tim has given me a tape recorder. I write a page or two by hand. It's like painting with words, and when I feel I've got it right I burble it all on to the tapes. These, I send to Tim, and he and his friend Jenny transcribe them. I am encouraged by their immediate feedback. They have been laughing and crying at the story, and at one point, Jenny is so upset she can't go on. I am possessed. Woken up in the middle of the night by my mother and Robin, telling me the stories long since forgotten. The veil is thinner in the early hours and the spirits are notorious for not being 'in time'. I work non-stop for the first six weeks and don't see anyone – I don't watch telly or talk on the phone – I'm a total hermit. At the end of it, I have written the main outline.

Meanwhile we've had the most frightful storms. Water is pouring down my chimney and coming up through my kitchen floor. I'm going to have to move out while my kind farmer sorts it out. I go to stay with friends. Tim has booked me for endless interviews and events to promote the book and to keep the pre-orders coming. I am now beginning to feel responsible to the many people who have ordered the book, and once again I am blown away by the generosity of the fans.

I'm loving the current series. Since David took over the role it seems even more magical. Watching an episode one night, one of my old foes is revealed... I'm shouting at the screen,
'Watch out Doctor! Macra!'

Tim's getting lost among all the 'inserts' I keep adding, and keeping track of the chronology is becoming a nightmare. Neither of us have done this before, but we are learning fast. At one point – horrors – we seem we have lost a large section in the recesses of the computer, but we keep going anyway and weeks later, the missing work turns up. My hair is now grey.

I go to the BBC in Bath to record a narration for a CD of *The War Machines*. I stay in a lovely old hotel in the centre. What a treat to enjoy this gorgeous city – never mind the shops! The studio has such a special atmosphere and Michael Stevens, the commissioning editor, offers to release *Self Portrait* as a talking book.

Tim is sending me manuscripts of the work so far, and I am freaking out because it looks like instructions on the back of a soap packet. I don't realise that all they have done so far is type the words, there is no design, so I am on the phone, flapping about the need for a professional typesetter.

'Anneke, don't worry. I can do all that on the computer.' I am totally unconvinced, but sure enough, when the next section drops through my letterbox, it looks like a proper book. My buddy Stefan and I are enjoying researching all the music. How powerful music is, how it sparks the memories. We spend hours on the phone, Stefan trawling the internet double-checking dates and singers, reminding me which programmes I had done. Half of them I'd forgotten – I did a lot of telly in the sixties!

We are keen that the book should look and feel right. We want it to be on good quality paper and to have pictures all the way through, and not just in a couple of separate sections away from the stories they relate to. It's going to cost us more money, but we feel it's worth it. Because of all my travels and the 'mishaps' that have happened to my photos, I have very few left. We gather up pictures from wherever we can and also include some paintings and drawings. Jas Wiseman has unearthed a stack of photos from the sixties, many of them from *Strange Report*. In the batch is a photo that I have never seen, and without any question, we all agree, that's the one for the cover. So much magic is happening around this book. People are popping up from my past and contributing to the story. I talk to old school-friends, old lovers, directors and actors I worked with so many years ago. The story becomes richer for this.

I'm writing about Tim Craxton and remembering the look in his eye when he spoke about his time as a Squadron Leader in the RAF. A moment later I look out of the window and I see, flying over the valley, a Spitfire. I finally make a pilgrimage to St Mawes and pass a

Riley Gamecock, the car Tim used to drive. Toots Lockwood finds drawings from when I was a child. I'm talking to Tony Gray and Jillybeans and a few old lovers who seem to want rekindle things. Dear Goddess... save me from the ever more desperate randy old men! My mother gives me back delightful memories... I'm four years old and playing in her calfskin 'cabin trunk'. It stands higher than me. Inside, her clothes are on hangers and there are drawers I open with peach silk underwear wrapped in tissue paper. I love this feminine world of perfume and pearls. I open her handbags and climb into her high heels. How I love the laughter and applause.

We have promised to launch the book at the third Regenerations in 2007, and already we are running out of time. I have never been in such a state of anxiety and panic. One of Tim's qualities is the art of placation, he's infuriating! We spend whole days on the phone to each other editing and further days in my kitchen, tweaking the story and designing the layout, often till the early hours, until I am shaking with exhaustion and I can't see anymore. During this process we become obsessive editors as we realise that less is more. But that's it. Now, I can't add another word. What a relief. I need to switch off the mind, slow down, I can get some autumn work done in the garden. The hedges may be 400 years old but they still grow like stink. We've had so much rain this summer. There is a permanent puddle in the porch, so my bamboo table wears little wellie boots. The bindweed has gone nuts, everywhere, and the weeds are taking over. The slugs are lolling about, satiated, the hedgerows are stuffed with blackberries, there's much to do. There's chutney and sloe gin to make.

Our print deadline looms. At the eleventh hour, we are still finding passages in the wrong place, Tim is running around London with manuscripts for Roger, Jim Broadbent and Angela Douglas, who has promised to give me a 'Foreword'. We can only give them a few hours to get back to us. Angela spends the last few hours before flying to South Africa writing her contribution. Nick Setchfield of *SFX Magazine* is going to give us a quote for the cover, and he reads it on the train. And in the nick of time, we get it to the printers. Tim and I adjourn to the pub where we fall gratefully into a vat of wine.

We are two weeks away from the launch. Tim has had to take time off work to sit with the printer, because the proof isn't right. He is in Southampton for hours on end, trying to sort it out, even as the printing presses are firing up. This delays the production by a few days. Tim daren't tell me, fearing my wrath. I've been put through a wringer and I'm swearing I'll never do this again. Ever.

I am travelling to Swansea on the train with a leaden heart. We have no books. Will they arrive at the hotel tomorrow? I feel like it's *The Emperor's New Clothes* – I'm going to have to stand up on stage, and wing it. During the evening we are totally professional, appearing calm and relaxed in the bar, but we meet up every half hour, in the courtyard, on the bench, where it all started this time last year. We chain-smoke and wonder what the fuck we are going to do. That night, I have a nightmare. I am sitting on stage with Colin Baker. He's asking me about the book, and as I'm telling everyone that they can come to see me at my table and I'll sign their copy, I look down, and realise, with shame, that I am naked. I'm doomily sitting at breakfast the next morning, when I see Tim's grinning face walking towards me.

'We have books.'

They feel like they are still warm, and smell delicious, and we unpack them on to our table as the queues are growing. Everyone loves the look and feel of the book, and I can't believe that I'm actually signing the first few copies. Tim and I have become an author and a publisher!

As Tim unpacks the books, Jenny arranges them on the table, and I look like a picture of contentment as I sign copy after copy, the queue never ending. Nobody has any idea of all that we've been through, and of course, we don't mention it. People start reading it at once, and amazingly, the next day, they are already telling me how they can't put it down. This is very satisfying. Julian Glover has nicked a copy, Sharon Willows comes with tears in her eyes to tell me how moved she has been and Sophie Aldred is demanding volume two. We've done it.

After Regenerations, we don't stop. On the Wednesday, I am in my kitchen, with Tim and the printer, Justin, surrounded by boxes and boxes of books, which we are stuffing into envelopes for the people who had pre-ordered. We are busy until the early hours. A genuine cottage industry!

On the Sunday we have the launch party. I had originally hoped to have this in The Troubadour, the coffee house which was so much part of my life in the early sixties. However, with only a few weeks to go we had decided that it was too expensive – we are funding it ourselves – so Tim has found a lovely pub-restaurant in Hammersmith. It's the most beautiful, warm October day. We gather outside in the garden and there are friends from every decade of my life, characters from the book, all coming together. Tim makes a complimentary speech and then Yogi stands up and speaks so glowingly about me that I am awash with tears. I had particularly wanted this party to have a family atmosphere - this wasn't for the press - which is partly why we chose a lunch-time, and it's lovely to see Sophie Aldred's two boys charging about the garden. Roddy arrives late, looking extraordinary in his white whiskers, because he's playing Francis Bacon in a play. Barney Broadbent is telling Yogi how much he loved him as a little boy, and he has called his daughter Polly. It's been a rewarding and emotional day, having been reunited with so many friends past and present. As they dwindle in the warm early evening, it is only the party loving *Who* friends who are left…

Roger Lloyd Pack

Jillybeans & Michael McManus

Yogi &
Barney Broadbent

Me, Nick Setchfield &
Steve O'Brien

Chris Burke, Mark and Nicky Ayres and Carlotta Barrow

Me and Carlotta Barrow

Jehane, Nisheeta, Rashid & Stefan

Me and Yogi

Gary Russell

Sophie Aldred & boys, me and Tim

In the days that follow I feel disappointed that in spite of our press releases and the work we had done to publicise the book, we haven't heard from any members of the media so the launch remains low key. But soon, '*Self Portrait*' is getting glowing reviews from many of the professional writers we know, from customers on Amazon, from various magazines, from the fans, and from some of my oldest friends, whose opinions I really value. Our pride in the book is justified, although the prospect of doing it all again for the second book fills me with dread. Hopefully we'll be able to build on what we have learned. Days later, on my birthday, I'm at Tenth Planet signing away, when they bring me a Tardis shaped cake, complete with a David Tennant made of icing - I can't bring myself to eat him! This event is the first of many in our nationwide tour, which we refer to as 'Anneke in the UK'.

I seem to have developed the habit of asking Tom Baker questions during his panels at conventions. We are at Invasion in Barking, when I take the microphone and ask him about his infamous gravestone. His answer is typically barmy. Before Christmas, Tim had given him and Peter Davison copies of *Self Portrait*. Their response was,

'Am I in it?' And now, Tom is telling me that he enjoyed my story and he thought it was a 'brave book'.

A big debt of gratitude to Tim. The miles he's driven, the hours he's worked, the cash he's invested. Even when I was finally at my most anxious and fractious, he has handled me with patience and honesty. After many gallons of coffee I have watched the steam rising from his head as he worked into the early hours on his computer in my kitchen. In spite of having a very busy schedule of his own he still found the time to manage and organise everything with endless cheerfulness. His enthusiasm and friendship has been such a gift; I couldn't have done it without him.

Chapter 28

Polly Returns

We are at a convention and David Richardson from Big Finish is telling me about the story that has been written for Polly, as part of their *Companion's Chronicles* series. It takes place in France during World War 2 and it sounds so interesting I can't wait to get the script. It arrives just before Easter but - oh dear - I am very disappointed as I don't feel that the characterisation is right. Polly hasn't been in *Doctor Who* for over 40 years, so it is important to me that this return honours her. The revived Polly is written as a meek second-fiddle to The Doctor, Ben and Jamie. My disappointment turns to anger. I am so upset because after all this time, I don't want to misrepresent my character and I feel I owe it to Pat and Mike and the writers who created her, to get it right.

The Gods have a sense of humour. I'm on stage at the Darwen *Doctor Who* day, and as part of the interview Tim asks me about the forthcoming audio play. I look at him with a pause, and say,

'Can I say this?' We had already decided that we probably shouldn't talk about it.

'Go on then.' And I launch into a tirade about how uncomfortable I am with the script, and why. I don't realise at this point, as I am ranting away, that the writer, Steve Lyons, is sitting in the audience. We need to talk! It turns out that Polly and Ben were his favourite characters and he had been particularly keen to write this story. The poor chap is then subjected to the full force of this 66 year-old woman's energy and he doesn't know what's hit him.

'Polly was SASSY! INTELLIGENT! Bright and plucky, and naughty with it! The Doctor relied on her. She wouldn't have worn white lacy boots on a battlefield! And Ben wasn't her hero, he was her buddy!'

Now, I have to convince Big Finish to make the changes. We have animated discussions, at one point David suggests that we pull the whole thing, and I agree. A few days later, David's back on the phone. He would like to meet with me and Lisa Bowerman who is directing, to see if we can iron out the problems. He suggests finding a room in a London hotel - I offer Roger Lloyd Pack's kitchen table. Lisa is very supportive and we work through the script until we are all satisfied. We all meet up in a studio in Brixton. Lisa has chosen a very attractive actor called John Sackville, who will play the part of the pilot. John's performance is making the script come alive. We both know that we are creating a cracking story and Lisa's direction is encouraging and to-the-point. Afterwards, just like 40 years ago, we are off to the pub to celebrate.

With Lisa Bowerman, David Richardson and John Sackville

We've had massive storms and the water is pouring out of the moors and down past back my back door there is a permanent river. I've built a wooden walkway over it, which helps. I feel like Winnie the Pooh, waiting for the water to rise, running out of honey. It's so damp my shoes have all gone mouldy and I've hurt my back doing the strimming. In the good old days there would be a lovely old Reggie or George who would turn up on their bikes, sharpen and clean your tools, cut your hedge and plant onions, in return for a couple of bob for a few pints. In this 21st century the old boys are wearing DayGlo spandex and going mountain-biking, replaced by young men with tattoos called tree-surgeons, with big trucks and noisy equipment, and charging you hundreds.

Derek Hambly has invited us to a big autograph event at the Birmingham Hilton. The guest list is astounding – everyone from Tony Curtis to war heroes, original astronauts, cosmonauts, and Bond girls. There is a drinks reception for the guests. An 80 year-old pilot tweaks his moustaches at me, a Bond actress who had survived Auschwitz, so beautiful and vibrant in her late seventies, a woman who left acting to become a priest, and what do you say to the man who did the first space walk?! I tell him that I've been on the moon. In *Doctor Who*. Jennie Linden, who I first met when she was in *Women in Love* with Mickgough, is here, and I love her, a soul sister. We even look similar and we have to be prised apart because we have so much to share. One of my favourite things is watching the show with a crowd of people - so much joy, seeing the children's faces as they root for The Doctor, and explain to me what's going on – it's so fast and full-on. Everyone is asking about the second book – they want to know what happens next. I had always planned two volumes, so we are considering the practicalities. Although we have sold over a thousand copies, like many creative wildcards it's been a labour of love and we haven't made a penny.

I am contributing to a documentary about the sixties for a Who DVD. They film me walking down Greek Street and arriving at the club that used to be The Establishment. This is the first time I've been here since the early sixties. We're going to film inside but the club isn't open yet so while we're hanging around I say that it would be nice to recreate the famous photo of Peter with an umbrella. It's a lovely sunny day so no-one has brought an umbrella but magically, in that moment, out of the corner of my eye I notice an umbrella lying against the railings. Thanks Peter! In 2009, English Heritage will honour Peter with a blue plaque at The Establishment.

The abridged script of *Self Portrait* arrives from BBC Audiobooks. I am in shock. My Work! My book! Three quarters of it, gone! I knew it would be edited but I hadn't realised how much I was going to lose. So much of my childhood, most of my mother, I'm devastated. When I've calmed down, I call Michael Stevens and he is very encouraging and reassures me that my story comes through strong and clear.

I am walking around Queen's Square in Bath at dawn, warming up my voice, because this is going to be a big moment for me. And then I'm in the studio, headphones on, Kate Thomas, the dynamic producer cheering me on. I meet the composer who is going to weave music through the story. Is this really happening? Am I really reading my story, for the BBC, more than half a century after I first worked with them as a 12 year-old actress? When the audiobook comes out I do lots of interviews with BBC radio stations all over the country. Some of the presenters have listened to the CD so their interviews are more in depth. Others simply present me as 'the Billie Piper of her day' – but I don't mind – I have a big, new audience to talk to and I love the experience. Judi Spiers of BBC Radio Devon, loves the CD so much she goes straight out and buys the book and gives me the phone number of Noel Harrison, our friend from the sixties who lives in a nearby town.

I have been working on *Naked* since the beginning of the year. We have learned a thing or two along the way, so this time it's a little easier. Again, I handwrite it. I find the train journeys all over the country are the perfect time to write – there is no escape. So with earplugs in and sandwiches and water to keep me going, I fill my notebooks, as I watch the bare trees and sodden fields turn into the sweet lime greens of spring. The memories come flooding back. Tim comes with his laptop and we create the book, editing and revising as we go.

August, 2008. Tim has been sleeping on my sofa for a week, eating home-made marmalade and drinking me out of coffee. We work sixteen hours a day. By October we're on the fourth draft and I'm grateful for having more time to let it percolate and simmer – it's an organic process of many layers.

The cover of *Self Portrait* was so strong and well-received, that we wonder how we could follow it. I suggest a little snap of me, standing in a Norfolk river.

'If Katy Manning can drape herself round a Dalek with no clothes on, then I can do this,' Sadly the photograph is too small and out of focus, but it gives us a great laugh to mock-up a cover and launch it to the *Doctor Who* world as a tease.

With Stefan

At a convention some years ago, I met Stefan Sundin, and we discovered we had a shared passion for growing vegetables, which sparked a great friendship. Although he lives in the north of Scotland, we speak often and I call him my 'confidante'. He supported me through the dramas of compiling the books, and spent hours on the internet researching dates, music and TV shows. He's a great big heart, and I am very lucky to have him as a friend.

With Tim and my fellow 'Troughton Era' actors; Nick Courtney, Debs Watling, Wendy Padbury and Frazer Hines

In the Tardis with Cary Woodward, David Bickerstaff, Tim and BBC Head of Drama Jane Tranter, with her children

Doctor Who colleagues enjoying *Self Portrait*.
Tom Baker, Peter Davison, Louise Jameson, Nick Courtney, Sophie Aldred (and Adam) and Sylvester McCoy.

Chapter 29

To Days to Come, and All My Love to Long Ago

In these two books I've torn the bandage off, sharing the experiences that have shaped my life, told of the beautiful human beings that I've loved along the way, and the antagonists, who I actually learned the most from. In the world of relationships you only ever meet yourself. I've cried all over again for those that I've lost. I've had to rewrite, edit and reread those stories all over again, and again. What a meditation in letting go. If it wasn't for the *Who* fans I wouldn't have done it. It feels as though I've put all the pieces of the puzzle together. Now I can see the whole picture. It's a sense of completion. A final healing of ancient wounds, to have relived the fun, the laughter and so many blessings. Bhagwan said his epitaph would be his people. Poona now has black pyramids and meditation halls set in lush parks. He told us to be weightless in the spiritual life and rooted in the ordinary life. I'm equally at home in a rowdy East End pub, talking to a guy with a two-foot blue Mohican about climate change, as I am talking mysticism with an Oxford scholar. Arthritis began way back when I was cleaning in California; the meditation is 'Here's the pain… and here's me gettin' on with it.' My hands, with which I have painted the picture of my life, are becoming weak and stiff at last. But I love my simple country life, tending this piece of land which I've borrowed. Walking in the woods pausing at a little sandy beach by the river, once again I am that wise child, dreaming of building a shelter, making a fire. I'm often alone but never lonely. The robins fly into my kitchen, the pheasants peck at my feet.

The suffering we endure can ennoble us. The simple kindness we encounter can humble us. The trust we need to cultivate can sustain us. Let's celebrate whatever brings us to our knees in gratitude. We are eternal spirits. We will see each other again… and again.

"The path leads home and we arrive… where we have always been"

Anneke
April '09

**A heartfelt thank you
to the following people
for pre-ordering this
book.**

Janice Adam
Thomas Adams
Carl Akers
Sophie Aldred
Darren Allen
Lee Allum
Mark Ambler
Nigel Anderson
Celia Andrews
Persephone Arbour
Anna Ashley
Shaun Ashton
Jodie & Shane Astbury
Jan Avery
Mark Ayres
Mark Bailey
Graham Baird
Prakash Bakrania
Garth Bardsley
Andrew Barrett
Enid Barrington
Carlotta Barrow
Andrew Beech
Patrick Bellis
Howard Bennett
Gareth Bevan
Todd Bielby
Jo Biza
Richard Black
Rosemary Blake
James Bland
Jon Bond
Rebekah Bond
Alexander Bond
Philip Brennan
Liam Brison
Ben Brown
Mike Brumpton
Kit Buckley
Russell Buer
Steven Bull
Shaun Butcher
Lesley & Rory Byrne
Allison Cadman
Martin Cadman
RJ & Tori Cadman
Jim Campbell
Stuart Cann
John Carr
Beverley Carrington
Kay Carver
Paul Castle

Lee Catigen-Cooper
Darren Chandler
Dino Charalambous
Mark Chilver
Neil Christie
Andrew Clarke
Jonathan Coley
Baz Collins
Mike Cook
Russell Cook
Wendy Cook
Mark Cooper
Paul Cooper
  & Sue Derbyshire
Barry Cooper
Steve Corke
Tony Cotterill
Alistair Cowan
Martyn Craigs
John Crocker
Nicola Crookes
Anthony Curr
Montague Curzon Herrick
Allen Dace
Pippa Dakin
Colin Dalglish
Manau Das
Denim Dave
Mike Davey
Paul Davey
Barbara Davies
Sean Davies
Ian Davis
Britt Dawes
Robert Day
Patricia Dempsey
Paul Deune
Rory Deutsch
Robert Dick
Madhura Dickeson
Jonathan Dickie
David Dickinson
Paul Dillon
Paul Doody
Patrick Dowling
Brian Doyle
Simon Doyle
Tim Drury
William Dyson
Phil & Jenny Edmonds
Carolyn Edwards
Trevor Ellis
Harry Emambocus
Paul Engelberg
Mark English
Stephen Eramo
Jon & Sharon Evans

Matt Evenden
Simon Exton
Rob Fairclough
Marty Fairgrieve
Angela Farren
Alan Fawcus
Michael Ferguson
Christopher Fewell
Michael N Flint
Kevin Gauntlett
Richard Geldard
James Gent
Janine Gibson
Gary Gillies
John Godbold
David Gogarty
Richard Gous
Tony Gray
Paul Greaves
Kevin Green
Aaron Gregson
David Griffiths
Stephen Griffiths
James Grizzell
Graham Groom
John Grunewald
Simon Guerrier
James Guthrie
Mark Hadlett
Joe Halliday
David Hamblin
Simon Harries
Simon Hart
Michael Harvey
Steve Hatcher
Tim Hawtin
Nicholas Hayward
Stephen Hedley
Matt Henricksen
Steve Herbert
Gary Heron
Simon Hewitt
Greg Hill
Stephanie Hill
Sean & Jenny
Holdsworth
Henry Holland
Laurence Holton
Carl Horne
Laurel Howard
Martin Hughes
Peter Hughes
Adrian Hulme
Daniel Humes
Gary Humphries
John Hurles
Alan P Jack

Maria James
Martin James
Nicola Jarris
Judith Johnson
Paul Joliffe
Tom Jolliffe
Brendon Jones
Jonathan Jongkind
Brad Joy
Shanie Joyce
Eeva-Liisa Kannikoski
Sheila Kay
Anthony Kendrew
Mark Kendrew
Kerry Kerr
Geoff King
Julian Knott
Gary Knowles
Stephen La Riviere
Ceri Laing
Moray Laing
Tim Lambert
Phil Lane
Richard Laskin
Richard Leong
Tony Lightfoot
Kari Limond
Gideon Llewellyn
Simon Lloyd
Julia Lockwood
Stewart Lowe
Thomas Lyles
Christopher MacAllister
Neil MacDonald
David MacGowan
Eleanor Maddocks
Andrew Main
Michael Maiwurm
Jonathan Mallinson
Gary Marsh
Sean Marsh
Stephen Marshall
Garron Martin
Richard Mascall
Alan Maskell
James Mason
Kenneth Mason
Diccon Masterman
Steve Matthewman
David May
Mickey Mayhew
David McCallum
Roddy McDougall
James McFetridge
Sean McGawley
Simon McGhee
Janette McGuire

Michael McManus
Robert McMillan
Phil McMullen
Ben Melberg
Andrew Melling
Trudy Messingham
Joseph Metcalf
Jonathan Miles
Glen Miller
Steve Miller
Aileen Milne
Chris Moore
Nathan Moore
Paul Morgan
Mark Morris
Cheryl Mosby
David Mullen
Chris Murfin
Paul Murthwaite
Maureen Neathway
Gill Nicholls
Paul Norman
Dave Owen
Isayc G Paine
Erica Pardee
John Parkhouse
Dylan Parry
Andrew Parsons
Dave Parsons
A Pask
Stephen Pasqua
Patricia Paul
Adrzan Pauley
Ali Pearce
Alister Pearson
Rhonda Poacher
Emma Potts
Francis Price
Robin Prichard
Graeme Pritchard
Mike Purser
Gerri Quilty
Gill Rainey
Philip Ramshaw
Flipper Reddolphin
Paul Reeks
Billy Rees
Peter Relton
William Relton
David Richardson
Anthony Robertson
Gary Russell
Judy Saks
Michael Sauers
Donnaleen Saul
Gavin Saxby
Karl Scarisbrick

John Seymour
Adrian Sherring
Graham Sherring
Neil Short
Hazel Shultz
Bryan Simcott
David Simons
Robert J.E. Simpson
Caroline Sinclair
Dickon Sire
Sharon Skinner
John Slater
Douglas Smith
Leslie Smith
Peter Smith
Judi Spiers
Mark St Andrew
Darrell Stanley
Chris Starr
David Stevens
Mark Stew
Andrew Stingel
Anthony Wells-Stubley
Robert Sturrey
Paul Swales
David Clifford Taylor
Kate Taylor
Hugh Thomas
Martin Thomas
Chris Thompson
Jackie Thompson
Jacky Thornton
Paul Towse
Adrian Traynor
Nick Trueman
Robert Turner
Michael Vernon
Tony Viney
John R Walker
Stephen James Walker
Wayne Walker
Chris Watkins
David Wharton
Neil Whiteley
Martin Wiggins
Alex Wilcock
Craig Williams
John Williams
Mag Williams
Mark Williams
Sharon Willows
Donald Wilson
Edward Wilson
Jamie Wilson
Stephen Wilson
Chris Winwood
Peter Wood
Cary Woodward